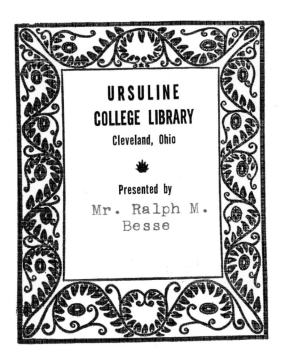

ATTIC & ELIZABETHAN TRAGEDY

ATTIC & ELIZABETHAN TRAGEDY

BY

LAUCHLAN MACLEAN WATT

KENNIKAT PRESS, INC./PORT WASHINGTON, N. Y.

ATTIC AND ELIZABETHAN TRAGEDY

First Published in 1908
Reissued in 1968 by Kennikat Press

Library of Congress Catalog Card No: 67-27661

Manufactured in the United States of America

INSCRIBED

TO

PROFESSOR S. H. BUTCHER,

LITT.D., LL.D., M.P.,

IN

GRATEFUL REMEMBRANCE

OF HIS

TEACHINGS, INSPIRATIONS AND ENCOURAGEMENTS

FOREWORD

In order to concentrate the teachings of certain passages, I have sometimes in these pages made free paraphrases, rather than literal translations, from the Tragedies. Such a method lies more along the line of my purpose in this book.

CONTENTS

CHAPTER I

ATTIC AND ELIZABETHAN TRAGEDY

THE Attic Tragic Drama survives to us in what are, after all, only a few fragments of the great body of material which once thrilled Greece—the works, practically, of the three great names of the Greek Tragic age; but of the quality of these fragments we need have no sentimental fear, for the Alexandrian critics took what remains as types of what the perfect Tragedy ought to be; and, further, they have the mark of approval upon them, for they all came through the ordeal of popular favour, in some form or other, and were preserved so, till scholarship finally embalmed them in undying print. These may be perhaps not the highest tests, but no man can afford to despise any fruit until he has tasted it.

Of the seventy tragedies of Æschylus, and one hundred and thirteen by Sophocles, we have only seven left for each writer; while of the ninety-two of Euripides but seventeen remain.

Æschylus, we may be sure, would have the spirit of his age in all he did, for he was intensely the son of his epoch and its needs; and, indeed, it is remarkable how the literature of an epoch hangs around a few great names. Æschylus fought in the glorious fight of Salamis, and so poured into his lines the inspiration of the liberties of Greece; while yet, being a native of Eleusis and his childhood having been passed in contiguity to the oracles and their spells, he set the liberty and the life of Greece in a great solemn background of the gods, till his drama becomes, sometimes, like a gigantic oratorio.

Sophocles, a lad of fifteen years, led the chorus of youths in the celebration of the victory; while, in the island whither the women and children had been conveyed for safety, lay Euripides, a babe in his mother's lap, all unconscious of the momentous issues for which his fellow-countrymen were battling away their lives. These three lived through the greatest period of all the national struggle of the Greeks, and, when they passed away, the glory of the Attic Tragedy faded with them.

Perhaps in all the history of the fluctuation, conflict, and yearning of the world, there are not recorded any periods more fraught with influences, environments, and provocations of greatness than the age in which Attic Tragedy rose and flourished, and that in which the genius of the Elizabethan era found its highest utterance on the English Tragic stage. With a grandeur, depth, and breadth never eclipsed, the national thought took up the most momentous questions —life, death, God, man, judgment, and all the huge ethical shadows that, on the skirts of these, haunt man's being and conduct; and, probing the deeps, or piercing the heights, tried to arrive at an understanding of the mysteries of the Eternal here in Time.

The Greek Tragic theatre was purely Attic in origin, and the master-dramatists themselves, whose plays survive as the sole fragmentary remains of that rich literary out-pouring, were Athenian. The general Greek mind, from all its sundered colonies, was content to look upon Athens and its passions of the gods as representing the highest conceptions regarding highest things.

Out of the dim unknown Asia, the myriads of the Persian invasion shook the waters and the land. The liberty of Greece—and, to the Greek, that meant the very life of Hellas—trembled in the balance. Darius and Xerxes —these very names darkened the outlook of the States. Self-preservation drew them together. Attica and Sparta forgot for a while their feuds, and their only rivalry was a rivalry of patriotic defence. Resolute, united, confident, the men of Hellas faced the terrible foe ; and at Marathon, Salamis, Artemisium, and Platæa, vindicated the cause for which they took the field. Now, the rebound from action is utterance. Success and failure, alike, in any enterprise, find their bard. Here, naturally, the heartstrings of Greece were drawn with a terrific tensity—so much depended on the struggle ; but, when the hour had passed, Victory swept the chords, and the soul of the people burst into great song.

So in Elizabethan England—the sixteenth century saw the misty gates of the unknown West falling apart. Men feared no longer to dare the unexplored. Whispers of adventure and of treasure-trove came across the waters, and, soon, venturesome sails out of English havens were following the setting sun. The growl of Spain only kindled the national pride the more, and the spirit of romantic adventure sailed the seas, and broke across the Spanish Main, clothed in the colours of national enterprise. Thus, even a raid of ragged buccaneers got set in a nobler background than mere burglary and piracy, when it became a matter of contest between Englishman and Spaniard as to the right to sail the whole wide seas.

Then, again, the giant threat of the Armada sent a thrill of unifying potency along the tide ; and Catholic and Protestant alike drew together, in an invincible integrity of patriotic resistance. When the pluck of English sailors, and the angry storms of our island seas had sundered and shattered the vast emprise of Spain, the reaction was bound, likewise, to be an utterance as great as the provocation which drew it forth.

Success or failure in any struggle of which the inevitable

issue is either national death or national vindication cannot escape the poetic cry. The teeth are too grimly set for sound while the struggle is going on ; but laughter or wail must follow the triumph or the defeat.

Now, Elizabeth's England had all the daring of a people in the growth, whose development has been disputed ; so, in the very spirit of the Sagas, she sought the enemy everywhere, and, heedless of everything but the repute of her right to the open seas and the open world, she flung her water-dogs at the heels of Spain, till she made that proud power stagger before her on the water and the land. The Tragedy of Elizabeth's time was the highest utterance of the thought provoked, struck out of the nation's heart in the hope of a dawning life, as the morning sun struck song out of the desert stone of Memnon ; but it had its beginnings in the rugged men of the Western seas, with the laugh on their lips, and the scars of fight on their faces.

But not alone was it this victory of Greece and England over threatened conquest that broke noblest utterance from the hearts of poets, and awoke deepest interest in the general heart of the people. Other influences also had their share. Freedom itself kindled heroic qualities in the soul of the Greek, for he felt that he had liberty as his right, which no man should dare to lay in chains. So, also, Elizabethan England, quickened to intellectual freedom by the magnetic throb of the Revival of Learning in Europe, which had shaken off the shackles of Scholasticism—and, further, having learned its muscular rights and potentialities, through the Reformation having pulled down the limitations and tyrannies of the Romish Church—was on a level which gave it such far-stretching views as made it vow to suffer itself no more to be dragged down into the shades and into bondage of any kind. The battle-shock and the victory smote, then, upon its heart, and the full chords of utterance were stirred to living sound.

CHAPTER II

THE DRAMA

THE Drama is the action of soul upon soul. It is philosophic in the deepest sense, and yet it is not a philosophic disquisition. It is the noblest preaching on the most momentous truths, yet never sermonising.[1] A noble, vivid aim, clearly and definitely acknowledged, must thrill and hold the spectator. The Tragic Drama is not for sport, nor to kill time. It takes up the moral sphere of human life's activity. In kaleidoscopic glimpses it flings a struggle before us, and it works out for righteousness. The contest becomes a great game between evil and good, with the triumph of good sure, even in apparent failure. It is the most artistic representation of the primal beauty of the soul, yet it is never mere sunset-painting, nor stained-glass-window work, but the living spirit conflicting with living spirit, and with its own lower self. It is motion and emotion, the passions in activity giving tangible reasons for themselves and for what they do, or abstain from doing. The practical Reason, with a definite purpose, moves like a monarch through the whole. The dramatic poet becomes creator of a world in order to explain the world of creation. The discontent, the questionings, the yearnings of the soul, set in living reality on the stage, is the true Drama.

The Drama, then, being the embodiment and utterance of the soul's explanation of the soul's struggle and conflict, the Tragic Drama is the solution and explanation

[1] " Quid enim in tota philosophia aut gravius aut sanctius aut sublimius tragedia recte constituta, quid utilius ad humanæ vitæ casus et conversiones uno intuitu spectandos ? "—JOHN MILTON.

of the highest and deepest agonisings of a nation or an
individual. Inborn native Liberty in grips with external
Necessity is the

" Shadow like an angel, with bright hair dabbled in blood,"

that haunts every tragedy which has ever held the world.

The crisis is the point of living intense contact of a
great personality, expressing itself in deed or word, with
a great environment of Destiny, Law, God, or Fate.
When the thunder and the fury pass, we listen for the
poet's voice; and we see upon the stage the embodied
sorrows, trials, and unanswered riddles of the life over
and around which have been raging the tides and storms,
the perplexities and bitternesses from which we have
emerged as questioners.[1]

Human nature is intensely dramatic, and the stage
Drama is the spontaneous growth of human impulse and
devotion. The dramatic instinct is at the very foundation
of human being. Watch children at play if you want an
explanation of the source of the dramatic. A child is a
born actor. Now, a child is so engrossed in the character
which he represents, that it matters little to him what the
environment may be. He is a ship, or a whale, in the
middle of a meadow; and he sees no inconsistency in
being a lion in a rowing-boat. The joy of living and the
happiness of Nature make him leap and sing for very
gladness of heart, which, at first imitative, becomes as
accurately representative as an attempt at costume can
make it. That is how the Drama becomes the truest
poesy or creation.

In its origin in Greece it arose from the outburst of
gladness over the ingathered harvest or the conclusion of
the vintage.

The childlike poesy of the Greeks gave the fields and

[1] Tragedy is the representation of the whole of life in a typical example. The
Tragic artist is one who can sum up the lessons of human vicissitude through the
delineation of a particular crisis. See Prof. Lewis Campbell.

woodlands over to rustic deities, whose care and goodness
they acknowledged in dance and song, the rudiments of
early worship ; and, through this point of view, the whole
universe put on a living meaning. Pensive, yet with periods
of passionate elation, the god Dionysus was the centre of
such adorations.[1] Along with Ceres he was the patron of
agriculture. His festival times were when the winepresses
were busy, or when the sunshine ripened the purple grape
throughout the land.

Now the first notion of worship is to compliment the
deity ; and in this, to the simple mind, imitation is the
sincerest flattery. Dionysus had his attendant train of
satyrs [2]—a wanton, mirthful, sylvan, hybrid tribe, half goat,
half man ; so the peasants, identifying themselves, in this
their worship, with these attendants, decked themselves with
goatskins, and danced and sang as they imagined the satyrs
of the woods would do.[3] From a somewhat similar
corybantic origin arose the popular Drama of Japan. A
master of ceremonies, having an intrigue with one of the
vestal virgins in the cult of the Sun-goddess, was dismissed,
and took to open-air performances in order to earn a liveli-
hood. One hears, as it were, an echo of the waggon-players
of Thespis, in the village fairs, or the creak of the door that
opened somehow out of the Mysteries and Moralities into the
later Drama of England.

The episodic narrative or comment of the leader of the
Chorus, emphasised by the choral dance and incantation,

---

[1] The cult of this gracious god came from Thrace, where he was worshipped as a
deity of vegetation and giver of earth's increase.

[2] Silenus is the oldest of the satyrs and the leader of them. Though riotous and
prone to wine-bibbing, he is yet filled with wisdom and knowledge. Even Virgil
did not think it out of place to put in his mouth a philosophic discourse on the
origin of the universe and man ("Ecl." vi. 31). Pan, the god of Arcadia, is perhaps
the typical satyr.

[3] The goat was sacred to the god, and was regularly sacrificed to him. Cf. " *Baccho
caper omnibus aris* " (Virg. " Georgics," ii. 380; Hor. " Odes," iii. 8, 6 ; Ovid, "Met."
v. 329). This goat was awarded later to the leader of the victorious chorus. The
derivation of τραγῳδία from τράγος, a he-goat, because that was the prize, has been
departed from in favour of that which takes the name from the goat-like appearance
of the chorus of satyrs. *Vide* Bergk, Donaldson.

would be a very natural origin of the different scenes. I question if it would be much different from the "Callaig" of the Highlands, when the man with the calf's skin in Skye went round the house, followed by shouting peasants, singing the "Callaig" song.[1] Its simplest form would be hymns to Dionysus—hymns of praise, with glad accompaniments of dance and laughter. But, once begun, the peasant mind broke open channels for the peasant mirth ; and the humour of the peasant people, all the world over, is sarcastic. It is wit at the cost of some other person. So, we can imagine, acting some mythical episode in the world-progress of Dionysus and his company, now the peasant players, and now one of their band, would give cry and retort, with grotesque enough gesture and dance ; yet, always, in the heart of the pageant, remained the sacred chant to the genial, pensive, and passionate god, who walked the woods, and blessed their fields with his care.[2]

This hymn, accompanied by dancing around a rude altar, was called the "dithyramb"—a name supposed by some to be derived from one of the many titles of the deity whom it praised,[3] but more probably signifying "the revel of the god." This dithyrambic song was also called the "cyclic chorus," a phrase taken to mean "a hymn sung by a Chorus standing around an altar." But the simplest idea of a

[1] "On the night of Hogmanay, the last night of the year, the carollers go round the township in the dark. One of them is wrapped in a calf-hide, or oftenest a bull's hide, with hoofs and horns attached. They run round the house sunwise ; the others beating the hide with sticks, while the man who carries it shakes the horns and hoofs grotesquely. Then, having repeated runes of the season, they are admitted to the hospitality of the house. The hide is kept through the year, and a part of the ceremonial is to singe the tail and carry it round, that all may smell it for luck. The meaning of the symbolism of this rite is lost, but it is evidently pagan and of remote origin." *Vide* "Carmina Gadelica," by Carmichael, vol. i. 148.

[2] The Dorians celebrated, in the "Revellers' Song," the birth and adventures of Bacchus. Arion the Lesbian changed the peripatetic band of revellers into a cyclic chorus, and so, with regular songs, reached Lyric Tragedy. Now the Ionian rhapsodists were wont to recite their epics at public assemblies ; so, with cyclic chorus and Ionian rhapsody united, it only needed Thespis to stand upon his cart, or anything at all, in the market-place, or elsewhere, and act the epic, to bring thus about the full Drama. *Cf.* Aristotle, "Poetics," iv.

[3] *Cf.* "Bacchæ," 520-30.

jocund song by simple people, peasants or rhapsodists, is connected with joined hands, and a "jingo-ring." I should not be astonished to find that the oldest and holiest things have lingered longest in the hearts of the children of the world, after all. It was accompanied by flutes, and was sung in the Phrygian mode. Out of this dithyrambic, serious, and religious part of the archaic festivals flowed the real stream of Greek Tragic Drama. The rest became the satyric play, celebrating the humours of the forest life, the sport of wine, the frenzies of the desert-possessed; [1] but the dithyrambic song, in which the deeper reasons of Nature-life and Nature-love found throbbing expression, kindled the great questioning spirit of the Tragic poesy of Greece, undoubtedly the noblest, most magnificently impressive creation of the human mind.

Tradition gave to Thespis and his strolling band the credit of the real beginning, when, from a cart in some village fair, he and his fellows, with faces all stained with the lees of wine, gave, in dialogue and chorus rudely framed, representation of some of the conflicts of the genial god, foe to all gloom, and giver of impassioned joy.[2] This mission of Dionysus identified him with the Bacchus myth, as it was found that wine stimulated an elation which had to be simulated before.[3]

---

[1] The orgiastic impulse arose from the cult of Dionysus, a peculiar form of Nature-worship, already referred to, which was imported into Greece from the East by way of Eleutheria, and fused with the rites of the Eleusinian Demeter. See Prof. Lewis Campbell.

"The Scythians reproached the Greeks because of their Bacchic ceremonies, for they say it is not reasonable to discover a god like this who drives men to madness." —Herod. iv. 79.

[2] Herod. i. 23. Arion is here named as the first conductor of a regularly trained Chorus—

"Ἀρίον τὸν Μηθυμναῖον . . . . πρῶτον ἀνθρώπων τῶν ἡμεῖς ποιήσαντα τε καὶ ὀνομάσαντα καὶ διδάξαντα τὸν διθύραμβον ἐν Κορίνθῳ."

Thespis *floruit* B.C. 536. See note on next page.

[3] *Cf.* Archilochus—

"Well can I reel the wild dithyramb
When the giddy wine booms through my brain!"

The development which gradually led to the evolution of a Drama dealing with mythical and national episodes remote from the Dionysian myths, and which finally led into representation and embodiment of thought that was really tragic in the ordinary acceptance of the term, arose, probably, from the love of variety and the kindling power of fancy, combined with the natural ebb of feeling and the reaction of emotion upon emotion.

There is an imaginative plea, undoubtedly, in that strolling band; [1] but the man who set Tragedy, however, in its proper sphere, was Phrynichus, a scholar of Thespis; and he dismissed the satyrs and Bacchus, and took up the events of history as topics of dramatic inquiry. Tragedy henceforward became the voice of Hellas and the struggle of Hellas, set against the background of the purpose, and sometimes the spite of the gods.

Of course the Satyric Chorus was not necessarily comic in the Thespian Drama, as the woodland deities were symbolical; but yet they were doomed to go out into the lighter department of Drama the moment grave dignity and solemn themes were given to the stage. Silenus and the wanton comic band of sylvan oddities were out of keeping with the conflicts of the gods and the godlike. They were more of pantomime than of Hamlet; and so they were relegated to the fourth place, after the trilogy was played, becoming to Attic Drama what the modern farce was to the ordinary play. The separation was usually attributed to

---

[1] Thespis was, without doubt, the founder of Tragedy. This is supported by all authority; but the revellers who went about the country, and ἔσκωπτον ἀλλήλους καὶ ἐλοιδοροῦντο πολλά (Schol. on Lucian, Ζεὺς Τραγῳδός, vi. p. 388), developed into Old Comedy. "The Waggon of Thespis must be shoved back into the lumber-room" (Gruppe, "Ariadne," p. 122).

Thespis acted himself, but Mahaffy holds that he was leader of the chorus, and only delivered a kind of epic recitations between the choric songs ("Greek Literature," vol. i.), while the more usual opinion is that he held a dramatic dialogue with the leaders of the chorus. Bergk ("Greek Literature," ii. 257) thinks the choirmaster delivered the speeches, and then that there was sometimes a dialogue between him and the choir leader. See Hor., "Ars Poetica," 257-58.

Alcman, about the seventh century B.C., composed antistrophic choruses which made a step towards dialogue, in effect, while Stesichorus added the epode.

Æschylus, and he further made a real p,ay possible by introducing a second actor, thus reserving the dialogue for the stage, and making the Chorus merely commentator and interpreter. He also it was that set up a background to the stage, with its three doors of entrance, and with the possibility of a later development of scenery. He, too, was the inventor of the Tragic style, a diction rich and heavy, which became the standard for subsequent writers until Euripides shook off its yoke.

The next great changes were when Sophocles brought in a third actor, still further separating the Chorus from the action of the play, and began to write dramas which hung around one individual interest, independent of trilogy sequences.

The closing step in Euripides [1] was the introduction of the prologue to explain the play, and the *deus ex machina* [2] to arbitrarily extricate the characters from insuperably difficult situations; while he clothed the Drama in a new speech, with the methods of the Schools of Dialectic which were so strong in Athens in his time, and with many archaic words and phrases, like stage echoes of the ancient days, at the same time separating the Chorus altogether from the action, making their work purely musical, lyrical interludes.

Of course, the Thespian myth probably arose quite naturally from the necessity which impelled the Greeks to account for things, to find origins and causes for existing institutions. It proved nothing more than that the Drama owed something, at least, to Thespis and his band. It is not asserted by Aristotle, but is found in a reference in the pseudo-Platonic Minos, later than Aristotle's time; while the

---

[1] The unconventional methods of Euripides arose, like those of the Jacobean Dramatists, from the demands of the people for novelty of situation rather than illusions of poesy, as much as from the poet's own point of view.

[2] Sometimes the *deus ex machina* is required, in order, as in the "Bacchæ," to justify himself and "lift himself above conflicts and adventures which might have lowered him in the minds of the spectators, rather than merely to get his people out of difficulties. *Cf.* Tyrrell.

existence of dialogue even before Thespis is referred to by the grammarian Pollux.

One result of the development from choral lyric and dance to dialogue was the use of the iambus,[1] because the dialogue became less of song, and nearer the ordinary speech of life. Undoubtedly the iambus was meant to be a compromise between ordinary conversation and the solemn religious chant. The frequency of the ictus gave a stately emphasis, and has always, everywhere, caught the listening ear by its charm. Some words also became exclusively dramatic in usage. This employment of a select vocabulary, making a standard like our Bible English, intensified and elevated the play. The sorrow that speaks in the iambic wave-beat utterance is no trivial pain. As time went on, the iambic verse became more fluid and passionate; fewer set speeches, and more cut-and-thrust of utterance came into vogue; until Euripides made it a vehicle of passion, while, at the same time, his influence tended to lower this apartness of tone, which was one of the marks of those priestlike poets who had preceded him.

It is thus evident that the ancient Drama was the unifying point of meeting of chant and incantation, lyric and dance, epic tale and sculpturesque art, of rhetoric and religion.

[1] The iambus was first used to any extent in the satirical verse of Archilochus and Hipponax, and then in Attic Drama. *Cf.* Hor., " Ars Poetica," 79—

" Archilochum proprio rabies armavit iambo."

The word is derived from *ἰάπτω*=to fling, from its whip-like throw in satire. *Cf.* Catullus (36, 5), " truces vibrare iambos."

CHAPTER III

THE CHORUS

THE poet is always the voice of his age. He gives in song what his age has given him in sorrow or gladness. And yet, while he is the voice of his age, he has tones which the age does not give him—which, indeed, the age does not sometimes recognise. His message, besides, is not a phonographic reproduction of the age's voice and clamour, but is an expression of interpretations, with now warning and anon encouragement, which the age very frequently finds quite beyond its grasp. The ordinary mind saw only, beyond doubt, broken ships and pride dishonoured in Salamis and the Armada; but the soul of the poet heard whispers of doom and judgment, and saw gaunt shadows on the tide, so that the voice and message of his age, for him, meant history, and the meaning of history, the eternal things in passing events, the philosophy of gods among men.

The mind of the Greek was not shadow-haunted, any more than the mind of the Elizabethan Englishman; yet the circumstances and the outlook of their times gave to them both a pensive tendency.[1] The laughter of the fields and woods, the song of streams, and the charm of shepherd life in Arcadia, were all very well; but, to face a struggle for existence against powerful foes, to wade knee-deep, and often heart-deep, through State complications and home-rule jealousies, made you frequently look over your shoulder as you pushed ahead. It begets a pensive habit. It teaches

[1] See " The Melancholy of the Greeks " in Professor Butcher's " Some Aspects of the Greek Genius."

your heart to remember, to anticipate, and to desire. The essence of the tragic in human life lies as we have seen, in the struggle of Freedom against Fate—Freewill against unbending Destiny. Yet all tragedies are not wrapt in inpenetrable gloom, though shadows brood above them.

Undoubtedly, of course, a greater tragic melancholy lay above the heathen outlook than above the later Christian. Wherever you moved, over the laughing water or on the sunny land, at home or in the fields of fight, that shadow, which gave back no answer, moved beside you, and the rest was silence. The surly ferryman, with veiled face, received you with no greeting, and the shore ahead was horrid with wailing shades. Hence the poet, who, in this background, set the conflicts of heroes, gods, and men, was sure of a sympathetic multitude reading his interpretation into their own. Here was something intensely human, yet superhuman. Here was a meaning given to what was beyond all meaning, a light cast over what must for ever remain dark beyond all penetration. Thus, the poet of Tragedy produces an ecstasy. He draws men out of themselves [1]—lifts their souls up to the applauding lip and the tearful eye, which are his certificates of success. So, vindicating the loftiness of his calling as a prophetic criticism and interpretation of life, the utterance of his creation must move along in loftier majestic cadence than the huckster's cry or the utterance of the streets; and the lyrical comment of some ideal spectator may well intervene to give spaces when the pent-up feeling of actor and of audience must have relief and rest. This was the function of the Chorus—one of the most remarkable adjuncts of any literary creation.

Its origin is absolutely lost in mystery, and can only be guessed at.[2]   Its dithyrambic rapture and rhapsody, with the

---

[1] This escape from self is, after all, the secret of the Bacchic orgies—the falling out of to-day into something fresh and strange—into an imaginary world.

[2] In Tragedy the Chorus was retained until the end.   In Comedy it was little used after B.C. 400.

mystic dance weaving its captivating dreamy mazes around the Thymele, were a survival of religious symbolisms. Its sacred origin preserved for it its place until the end—was, in very truth, the real secret of its continued existence and popularity. The dialect of the Chorus which persisted was Doric—but a conventional Doric, and not the living patois ; just as the Coptic prayers are embalmed in a tongue the very meaning of which is sealed even for the priests who read the liturgy.

The Chorus rejoiced in the triumph of good ; it wailed aloud its grief, and sympathised with the woe of the puppets of the gods. It entered deeply into the interest of their fortunes and misfortunes, yet it stood apart, outside of triumph and of failure. Only very seldom does it, as in the "Eumenides," come forward with individual remarkable effect.[1] No gladness dragged it into the actual action on the stage, and no catastrophe overwhelmed it, except in storm of sympathetic pain. It was the ideal spectator, the soul being purged, as Aristotle expressed it, by Pity and Fear, flinging its song and its cry among the passions and the pain of others. It was the " Vox Humana" amid the storm and thunder of the gods.

In the Elizabethan Drama the feelings of the crowd are represented by nameless individuals, such as "First Gentleman," or "First Lord," and so forth, expressing emotions and opinions similar to those of which the Chorus of the Greeks was mouthpiece.

The Chorus showed its origin, partly, also, by dressing like the chief actor.[2] When that was a woman, the Chorus were women, except in the "Antigone," where splendid isolation sets the trials of the Protagonist against the background of a stupendous grief.

The Chorus has been censured as an absurdity, inasmuch as, representing a crowd, it shows a secret transaction of the

[1] *Cf.*, however, the close of "Agamemnon," and "Hercules Furens."
[2] The success of a play hung largely upon the successful get-up of the Chorus.

soul being carried on before the public—an objection which, of course, might be applied to the condemnation of the whole Tragic Drama, whereby the inmost agonies of contending souls are laid bare to crowded benches. The Tragic Chorus represented with wonderful truth the Greek inquisitive crowd, and was essentially Athenian in conduct and in spirit.[1] Indeed, it was more—it was intensely human!

I question if the assertion that the chief motive of ancient Tragedy was the warning spectacle of retribution following upon some exaggeration of self is even a half truth. We humanly love to see into the lives of others, and, in a tragedy, we are not like indifferent spectators lounging on a balcony. We enter into the sorrows and the pathos all through the action; and the Drama would be more than half a failure if it only sent the onlooker away with the verdict, "Serve him right!"

The Greek Tragedy was the child direct of the Greek Epic. It made the story stand out in a sort of bas-relief. It lifted the curtain of the gods, showed the hidden cords which moved events, revealed the progress of the invisible, and always with a bias on the side of good. Hence, exhibiting on the stage the nobility of heroic endurance and courage, or the awful accumulations of difficulties and despairs which dog the trail of sin, the Tragic Drama became a school of conduct for all the State and for all classes. In Athens, under the shelter of religion, it was untrammelled and unrestrained, and it created a public morality so pure and lofty that its own morality was braced by the very atmosphere itself had made. The Greek Tragic stage was the secondary school of applied ethics, the platform of history's vindication.

Plato, though his soul moved in an atmosphere of highest poetry, felt somewhat afraid of this soul-shaking art; and, very remarkably, proposed to exclude dramatic poets from

[1] See Schlegel's "Lectures on the Drama."

his ideal Republic, on the ground that they tended to develop sentiment at the cost of the practical side of the soul. But this is, indeed, a narrow view. The Drama is the most practical of all the poetic utterance. It is the creation of the practical Reason, and it issues in a practical life; for the sympathy with the passions, trials, conflicts, and wrongs represented on the stage, awakens mutual sympathy in the audience, and kindles humanity in the heart. Aristotle, who, in his philosophy, set before him as his quest the understanding of human nature rather than the transformation of human life, in replying to Plato's charge, defines Tragedy as "an imitation of a serious and complete action, which has magnitude . . . and it uses the agency of pity and fear to effect a purging of these, and the like emotions."[1] The soul is purified by the power of pathos, and is ennobled in the purifying. It learns to pity others; and, taking self-pity, it diverts it outwards to the pangs of the world around, which is also under trial by the gods. At the same time, the vision of things makes us go warily, remembering our humanity. This "katharsis" steadies the circulation of the passionate constitution, gives us patience with our own lot, and sympathy with the lot of others, helping us at the same time to see life clearly, and to understand it as a whole.

[1] See Prof. Butcher's "Poetics of Aristotle," *in loc.*

CHAPTER IV

DRAMATIC CONVENTIONS

Naturally and obviously, an institution like the Drama, which was an evolution from a remote religious origin, must carry with it certain elemental components which should resist all change. The agonising souls whose conflicts were embodied on the stage, with the struggle of their lives, were more important, by far, than their environment. Certain conventions, therefore, remained throughout all the unfoldings and developments of the Drama.

The first important convention of the Greek dramatic art was the fact that the source of the story was prescribed by religious tradition. Homer was the source of all the figures.[1] The myths of the passions of the gods, and of the great legendary houses of the heroes formed the material. The stories were, in general outline, familiar to the vast multitude that filled the theatre; but this never palled on either dramatist or beholder, for the fact rather drew forth the higher imaginations of both, and strenuously served the purpose of Tragedy, by showing how even the loftiest greatness could not escape the blessing or the wrath of heaven.

In the eye of the Tragic poet a man is never free from the pursuit of the gods, and he knows not what lurking, invisible

[1] "Homer, than dramatists more dramatic, was founder of the theatre, and peopled the stage. The Greek Tragedy is Epic re-cast, the narrative being broken into dialogue, and the poet disappearing in the chorus."—Willmott, "Pleasures of Literature."

The Homeric cycle, however, does not mean the "Iliad" and "Odyssey," which may not have been popular in Attica at this time, but was the vast library of poems and legends inferior in quality but living in intensity of interest, dealing with the adventures of the Trojan heroes and their hosts. See Paley's "Euripides."

curse besides. The gods, amidst and above all chances, are absolutely sure. The curse seems hard perhaps, and a man seems involved in inexplicable, inevitable destiny; nevertheless, it is his own proud hand, smiting the impious blow, which, in that fatal moment, firmly and finally rivets the chain of doom upon his life.[1] It is the voluntary, insatiable inquisitiveness of Œdipus, for example, that drags him to the revelation of what heaven has mercifully been hiding. Pride blinds him, then, against the recognition of the terrible truth that peeps from behind the veil; for the worst he can think of is humble birth, and obscurity of origin, which have been surmounted and overcome by his own ingenuity. Suspicion next begins to circumscribe his outlook. He imagines he sees enemies lurking everywhere, and so he finally discovers them, just where he fancied them to be.

The Tragic truth largely is that Character and Fate are one—

<blockquote>
"Our acts our angels are, or good or ill;
Our fatal shadows that walk by us still."
</blockquote>

In Sophocles, Fate remains only to signify that element of Cause inexplicable and unexaminable, beyond the pale of human control.[2] This is found also in the Elizabethans. Neither Hamlet nor Orestes, Macbeth nor Œdipus could extricate their conduct and life from predisposing, predestinating antecedents, nor from existing environment utterly beyond their mastering control. The test of the Tragic artist is indeed most highly met, when, recognising these circumstances, he makes Tragic action flow naturally from environment and character, not harshly contradicting human impulses and purpose, nor suffering either artifice or novelty to weaken or destroy the great ends of art. What

---

[1] After Hesiod, who spoke as the mouthpiece of his country's gods, a wave of revival stirred religious ideas among the Greeks, and awoke the questioning sense of sin, under the influence of which the Tragic poets became really prophetic preachers. See Barnett, "Greek Drama."

[2] His gods carry out their inexorable purpose by what seem to be merest accidents, and the pathos of the Tragedy is intensified by the sight of the blind creatures, of their own will stepping on the skirts of Doom.

must life mean to us, when we see how even the greatest have been tossed and torn by angry, malignant, and unswerving destinies, revealing the vengeance of the stars against human pride, the jealousies of Olympus against the godlike in mankind? Even the purple cannot hide a broken heart, a soul in pain, or protect a kingly spirit from deepest suffering and trial.

This convention of the myths is not so remarkable as at first sight appears. To Christians in worship, the whole familiar phrase and episode of Holy Scripture never become stale. The great ethical problems and qualities which they illustrate are for ever hung upon them, interestingly, thrillingly, and with purpose above the commonplace. Further, of course, the myths did not survive in one fixed stereotype. They had passed through the crucible of Pindar, Stesichorus, and others; the influences of hosts unknown, lost to our day, had played upon them. Details, consequently, often differed, just as in the Macbeth legend, where, in one version, it is told that the ambitious king did not perish at Dunsinane, nor even by the hands of Macduff. He retired to Lumphanan, to try the last throw with Destiny, and rode forth from his fort there, to precipitate the final test. Mortally wounded, he was borne by his charger away into the mountains, and no man saw him die. His cairn still stands where they found him dead. Opened some hundred years since, it held a few handfuls of mould, some feather-quills, and some rusted bits of iron! So, too, in the common version of Lear's sad fate, Cordelia survives and triumphs, whereas Geoffrey of Monmouth makes her hang herself. Shakespeare took the version which fitted best his own conception of the Tragic stage. The artist was greater than his subject. In the Attic Tragedians also, we find, as for example in their treatment of Iphigeneia and Orestes, each man's artistic idiosyncrasy suiting itself. Further, the streams of national and international legend are fed, often, at most, from one or two widely-separated wells ; and frequently the same motive, with the same tragic issues, and very frequently the same dramatic artifices, are found attached to a multitude of different names, in widely varying circumstances, literatures, and lands. Gipsy folk-lore and Gaelic tales, told by peat-fires in far Hebridean hovels, use material for their development identical with Homeric and Euripidean schemes, though never a word of either had come across the distant seas to set such fruit agrowing in soils so widely sundered.

It was not considered legitimate for the dramatist to use historic material of recent or contemporary date, as the function of the stage was first religious, and then national, in a big sense. Yet there are, no doubt, contemporary references in some of the Tragedies.[1] Æschylus certainly refers to Aristides, to the discussion of the fate of the walls of Athens, to the alliances with Argos and Egypt, and the questions of the time affecting the privileges of the Areopagus. Euripides seems often to make a shadow of some contemporary walk across the stage, if not to show himself how others see him, at least to make others see more plainly than they do what he is really like. But the tragic tide and passion of the play lift it quite out of the level of things like these.

Nearness, of course, does not give the possibility of a good perspective, or indeed any certainty of proportion. The experience of Phrynichus, who represented to the Athenians a tragedy based upon the disasters of Miletus, is familiar to us all.[2] So deeply did he pain his audience that his reward was a heavy fine, perhaps the strongest compliment to the truth of his conception which he could have received. He profited from his lesson, and laid in the Persian kingdom the scene of his " Phœnician Women,"

---

[1] The tragic agony of Œdipus may have been intensified by the thought of Pericles, that supreme ruler of the State, belonging to the family of the curse, whose children were decerned to be illegitimate by the very law himself had framed— whose glory was eclipsed in its meridian height, and who died a victim of the plague. *Vide* Herod. vi. 131 ; Plutarch's "Lives."

[2] Herod. vi. 21.

which dealt with the defeat of the Persians. The composition of the Chorus was what gave its name to the play, but even then he risked the reward of the innovator, the bitterness of which he had already tasted. Æschylus, also, ventured something in his "Persians," but he evaded disaster by laying the scene in Susa, and evoking the spirit of Darius himself to testify to the glory and courage of Greece.[1] Besides, of course, the play celebrated the immortal triumph of Salamis, only eight years before, and touched upon a question which was before the people, namely, the proposal by the Persians for a final peace, upon most humbling conditions. It had its basis, too, in the teaching of the evils of obstinate pride and the invincible potency of national and individual integrity. The remote scene of the play, and the presence of the supernatural met the demand of stage convention.

This, of course, is quite appreciable. A contemporary play, for example, on the Scottish Church Case, or Chamberlain's Protection Policy, would be at the moment not only questionable taste, but would rouse party passions, and utterly thwart the purpose of the Drama—would, in fact, be journalism rather than literature. I fancy it would take a hundred years before Gladstone or Beaconsfield could with propriety be brought upon the stage. Age, like distance, ennobles and abstracts. Antiquity colossifies Tragic virtues and vices alike, removing the hero from the familiar contact with his period,[2] and preventing the Drama from being merely a reporter's interview with a celebrity. The crimes, sorrows, and soul-disasters of the heroic age can hurt no one's feelings, and of course, in those distant periods of history, great tragic shiftings of Fate's chessmen must have been not uncommon. The power of a great kingly

---

[1] Æschylus was, however, a poet of the heroic ages. He aims at giving weight to his characters, judging that this peculiarity, the magnificent and heroic, was of the antique stamp. Hence he is ridiculed by Aristophanes for the excessive heaviness of his characters, ("Frogs," 911.)

[2] A man, after death, *may* become a hero to his valet!

" sorrow's crown of sorrows " moves the soul to sympathetic tears. Littleness is lost in the general survey, and even a character which had rugged and debatable points, becomes mellowed by the years through which it is looked at, as the gloaming in the hills clothes squalid huts and ruined bothies with imaginative charm. Thus, take the feelings with which the soul thinks of Jerusalem or Damascus afar. These become ideal cities, casquets of poetic memories, chivalry and emotions most divine, which, near and moved among, in closest contact, are places of mean streets and evil odours. So, too, Thebes, with its ruined gods, maimed, knee-deep in the marshes, is greater to the soul, in poem, epic, or play, than with its temples all complete, and filled with worshipping priests. The heroic myth soon deeply encrusts a leader's name with awe and romantic interest. Cromwell, Kentigern, Wallace, the Cid, Orlando, Alexander —how their warts are forgotten, their lusts and passions modified, and only the great power of them on the ages keeps moving the dreams and emotions of men! How Wallace became almost a mythical demigod, to his own people, can be seen by a perusal of Blind Harry's romantic history. These great leaders became pre-eminently Tragic subjects; for men saw how they had been tried by judgments, strifes, and agonisings, through which they tore ways wide for social and religious freedom, and dragged the remote ends of the world nearer to the knowledge and use of men. Think what that means for us, the lesser creepers, nearer the dust, in the trials that make us cry aloud.

So, in the Drama of Elizabeth's age, we find the poets wisest in their art, cunningly following similar traditions. The terrible judgments of God and man on blood-guilty ambition find their best illustration in the passion-driven king and queen, in a far-off age, only remembered in the haze of a Scottish tradition. The contemporary, tempest-clouded, staggering politics find their moral and their meaning wonderfully reflected in the Court of Elsinore; and the love-sorrows of all time are moved and comforted, even in their awakened tears, over poor Ophelia, all distraught, with faded garlands, dead in the woodland stream; while Marlowe's "mighty line" thunders the very anger of the gods on the intellectual pride which blinds those whom it enslaves, hiding from them the downward path to hell that yawns before their feet.

And not only were the figures of the Tragic stage conventional, but they were clothed in conventional attributes.[1] Agamemnon, as he entered, brought with him at once heroic greatness, marred by personal, imperious ambitions, dragging doom with them. Cassandra's ravings of truth unheeded warned the ear and heart to listen and to wait. The ghostly name was hung above the teaching voice, and the nation recognised, looked around, and then, looking within, began to learn.

The myth explained either the phenomena of Nature, as in the beautiful story of the young Adonis, or the origin of historical and national customs, or was a reconciling medium between the highest moral code and the discrepancies in daily life, or in the Sagas of the gods. So, gradually, there evolved from the stories of the intrigues of Zeus a higher conception of the king of the Olympian crowd.

The dramatic use of the myth also touched the nation's pride. Every city had its founder, whose name and story lifted it into contact with the gods. Thus the Argives' retrospect touched their hearts with pride, in recalling Perseus, the offspring of the golden shower of Jove, and reminding them how he journeyed to the land of the gloaming, and slew the gorgon. Laius and Œdipus also

---

[1] Sometimes the poet, by his genius, illuminated the dark and sombre depths of some gloomy legend. Both in ancient Drama and in Elizabethan Tragedy we see how the poets had a repertoire of great antiquity, with certain remarkable similarities—as, for example, the legends of Œdipus and Macbeth, of Orestes and Hamlet, of the sons of Œdipus and the daughters of Lear, all tinged by the spirit of the age and the individual point of view of the poet.

told of the great past of Thebes. Through the myth, Athens, and institutions like the Areopagus, which were its pride, with all the tribes and clans of Greece, were lifted into nobleness.

The titled sorrows on the stage moved the people deeply. The trials of our equals do not always impress us so much as the agonising soul-conflicts and despairs of kings and queens. The simple mind likes to look in at windows of palaces, and into the hearts of monarchs and of nobles.[1] The factory girl does not understand the halo of a tale of simple life, but loves to read the hysteria of romance of dukes and countesses in the " family novelette." Œdipus, Agamemnon and the rest of the great national sculpture-gallery of the poets' creating were immense, to the mind of the multitude. And, lo! the sorrows that were theirs— the shadows that stalked behind even such as they! The Greek literary mind, besides, was essentially retrospective, following clues away back through the days of yore, beginning always from the group of human pathetic statuary on the stage.

The idea of action itself in the Attic theatre was unique. It was rather " action in suspension." The stage was not the place for action so much as for explanation and commentary. Hence Agamemnon, Cassandra, and the rest are slain behind the scenes.[2] The awfulness of the hidden transaction of horror is intensified by the cries from within, and by the helplessness of those without ; and then the scene falls apart, and the poor slain victims are beheld, fresh from the baleful slaughter. Undoubtedly, in many cases this deepens the tragic emotion. I remember thinking so especially in a play where a Christian slave was lashed upon the stage.

---

[1] " The Drama is the manifestation of the invisible mind of man,—the mirror in which, while we think we are looking at others, we unexpectedly see ourselves reflected "—PALEY.

[2] Such horrors as the putting out of Gloucester's eyes in "King Lear," or the murder of Banquo in " Macbeth," would have been done off the stage. Evidently, however, Ajax and Alcestis die *coram populo.*

Had we heard the lash, and the scream of agonised terror, as it fell, from some place off the stage, I question if we could have borne it without swooning or crying aloud. On the stage it was impossible to be illusioned. Thus, the hellish terribleness of the crime in "Macbeth" is made immeasurably more a red-hot burden upon us by the washing of the hands so late imbrued in Duncan's blood, and by the soul-chilling, pulse-arresting knocking at the gate, than if we saw the dagger driven home into the sleeper's heart.

The result of the Greek conception was that a scene was like a vast sculpture of a passion. The dramatist flung his creation against the stage, with the greatness of some group in marble, teaching the lessons of the ancient ages, whose shadows had meaning of their own alongside the glories of the Attic people. The crowd hung hushed, upon the sufferings of an idealised life, charged with the magnificent hugeness of ethical crises, far remote from common experience.

Another somewhat remarkable circumstance of the Attic stage arose from the religious origin of the Drama. It was a national, democratic institution. The theatre must be so large as to be able to accommodate every citizen who cared to come.[1] Hence, imagine an edifice fit to hold, say thirty thousand people, and at once it will be seen how impossible it was to express in features, or in voice, soul agonies or imperial passions. The actor must be so far away from his audience that by-play of lip or eye would be quite impossible. The features themselves, indeed, must appear indistinct. In order to somewhat overcome this difficulty two conventions arose in Attic Tragedy, namely, the cothurnus and the mask—the former a kind of clog which lifted the actor to a more heroic stature, and the latter a boldly painted and carved representation of the feature

[1] By a law of Pericles, the cost of the admission to the theatre was provided by the State to the poorest of the citizens

of the character typified.[1] In this latter, also, a megaphonic arrangement was used, whereby the words of the play were made to resound throughout the vast auditorium. Any striking discrepancy or oddness of appearance arising from these methods was avoided by the use of the actor's flowing robes. Great skill was expended on the preparation of these masks, and the mind of the spectator did not feel disturbed by the knowledge that they were used. Of course, any convention whatever, though it may seem remarkable to another age or people, may seem the most natural thing in the world—nay, indeed, the most necessary, to the age that has agreed to look upon it as a regular thing.

On the narrow Attic stage the groups were practically the representation of a passion, the pathetic moment suspended as if in bas-relief. It was enough for the Greek if the Tragic artist displayed the momentous impressiveness of the situation, as it were, in perfect sculpture; and if the great, deep, dreadful, tragic burden of the passion whose moment was portrayed, was revealed, and insisted upon, in all its inevitable consequences.

[1] " Undoubtedly invented by Thespis to enable the reciter to assume different parts. On the Roman stage the mask was first used (according to Donatus) by Minucius Prothymus about B.C. 120 to 100. This distinction was also claimed for Roscius. The spectators were, however, nearer the actors in Rome, and the mask was disliked."—WILKINS.

CHAPTER V

THE THEATRE

THE theatre in Greece was at first simply the open market-place; but after the year 500 B.C. the great theatre of Dionysus was built over the place of the winepress or Lenæon. The upper seats were hewn out of the rock, so that the effect would be pretty much like a Highland Communion in Scotland, where the people sit around the side of a hollow place in which, often, Nature has been helped, and the slopes been made more suitable for rows of sitters. The analogy is, indeed, closer than is apparent, for the Greek theatre was really a place with worship associations looming like ghosts behind it, and Tragedy was a sacred thing. The maintenance of the theatre was a burden on the citizenship, and a duty which the leading men of a State were proud to perform, as the Greek stage was a phase of life which had become nationalised. Every member of the State was liable for the upkeep of the Chorus, either by singing in it or by paying for it.[1] Nor was this accounted a hardship, but an honour; the same feeling, doubtless, which in our later Elizabethan England prompted leading generous nobles, like Leicester, to support with their patron-age companies of stage players. The new tragedies were produced at the Greater Dionysia;[2] and citizens chosen out of the ten Attic tribes paid for the Chorus, sometimes as

[1] All persons possessing property which exceeded in value three talents (about £732), subscribed for the maintenance of the Drama. He who provided a Chorus was called the *choregus*, and the Chorus was usually trained by the poet himself. The public duty was called a *litourgia*, which was the origin of *liturgy*.

[2] Founded by Pisistratus as national festival of Greece, latter half of sixth century, B.C.

28

much as one hundred and twenty pounds. It was this pride
of State service which impelled the Athenian first to create
the Drama, and then to make it a complete work of art. It
was like a rainbow above Attica. All over the glory of her
best life it shone, rising from the deep, as her history rose
out of the fight and the victory of the Athenians, and
sinking when the power of Athens sank in defeat upon the
waves; for, when the curtain fell on the glory of Attica,
the stage itself lay dark and silent.

The scenery was of the very simplest description. The
real "scene" was the high wall at the back. In Tragedy
this represented a temple; in Comedy it was a street. The
theatre itself usually occupied a beautiful position. The
plays, which were customarily three tragedies and one
satyric play, were performed in the daytime. The theatre
was not roofed over, nor did exigencies of climate demand
such a necessity. If a storm broke, the players waited and
began again. This was in conformity with the open-air life
of the Greek State. Nothing would have been more absurd
than to enclose the struggle of typical national heroic
characters in a room. Even the secret conflicts of souls
should be visible to all Olympus at any rate. Indeed, this
open-air scenic surrounding was, if anything, an aid to
dramatic illusion. It was not majestic, nor in accordance
with the spirit of the Ionian Sea, and surge and drift of
the life of Hellas, to think of the development of the heroic
in a roofed-in place, no matter how gorgeous or how
vast.

Immense though the theatre was in the Greek Drama, the
stage had the whole breadth of it, but depth of platform
was not demanded, as the actors were not many, at most,
three. The chief actor—sometimes the only one—spoke
from the middle. The vistas of remote scenery lay naturally
at the sides of the conventional wall with its three doors,
the central for the chief, the sides for the secondary figure.
On the left lay the town and the sea, on the right the rural

districts;[1] and, naturally, the beholders were thus enabled at once to guess whence the actor came, what kind of tidings he carried, and on which side he might be. There was no painted scenery, as we call it, but a few conventional articles of dramatic environment told the tale. Thus, some rocks gave suggestion enough of Caucasus; just as, in the Elizabethan theatre, a table or a chair was enough to signify a council-chamber; or even a blank stage with " Bohemia " written on a card was quite sufficient. The concomitant costumes were according to convention, allegorically significant rather than historically correct; as when, in "Hamlet," a simple sheet was quite sufficient to enclose the haunting secret of the Court of Elsinore. The mechanical and artificial subsidiaries were few. Chief among these was the apparatus for the suspension of the god, so often called into practice by Euripides, the earliest use of it being in Æsthylus, when, in the " Prometheus Bound " Oceanus comes through the air with sea-nymphs to sympathise with the tormented deity. The English stage was not above similar devices, as we can see from the stage directions in Greene's " Alphonsus, King of Arragon," where we read

" [*After you have sounded thrice let Venus be let down from the top of the stage.*"

So at the last exit the direction also is—

" [*Exit Venus, or if you can conveniently, let a chair come down from the top of the stage, and draw her up.*"

There also were the " Charonic," or stair by which the spirits of the dead returned ; the " Exostra," or representation of the interior of a house ; and, in front of the stage, the "Thymele " or altar, the lingering residuary symbol of the ancient worship-associations of the Drama.

The Elizabethan stage had, in its beginnings, just as simple an environment as that which satisfied the earliest

---

[1] That the Attic stage commanded a real view of the sea, *cf.* Aristophanes, "Equites," 170; Æschylus, " Suppl.," 693. See Haigh's " Attic Theatre."

Thespian band. Wherever a place was found suitable for representations, the players sat down and set imagination free. The old inn yards were especially adaptable for such a purpose. The inns were built around a court, along the sides of which hung galleries for access to rooms. A rough stage, built up against one side of the yard, became, at the will of the players, a street in Venice, or a field of valiant battle. Tamburlaine thundered over the creaking boards, or the Jew cringed and sneered, or kings and warriors made history stalk before the listeners' hearts. The gallery at hand became a castle or a balcony, or the battlement of heaven itself. At the third blast of a trumpet the curtain was drawn aside, and fancy clothed the scene. Holidays and Sunday afternoons were the players' opportunities, and the kingdom of Make-believe swayed the hearts of the fashionable onlookers on the upper floors, and won or lost the sympathy of the common crowd standing on the cobbled stones of the court. These circumstances of origin determined the arrangements of the theatres when they were built, and they are found still in the playhouse of to-day. In fact nothing better could be devised. The galleries, the private boxes and the pit simply take us back to the old inn yards, where the ladies and gentlemen, the rough apprentices and their sweethearts had their fancy kindled and their hearts moved by the great names whose fury, love, or sorrow fretted or wailed, stormed or prayed before them on a holiday afternoon. The same open-air playing as with the Greeks, and the acting all over before the dark, with the appeal rather to imagination than to sight, ruled the English stage, likewise, in its beginnings.

The reason for utilising Sunday and saints' days for dramatic representations was not far to seek. The plays were acted during the day, and consequently there were many whose only opportunity of seeing the Drama at all was on the Sunday between services, and on the other "holy days," which so soon became "holidays." The Reformation,

however, deepened the sense of religion in the land, and
made its votaries, especially the Puritans, insist on the duty
of absolute holy rest on the Sabbath, and of devotion during
that day to the study of the Scriptures and religious exercises. But the trumpet-call of the players brought a readier
crowd together than the bells of the preacher could gather.
And when, in Paris, on Sunday, 13th January 1583, the
galleries gave way, grievously crushing many and killing a
few, it was looked upon as a direct judgment of most high
Heaven. With this as an incontrovertible argument, the
Lord Mayor of London succeeded in having stage-plays forbidden absolutely on the Sabbath Day.

The Puritans, of course, vigorously and incessantly opposed
the players; and indeed most of the contemporary portraiture
of the theatre and the tragedians must in fairness be read
as lighted and guided by the estimate of bigotry and narrow
zeal, rather than truth or charity. The fear lest the plague
should be spread through this contact of the crowds, the
disturbance of the sanctity of the Sabbath and holy days,
the risk to the balance of morality through the promiscuous
concourse gathered to the inns, the chances of sedition being
promulgated among the people, and countless other objec-
tions, were detailed against the struggling Drama and its
exponents. Indeed, the City Corporation of London in
1575 argued that, as the weekly death-rate, without the
plague, was forty or fifty, there was sufficient ground to
forbid what brought so many people together from all
places.

Stage-plays were interdicted in London City as ungodly;
and the authorities tried hard to have their prohibition
applied to all places near the City. Naturally the Queen's
Players, struggling for their life, and supported in their fight
by the active help of the Earl of Leicester, and others intensely interested in the Drama, appealed to the Privy
Council; and in 1576 the City desired that these alone be
licensed, and that the names and numbers of them be

registered; while plays should only be acted in private houses, or, if in any other place, only on condition that the death-rate had not exceeded forty in the twenty days preceding the representation. Driven, by this opposition, to parts of London outside the domination of the Common Council, the players got James Burbage in 1576 to buy a site for "The Theatre." The same year a second theatre, known as "The Curtain," was built, also beyond the walls. The name of this James Burbage is in the list of Leicester's players in the patent of May 1574, licensing them to act in any part of the kingdom.

In 1583 Elizabeth appointed twelve players, selected from different companies, to be her own party, and to be called "The Queen's Players." In this she was simply using the custom of her lieges among the nobility, notably the Earl of Leicester, under whose patronage were companies of players who called themselves by their patrons' names. This, again, in itself was a survival of a habit as old as the time of the Miracle and Morality, when great lords kept servants to provide themselves with amusement. The Records of the Priory of Bicester in 1431 have a note of the visits of minstrels serving various lords; while, in other records before 1461, these entertainers are called Mimes and Players.

Mary, herself, had spent as much as two or three thousand pounds yearly on her theatrical and musical companies, though she had devoted her attention also to the encouragement of Miracle Plays, rigorously repressing, however, all such as reflected on the Romish Church.

The charge, so often brought against the Elizabethan players, of breaking Sabbaths, and disturbing holy days, was no new thing, but had frequently been the fortune of their predecessors.

That the Drama was popular is plainly seen from complaints by churchmen against it. Thus, one, writing in 1556, probably with a touch of exaggeration, says: "Woe

is me !—The playhouses are pestered, when Churches are
naked. At the one it is not possible to gett a place; at the
other, voyde seats are plentye . . . It is a woeful sight to
see two hundred proude players jett in their silkes, where
five hundred poore people sterve in the streets."

The play usually began at three o'clock. The theatre
even in Shakespeare's time was a poor building, circular, or
hexagonal, of wood, open to the heavens, except for the
stage. A signal flag was conspicuously displayed; and, on
the third flourish of trumpets, the performance started. At
the end of each representation a clown recited a jingling
composition called a jig, usually with topical allusions, as a
sort of Satyric survival. The nobles and ladies had seats in
boxes, or sat on stools on the stage, while the rabble stood
in the pit, or yard, as it was called. The stage was a bare
chamber, rush-strewn. "Imagination's artful aid" alone
clothed its nakedness to the beholder, so that now the castle,
now the arena of knightly conflict, now my Lady's bower,
and now the forest of Arden, became the scene of the
passion and pleading of the playwright's creations.

> " The air-blest castle, round whose wholesome crest
> The martlet, guest of Summer, chose her nest;
> The forest-walks of Arden's fair domain,
> Where Jaques fed his solitary vein,
> No pencil's aid as yet had dared supply—
> Seen only by the intellectual eye."

As with the Greeks, the female parts were played by
boys. It was in the little theatre of Vere Street that the
first actress is believed to have come upon the stage, on
Saturday, 8th December 1660. Her name is not known,
but she played Desdemona.[1] In the Prologue, written by
Thomas Jordan, occur the following lines :—

[1] The first who was known was Mrs Saunderson, who, at the opening of Davenant's
new theatre in Lincoln's Inn Fields played Jane, in the "Siege of Rhodes." Probably
the innovation was demanded because the boys who had acted female parts had, during
the Puritan times, grown up to manhood.

" Do you not twitter, gentlemen ? I know
   You will be censuring ; do it fairly though:
   'Tis possible a virtuous woman may
   Abhor all sort of looseness, and yet play :
   Play on the stage—where all eyes are upon her :
   Shall we count that a crime, France counts an honour ? "

Coryat, in 1608, had wondered to see women acting in
Venice, and says that he had heard " it hath been sometimes
used in London," a statement of which there seems, however,
to be no recorded corroboration. It was only after 1660
that scenic effects and illusions were regularly introduced,
and women actors regularly appeared upon a much-degraded
Stage, and to help a much-lowered Drama.

An opportunity was recently given us by the Elizabeth
Stage Society, of seeing for ourselves the effect of this
simple stage-setting, where only the passion or the sorrow
pleaded with the heart, or kindled the emotions, with a brave
independence of stage tricks and ocular illusion. Marlowe's
" Faustus," and some other representative productions,
walked the boards in the simple dignity and sincerity which
lifted them above the poor mean setting of an Elizabethan
age. Of course to the unimaginative mind, or to the person
who is outside of the history and literature of the time, and
who, therefore, cannot understand a stage without painted
scenery, or with men and women playing in their own
English Elizabethan dress, with their swords and daggers,
irrespective of whatsoever nationality or period is represented
by the play, the effect must be absolutely grotesque ; but,
to the literary and dramatic student, with sympathy and
knowledge, the effect from the opening to the closing scene,
when six of the players, kneeling together, prayed for Queen
Elizabeth, was undoubtedly enthralling.

CHAPTER VI

ENGLISH ORIGINS

LIKE the Greek stage, the roots of the English Tragic Drama stretch away back to the religious festival. The origins of the Elizabethan Tragedy, the unparalleled manifestations of the stupendous genius of Shakespeare, lay far up along the head-streams of English religious and social history, in the efforts of the monks to teach a people ignorant of letters the mysteries of the revealed faith and the miracles of the saints. The Miracle Play, the Mystery, and the Morality were the three steps of the evolution which issued in the Elizabethan Drama.[1] The secret, indeed, of the marvellously rapid culmination of that Drama in the perfection of William Shakespeare, is the fact that, from the eleventh century, dramatic representation, of no matter how rude a kind, had been the most widespread and popular form of entertainment at the holiday festivals of the people. Chaucer's "Wife of Bath" tells us how fond she was of entertainments and gatherings; and includes amongst these, vigils, pilgrimages, and miracle plays. Absolon, also, the Parish Clerk in the "Traveller's Tale," is a capable performer in the Miracle Play, and a master of the part of Herod. It is evident from Chaucer's page that, in his day, the Miracle Play was popular all over the country, that it was enacted on a platform in full view of the people, and that the Church retained the patronage of it. The medium

---

[1] The Miracle Play dealt with legends of the saints; the Mystery, with the Nativity, Passion, Resurrection, and Redemption, and the spiritual facts founded thereupon; the Morality, with allegorical representations of the Virtues.

of expression, however, was now the vernacular instead of
Latin, which had made the transaction, for the people, at
least, virtually a mere mummery in pantomimic dumb-show.
The purpose of the clergy in having these plays acted was
to accentuate the teaching of the Church, in amplification of
that which was effected through the pictures of the holy
miracles or the saints. They stood, roughly, in the same
relation to the sacred Art of the Middle Ages as did the
Greek Drama to the Greek Sculpture. So soon, however,
as the vernacular came into use in these dramatic representations, the familiarity which generates contempt came with it.
Broad farce, so easily understood of the people, took
possession of the stage; and soon the whole thing passed
into the hands of the laity, while the clergy shut the Church
door against it, debarring the players even from the
churchyard.

From the year 1110 when, in St Albans, the legend of
Saint Catherine was represented as a sort of spectacle with
Latin accompaniment, until the fourteenth century, when
the dialogue was English and the players laymen, the
Mystery or Miracle had won a growing hold upon the
heart of the people, and become the central interest in
Whitsuntide, Easter, and other holidays of all the Crafts
throughout the land. These Crafts or Guilds appointed
actors, who were assisted by friars evidently possessing
more liberty than their brethren under monastic rule. They
further provided each an act or scene. Some of those
plays extended to forty thousand lines, which proves how
intense the interest and enthusiasm must have been that
held the audiences patiently for several days together.
This interest and enthusiasm, fostered by the Miracles and
Moralities, was what secured the future of the Elizabethan
Drama, and prepared for its phenomenal success. Long
after the rise of the literary play, these crude productions
held their own in the provinces. Even in Newcastle, in
1599, the "Three Kings of Cologne" was performed.

Four famous sets of those plays survive, called respectively the Chester, Wakefield, Coventry, and York sets, from the places in which they had origin. They are primitive to a degree, and their point of view is that of the people of the time in which they were produced; hence they bristle with anachronism, just like those pictures of the Finding of Moses, and other Scriptural episodes, in which all the ladies and gentlemen are in the Court dress of the painters' period. They further display very strikingly the irreverence which had invaded the stage.

The Craftsmen's great festival was that of Corpus Christi, founded in 1264 by Pope Urban; and this became the chief midsummer holiday of the people, of which the Miracle Play was the central attraction. The number of plays in a set depended on the number of Guilds to be represented. In York there were forty-eight. The Tanners, Armourers, Coopers, etc., all bore their share, some with the "Expulsion from Eden," some the "Temptation and Fall," while the Fishers and Mariners acted "Noah and the Flood," the Shipwrights, "The Building of the Ark," and so forth. Many uncanonical episodes crept in, as, for example, the ridiculous scene of scolding and quarrel between Noah and his wife; through which, and similar matters, the Miracle Play was brought into contact with the life and humours of the listeners and observers, though at the same time removed, by a vast stretch unspeakable, from the old level of its religious origin.[1] The immediate parent of the Elizabethan Drama was, however, the Morality Play, which sprang from the Mystery, and was very strongly in evidence in the fifteenth and sixteenth centuries. Life, in any phase, but with relation to some abstract moral principle, was the theme of the Morality. Poverty, Death, Contemplation, etc., gradually began to

---

[1] Nevertheless, the Church jealously guarded for a while its monopoly. In 1278 the choristers of St Paul's petitioned Richard II. to prohibit ignorant persons presenting the Old Testament to the great prejudice of the clergy of the Church.

appear upon the stage, and development slowly but surely passed along.

A very good type of the old Morality is "Everyman," which we recently had the opportunity of seeing revived. "Everyman" is, as might be conjectured, a type of ordinary humanity, and the story is a kind of allegory of human destiny. The characters include, God-Speaketh—a kind of realised Conscience—Death, Riches, Good-deeds, Knowledge, Five-Wits. The play opens by showing how "The High Father of Heaven" sendeth Death to summon Everyman to come to Him. Everyman's ingratitude is bewailed : Death and Everyman engage in a dialogue, from which Everyman's state of unpreparedness is only too evident. He appeals in his distress to Kindred and Fellowship, next to goods and riches, but they neither can nor will help him in his present strait. So, also, when he turns to his good deeds, he finds them so few in number and so feeble withal that they could only be of small avail. Then, through Knowledge, he is led to appeal to God for forgiveness ; and at last, acompanied by Good Deeds, Knowledge and Discretion, and Five-Wits, he goes to his grave, assured of his pardon.

The burlesque element in these old productions lay always between the Vice and the Devil—the clown and the pantaloon of modern Pantomime. The joke was always at the expense of the Devil, and some moral principle was sure to emerge as victor. The advance made by the Morality arose from the fact that its theme was no longer confined to Scripture, or the legendary lives of saints ; while some attempt at individualisation of character, and at the unfolding of a plot or story, was necessary to awaken and maintain the interest of the people. Nevertheless, in order to hold the audience, the interjection of the "Interlude" or humorous scene, usually embodying some anecdotic episode, was devised, and helped to develop the popular Drama. Some of these Interludes, separated from the Morality Play, were acted by themselves, the village fairs and festivals demanding secular as well as sacred amusements.[1] Heywood's Interludes were famous, above the rest.

But, meantime, giant influences unseen were at work. The tide of the Renaissance was stealing over the world ; and in England, as elsewhere, the plays of Plautus, Terence, and Seneca were being read in schools, represented by the scholars, and were becoming models for English play-writers, with comic interludes thrown in, for padding and gilding. And, at last, in the middle of the sixteenth century, the unfolding of the modern Drama, in the birth of the three sisters, Comedy, Tragedy, and the Historical Play, began with the works of Udall, whose adaptation from Plautus, called "Ralf Roister Doister," appeared about 1551, though it was licensed probably only in 1566 ; and "Gammer Gurton's Needle," attributed to Still,[2] afterwards Bishop of Bath and Wells, the first English play acted at either University, a coarse, literally realistic transcript of low life and its humours. These two comedies follow no slavish model, but are simply based on human nature. Sackville and Norton's " Gorboduc " or " Ferrex and Porrex," founded on an old British myth, and modelled on a tragedy of Seneca, appeared in 1561 ; while " Kyng Johan," by Bale, a Morality Play, blended with history, written probably during the reign of Edward VI., was in 1562 adapted for representation by having a few lines added to its second part. " Gorboduc " was notable as being our first English tragedy, and, at the same time, as having been written

[1] The Act of 1543 against anyone playing in Interludes, or rhyming any matter contrary to the New Religion, has a proviso in favour of Songs, Plays, and Interludes, which have for object the rebuke and reproach of vices, and the setting forth of virtue, so always the said Songs, Plays, or Interludes meddle not with the interpretation of Scripture.

[2] Bricked up in an old chimney corner, on the stone settle where the reader of long ago had laid it down till it was forgotten in the dust, was discovered not long since a copy of " Gammer Gurton's Needle." It may have lain where it was found for 300 years. In August 1906 at Sotheby's this book was sold for £180 to Mr Thomas Wise. The last copy in the market belonged to George Daniel, and was sold for £60 half a century ago. No copy of " Gammer Gurton's Needle " of earlier date than 1575 has been known.

in blank verse, which, though a stiff, poor instrument in Sackville's hands, became soon, in Marlowe's, the marching music of the tragic utterance ever after.

The period, however, between " Gorboduc " and Marlowe's " Tamburlaine," extending over five and twenty years, was one of vast and rapid development. A rude people were trained to a finer sense of intellectual appreciation ; the theatres were got into shape ; and the dramatic advance had compelled a reasonable recognition of its liberties within certain well-defined limits ; while, above all, the poetic utterance no longer was a childlike stumbling thing, but had learnt to leap and march in full-vigoured manhood. Nevertheless, " Gorboduc " opened the door for a marked progression towards the possibility of the higher Drama, and especially did it secure this by its use of blank verse. This medium Marlowe developed ; and by his " mighty line " established it forever. To him is due its adoption on the popular stage. " Gorboduc " had only been written for representation at the Inner Temple ; and though blank verse was used also in the closing acts of Peele's " Arraignment of Paris," that also was for private use, having been composed for the Queen and her Court circle. But Marlowe struck out a note for all the world to hear, and set before him an heroic ideal. Thus, in his Prologue to " Tamburlaine," he says :—

> " From jigging veins of rhyming mother wits
> And such conceits as clownage keeps in pay,
> We'll lead you to the stately tent of war "—

thus banishing not only the popular doggerel jingle, but driving the episodic Interlude clown out of the Tragic stage. The usage was strikingly parallel to that of the Greek Drama, for it seemed to be growing into recognition as a loftier vehicle of expression. It breaks away in the " Arraignment of Paris " from the rhyming sequences, whenever Paris has to defend himself in the presence of the Council of the gods, and it developed a poetic phraseology, a kind of English Tragic dialect, above and apart from the common tinkle of other measures. "Kyng Johan" is of capital importance : as, though it had Vice, Dissimulation, and other characters of the old Morality in it; and though it is, after all, but sorry enough doggerel verse, it was the first of the great Chronicle plays, which were the fount of inspiration for the genius of Shakespeare, whence originated his great creation of dramatic history, unparalleled in any literature.

Poor enough were these beginnings, wherein Pegasus limps lamely, to little music ;—and that, often, a very poor accompaniment indeed. Difficult, too—nay, impossible—to determine when the hands of the clock led at last into the new full day. Elizabethan literature dawned like the day itself dawning over English fields and seas. Here and there a crescendo, a cry, a glamour, till the fullness of poetry is heard and felt in scraps of Greene, and Kyd, and in the unsurpassable moments of Marlowe. And then, into the full light floats, like an island with serrated, lightning-blasted peaks, quiet green glens, and soft, still, wave-washed shores, as the mists pass off, Shakespeare, king and creator of a crowd of eternal shapes.

Where the forerunners of the Attic day have passed, into what oblivion undisturbed, no man can tell, if such indeed there were, worthy to be spoken of; but the literature of no age entered into its heritage ushered in by such a line of electric personalities as this of the Elizabethan age in England. That age of Literature extends from 1558, the year of the accession of the great queen, till, say, 1610, when the tide of wonder ebbed, mingling with other voices. Its glory was the dramatic utterance, the sudden creation of a new world of Imagination bodying forth the form of things.

The birth of the Elizabethan Drama fell upon times full of opportunity and augury. The printing-press was ready to make all worthy utterance eternal. Marlowe's "mighty

line " cried the advent of true English native Drama, freed
from Morality and Interlude, and from the Senecan Tragedy,
which had failed to establish itself on the English stage.
Alongside of Shakespeare, we see, over all the ages, Ben
Jonson, Chapman, Marston, Dekker, standing out from
amongst a crowd of dramatic poets, of merit inferior only to
these. Later, we see Beaumont and Fletcher, Middleton,
Webster, Massinger, Ford, and Shirley. These represent a
large volume of thought, fire, and passionate splendour of
art. That group stands out, making the period itself unique.
It was, as we saw, a period of thought-quickening, history-
making enterprise, story and ballad springing up everywhere,
tales of world-sailings with Frobisher and Drake thrilling
the heart, till the tides around the island became as imaginative music to the soul, with an inviting glamour calling the
spirit away to follow Imagination over the free, wide world ;
making England and England's history the sowing-ground of
Masque, Pageant, Interlude, and Play, song and cry of love
and patriotism.

The influence of the European Renaissance, too, gave men
the knowledge and taste to discern a good thing, to recognise
a new genius, and to take its measure ; and it lifted English
Drama out of the ruts of mere classical influence and imitation. The impulse given thus by the frenzy of Marlowe's
genius carried on the development, till human-hearted
glamour of love and sorrow, with the ambitions and selfishness of man's nature, flowed over into such full utterance
as is found in " Romeo and Juliet," "Hamlet," and "Lear."
The activity of the Drama, especially in Elizabeth's time,
was strikingly noteworthy. Between 1580 and 1596 four
out of eleven companies of players played no less than one
hundred different plays, some in prose, some in rhyme, and
some in composite form of prose, rhyme, and blank verse,
till Marlowe's thundering splendour in "Tamburlaine" in
1587 made blank verse the monarch of all Tragic mediums of
expression. Lyly's influence lay in the direction of fixing

the proper place in the Drama of prose and lyric Interludes, so exquisitely brought to perfection by the master-playwright of all. The early Elizabethan Drama was the work of the so-called "University Wits" like Marlowe, Peele, Greene, Lodge, Nash, and Kyd. The later was the work of the "Theatre Playwrights," who added to the merits of their predecessors knowledge of the stage and men, and whose minds were full of imaginative vistas, through which moved all that they had ever known or fancied—village clowns, half-mad dreamers, frenzied scholars, and all the kingliest figures of romantic history.

CHAPTER VII

THE MYTH-CYCLE OF THE ATREIDÆ

WE shall see, in the treatment of the Myth-Cycle of the Atreidæ, by the three great Tragedians of Greece, the best proof of the elasticity, within bounds, of the conventional material put into the hands of the poets, as well as the freedom of teaching possible to each.

This Myth-Cycle may well be called the Hamlet episode of Attic Tragedy. In the Court of Denmark and the Court of Argos a woman's unfaithfulness breeds murder, and the pious duty of retribution at the hand of a son tears his soul asunder, and plunges him in a sickness of the brain, perplexing him amongst the different ways that seem to beckon him to enter for an answer to his quest. But here the ancient poet strings the dark fortune of the race upon the thread of heaven's wrath against the blood of Pelops, for a deed of most atrocious horror—the banquet of treachery given by Atreus, the father of Agamemnon, to his own brother Thyestes, whom he feasted on his children's flesh. Clytemnestra, Agamemnon's queen, during her husband's absence in the expedition against Troy, took Ægisthus, son of Thyestes, as her paramour, and their guilty consciences could not face the return of the great king. They determined to murder him, first, because of their own guilt, and secondly, because of the wound his selfish ambition had made in Clytemnestra's heart, through sacrificing their daughter Iphigeneia to satisfy the injured pride of Artemis, who had stayed the winds at Aulis, holding the Greek fleet idle on their way to Troy. But Agamemnon had himself been unfaithful, and had brought home with him Cassandra, Priam's daughter, out of Troy, to be his concubine.[1]

To avenge his father's murder, Orestes had to take upon himself the burden of a son's duty ; and killing his mother and her paramour, brought back the circle of the will of heaven to its beginning, working out, in his own sufferings at the hands of the Furies, atonement for the crimes of his race, and finding peace alone at the feet of the Athenian divinities in the highest Court of Athens.

[1] The returns of the Trojan heroes formed favourite topics of heroic lays, and notably those of an old poet, Agaias of Trœzene, summarised by the grammarian Proclus. From these mostly, though the subject is mentioned in the " Odyssey," book xi., the particulars of the fortunes and the misfortunes of the house of Agamemnon have been taken. The " Iliad " gives no curse to the Atreidæ. In the " Odyssey " it is Ægisthus that murders Agamemnon, and Clytemnestra is not spoken of in that connection. As distinguished from later versions even, Orestes murders Ægisthus simply as an act of retribution, while he is not mentioned as having slain his mother. The combined influences of the Cyclic poets and the Delphic priests developed the story. In later authorities Atreus is grandfather of Agamemnon ; and there are many minor differences in the story, but, in these pages, it is the tragic myth-form which is dealt with.

CHAPTER VIII

THE ORESTEIA OF ÆSCHYLUS

ÆSCHYLUS takes up the theme in his "Agamemnon," "Choephoræ," and "Eumenides." And in these plays we view the crown of the poet's work. There we have a complete trilogy—the god-haunted, doomful story of the house of Atreus, a cycle of plays strung upon one thread of destiny, the ripest production of his ripest age—for the last dramatic contest of his life in 458 B.C., two years before his death.

The first of the three is the grand tragic "Agamemnon." And here the poet rises to the highest manifestation of true genius. Quivering with passion, and strongly conceived, an unspeakable greatness clothes it as it moves. The interest and attention are held all through with keenest grip. It is the murder of a king. It is a tragedy of giant figures, and it is but a narrow step at last into the judgment-presence of the gods themselves. Moreover, the stern retribution of a prince involves the murder of a queen. The eyes of the watchful emissaries of the gods glare through the shadows of the sin-stained house, and heaven lets men kindle on their own hearth-stone the flame of their punishment. But is this all the poet's mind reveals—doom, and never a hope behind it? No; atonement is possible, but always through suffering. A soul trembles under the shadow of ancestral sinfulness and crime, but is led through pain by the hand of an irresistible, crucifying predestination into the house of the gods again.

One feels a kind of strong cousinship between the sentry's

platform at Elsinore and the roof of Agamemnon's palace, where the watchman waits for the gleam of the signal-fire that flashes from Troy, the message of the king's returning; while castle-halls of old Northern Scotland are recalled by the dark hints of a doom-shadow that sits by the palace fireside here. The Chorus of twelve old senators, in an ode of great beauty, disclose the reason of this gloom. Artemis, averse to the expedition to Troy, had stayed the breezes.

> " Idly flapped the sails—
> The great ships idly lay
> Bound fast by envious gales
> In Aulis Bay."

And when, to assuage the Virgin-goddess's delaying wrath,[1] a virgin-sacrifice was demanded by the seer, Agamemnon bowed to necessity's hard yoke, and gave his daughter to the sacrificial knife.

> " Her prayers, her pleadings, little did they heed,
> Or when the sweet name ' Father ' did she plead . . .
> She heard the monarch's dire commands,
> And silent stood,
> Patiently folding her sweet lily hands,
> And for her country's glory gave her blood."

This terrible deed of a father, god-driven, preferring the battle-path to the life's blood of his daughter, brought him under the shadow of the curse of impiety. He had won his will from a goddess, but he dragged the haunting curse of the gods upon himself; and expiation must be made. As they tell of this, the Chorus turn to ask about the heavenly powers, in whose hand lies the destiny of things. It is Zeus who sways them all. He has brought down underneath his feet two dynasties of gods, and the lesson of his rule over men is that knowledge only comes through pain. As the herald puts it—

---

[1] Sophocles, in the " Electra " (l. 566), describes the offence against Artemis as the slaughter of a doe in hunting.

> "All, each in turn, must suffer,
> But at last All's well."

These are words of portent on the entrance of the king,—
fear of too great triumph, and of the disastrous pride and
elation which success brings with it.

His wife Clytemnestra welcomes the thought of his
advent; but beneath her gladness is a sinister touch. The
dagger gleams in her smile, and the Chorus is full of dark
hints of fate. Agamemnon, entering, with a sense of
success and strength of personal triumph, fears the gods,
but he is greeted in extravagant address of powerful eulogy
by Clytemnestra. In Agamemnon's reply, slightly chiding,
the popular note of belief in regard to the envy of heaven
again is struck.[1]

> "Drag not on me the anger of the gods,
> Making me walk on purple glory strewn;
> I fear to tread on so much treasure now.
> Treat me like man not god."[2]

The double meaning of Clytemnestra's prayers deeply
intensifies their tragic potency.

> "Bring all my vows to completion.
> Finish thy purpose;
> Hear me, O Jove!"

The absolute power of the spell of the spoken word, which,
in the popular Grecian conception, had an undivertible fatality,
makes these prayers of hers, like winged arrows of doom.

Fate marshals her shadows nearer, and the shivering
Chorus feel the chill despair draw down upon them, when
Cassandra, scorned by Clytemnestra, begins to call upon
Apollo, asking whither he has led her,—to what roof? The
Chorus replies

> "To the Atreidæ's roof,"

a word fraught with doom to her prophetic soul.

[1] "To mythology belongs the poetic privilege of representing the glory of her heroes
as the occasion of their fall."—Curtius, "Hist. Gr." i. p.102.

[2] "As Clytemnestra has feigned affection, so Agamemnon feigns humility. They
are a pair of hypocrites, each endeavouring to outwit the other."—PALEY *in loc.* See
"Envy of the Gods" in chapter xvii.

D

And then the terrible horror of the curse-begetting sin of Atreus shudders across her soul. For Agamemnon's father, was Atreus, whose mother had murdered his father, Pelops: and whose brother Thyestes debauched his queen, who had two children by him,—what tale in all Greece was more fraught with horror than this?   How Atreus, to avenge himself gave Thyestes a sumptuous feast, serving up to him the children of his lust, and convinced him of what he had feasted on, by producing the heads and hands of the murdered babes.   The very sun is said to have shrunk from its course at the bloody sight.   Incest, adultery, murder, left their footprints on the threshold, and shadowed the god-doomed house, with the sense of the added crime that is to stain the hearth.

> "There's a Chorus that sits by the fireside here,
> And courage it quaffs from the life's blood of men :
> And it croons the old curse, the beginning of curses,
> The starting of grief for the race.
>
> And never the band of the curse-ghosts, alas,
> Will say a good-bye and go ;
> They range through the desolate rooms, and they cry,
> Till the echoes seem speaking forever of horrors,
> And secrets unclean, of the house."

She warns the Chorus of the impending murder, which is anew to link the house of Atreus on to doom.   And next, in vision, she beholds her own sad fate.

> " This lioness that with the wolf in lust
> Couched when the lordly lion was far away
> Will have my blood . . .
> But the just gods will never forget us,
> We die, but this ill woman's son
> Shall smite our bitter atonement
> Out of her deepest heart.
> He comes, and revenge for his father
> Is the breath that is filling his sail."

The vengeance of heaven must fall upon the murderess and adulteress; and so link goes on to link along the endless chain. But yet Cassandra cannot herself escape fate. Irresistibly it draws and entangles her over the threshold to her doom. Nor can the Chorus help reflecting on the price paid for fame ; and what is the worth of the exchange ?

> " What is the price of his triumph—
> Proud Troy in disaster o'erthrown,
> His arms crowned with glory of conquest,
> And he glory-clothed by heaven's favour,
> Yet, if, for blood poured, his must pour,
> If for all who are dead, he must die,
> He buys glory too dear for its worth."

The cries of the king in death agony are now heard from within ; and then Clytemnestra is seen, proudly, disdainfully, queenlily glorying, standing beside her crime,—murderer of her husband and her king.

> " No hurried act of scrambling rashness this :
> Long has my heart he hurt designed its scheme ;
> Grateful, as to earth's weary flowers to feel
> Heaven's showers descending, that rich rain of blood
> Which from his death-wound warmly gushed on me !
> His cruel pride
> Filled my sad cup with bitter loneliness,[1]
> Some bitter dregs were left himself to drain.
> There lies my husband slain, and slain by me.
> Mine is the deed. I claim it justified." [1]

There is here the terrible picture of a woman red-handed, with the vengeance of the gods on human pride. Her mother's heart hurls its reason at the astonished Chorus.

> " Wilt thou revenge and Exile's cruel hate
> Denounce on me because my lord I slew ?
> Shall he escape, who, for the winds of Thrace,
> His child gave up to sacrifice,—mine own
> Iphigeneia, daughter of my grief ? "

This is the note which is heard again and again all through

---

[1] " Subtle, proud, daring, resolute, and an accomplished hypocrite, she glories in the deed as an act of just retribution. With all this she is not the abandoned and shameless adulteress, but the deeply-injured wife and mother; not the merely vindictive and ferocious homicide, but the sophist who can justify, and the moralist who can reason upon her conduct."—PALEY.

the Dramas, dealing with this destiny-devoted house. One hears it more human, more pleading and piteous in Sophocles. It is the mother-love that is in her heart, like an unsatisfied savage hunger for her poor Iphigeneia slain for a superstition, that makes her relentless; and even the real affection she feels for such a mean vain creature as Ægisthus, son of Thyestes, lifts Clytemnestra into the level of a truly tragic queen.

But the Chorus sees further,—

> "No longer drop by drop.
> Now 'tis a full flood tide,
> And the crimson stain shall bide;
> And no man's hand can stop
> This murder-torrent shaking the solid walls
> That should have steady stood throughout all time;
> While Vengeance whets her blade for further crime.
> Murder on murder calls.
> What a succession, each to each claiming heir!
> Who can the horrible haunting horde out-scare?"

Clytemnestra does not, in her blinding pride, see how futile it is to attempt to stem murder's stream with murder. It but makes it overflow its banks. To deepen the horror of murderous vaunting, Ægisthus enters, proud to see this man suffering for the crimes of his fathers.[1] The tragedy closes with hint of more to come; but with the Chorus indignant, threatening the certainty of doom upon the murderer, and mentioning the name of Orestes,—a word of fate.

The thread of destiny is resumed in "The Choephoræ," in which Orestes slays his mother Clytemnestra, an act of piety, and duty to his father's memory, yet, at the same time, an act of atrocity. As the former, it was laid upon him by necessity of his position as a prince, whereby he was bound to punish his own household for crimes committed by them; while, as the latter, his deed being a murder, he had to flee for sanctuary to Delphi. The complication reveals the Greek idea of a truly tragic knot. Blood drags blood in its terrible

---

[1] Cowardice, vanity and spite are the graces of Ægisthus.

train.   Crime begets crime, till the whole issue is completed
by heaven.

The right of the next of kin to exact blood for blood [1]
became, as time passed on, a sacred duty laid upon him, from
which he could not possibly escape.   No matter by how
trivial an accident death intervened, the only way of escape
for the slayer was instant and headlong flight.   So closely
interwoven with the general texture of Hebrew family life
was this idea, that the same word means both " next of kin,"
and " avenger."

One of the consolations in death was, with the Greek of
the Homeric age, the thought that there was left one who
would exact revenge from his foes.   Thus Orestes was laid
upon the cross of a double agony, for he was bound by this
ancient Vendetta law to become avenger of his father's
blood, but in obeying the one, he outrages another code of
piety, for he has to make himself the murderer of his mother.
The ancient law of blood for blood, hate for hate, and a
blow for a blow, was encrusted upon the conscience of the
nation.   Both public opinion and the law of national conduct
alike demanded and justified his act ; but, at the same time,
nothing could save him from the red reeking horror of his
tragic deed.

Shadows of Lady Macbeth, of the suppressed passionate
soul-indignation of Hamlet, flicker over the whole Trilogy.
In this second play the tragic interest is centred on the anger
of the gods, and the heaven-impelled revenge of the murdered
man's son.[2]   The scene opens with Orestes and his friend
Pylades, like Hamlet and Horatio, standing by the tomb of
the great king who had been slain in the height of his home-
returning pride.   The Chorus of Trojan dames, bearing gifts,

---

[1] *Cf*. Numbers cxxxv.   The right of the Avenger of Blood was a phenomenon of all
semi-civilised States.   The Jewish Code was uniquely humane in providing Cities
of Shelter against thirsty Vendettas.—See Numbers v. 8, Leviticus xxv. 25.
The Arabic equivalent means impartially a friend, kinsman, protector and avenger
of blood.

[2] This anomaly of Duty contradicting Duty made such a tragic knot the most
popular of all topics with the poets.

enter.   They do not conceal their feelings of indignation and
horror : and later on, they disclose the reason for these gifts,
in the dream of Clytemnestra's conscience-stricken soul, that
she has suckled a new born dragon with her blood [1]

> " Shaken by fear,
> She, hateful, called me near,
> These gifts to bear, and lead with reverent tread
> These to the tomb, to soothe the kingly dead :
>   But will his shade accept the gift of hate ?
> When Pride, elate,
> Upon thy breast, O earth, the blood has poured,
> What shall atone for the black deed abhorred ? "

The terrible certainty of heaven's just revenge, though long-
delayed, is emphasised ; [2] and Electra asks how these offerings
are to be made, seeing they come from her whose hands
were imbrued in the blood of the dead husband whose dust
sleeps below.   "Pour it," say the Chorus, "with a prayer
for blessing on the dead king's friends, and that some god
may come to repay upon his enemies death for death ; and,

> Though distant far, remember poor Orestes ! "

She stands there, the embodiment of filial grief, and prays
beside the grave of her murdered father,—[3]

> " O bring Orestes back, and be his guide,
> Good Fortune ! "

And now, as she pours the libation, with the invocation
of the gods,

> " May thine avenger rise, and from our foes
> Ask blood for blood ! —"

---

[1] This dream had been sent by the dæmonic influence of Agamemnon.

[2] The vengeance of the gods is their surest vindication and apologetic in the mind
of the Greek.   *Cf.* the warning by Teiresias in "Antigone."   And again in the
"Bacchæ," verse 882.

ὁρμᾶται μόλις, ἀλλ' ὅμως κ.τ.λ.

> Slow but sure is the vengeance of heaven.
> To the proud and the impious given.
> Yea, the gods lie in ambush through slow-moving time,
> Hunting man down for his folly and crime.

[3] The dead hero has still power in Hades to influence those he left behind.   The
irony revolves around the fact of two different parties attempting on the same day
to propitiate the shade of Agamemnon, and for different purposes.   Agamemnon is
still, though invisible, a principal agent.

she suddenly perceives the " crisped locks " which Orestes
had laid upon the tomb; and after much surprise and
conjecture recognises whose they are, for the locks are like
her own in colour, there are footprints like her own, leading
to the tomb; and while she reasons, Orestes reveals himself
to her, and declares his mission, showing, in proof of his
identity, the very garment her own hands had wrought for
him long ago. He tells how he is here, defying the danger,
upon the instigation and by the command of Apollo himself,
at the risk of the most dire penalties should he refuse.

And now the Chorus, replying to the cries of Orestes
and Electra by the tomb of their father, teach the deathlessness of the soul, which makes retribution follow the deed
and the doer alike. For the transaction is not ended when
the blow is struck. There is what lives, and will not be
thrust aside by violent deeds.[1]

> " The fire that eats away
> The dead man's clay
> Can never touch the soul,
> Whose wrath in fullest time shall on his murderers roll."

Sad Electra's lamentation over her father, bursting forth
into impassioned wail, seems like the mourning, brooding
love of Hamlet, a great proud picture of a loving child, and
with the cry of the Chorus makes a complete threnody for
the King.

> " Yet, father, hadst thou fallen 'neath Ilium's walls,
> Peirced by the thrust of some bold Lycian spear,
> How had thy house been glorious through thy name,
> And thy proud tomb beside the waters stood.

> " And even in death's dark kingdom down below,
> Among the shades of all the illustrious dead,
> How hadst thou lorded it, in highest pride,
> Kinglike as those who rule that awful realm.

> But not by Ilium's walls death claimed thy crown;
> Nor stands thy tomb beside Scamander's wave ! "

[1] *Cf.* Sophocles's " Electra," 909 : κ.τ.λ. Also Euripides's " Electra," *in loc.*

The Chorus now rise above the popular idea of a blind Fate swaying the life of man. They turn away from the folk-tales of Jove, the amorous and wilful god, only saved by his thunders from the level of the wanton Satyrs. He is appealed to as a god of retributive Justice; and heaven and hell alike are called to condemn the unclean and treacherous slaughter. An impassioned prayer for the presence of the very dead at the planned revenge follows. And then Orestes presents himself at the palace gate, and is received by Clytemnestra with simulated grief, while he tells the message of his own death far away. She enters to convey the tidings to Ægisthus; and the Chorus, while praying that this bloodshed be the last, become undisguised accessories and instigators of murder.

> " Remember how thy father fell.
> Let not her cries " My son! " against thy purpose tell.
> Heed not her plaintive breath ;
> And him who dealt thy father's blow of death—
> Fling him to meet thy father's rage in hell ! "

Meanwhile Ægisthus appears, elate, a terrible figure of poetic irony, on his way to personally interview the messenger. Just as he enters behind the scene his doom meets him in the face, and his terrible death-cry is immediately heard—

> " Θ I am slain ! "

The queen returns to find the reason of the clamour, and her inquiry is met by enigmatic answers from the servants :—

> " They that fame called the dead, have slain the living ! "

The truth flashes upon her suddenly awakened conscience

> " I know the meaning of thy darksome words.
> Lo ! in the net we spread, ourselves must die."

She knows the awful retribution which has crossed the

---

1 The irony of the Greek Tragic Poets would form a topic for an interesting book. They were precluded from introducing unforeseen issues, as the fable and its move- ment were of course prescribed to them ; but they created situations by means of this irony,—the contrast between the agent's real position as seen and known by the audience and by heaven, with his own conception of that position.

threshold; and she goes in. And now, face to face with his mother, filial piety distracts the avenger. He turns for advice to his friend, Pylades, who speaks, here, for the only time in all the play, breaking his most terrible silence.

> "Where then Apollo's oracle? Your vows?
> Make foes of all the world: but please the gods!"

There is, in this silent man, who stands beside Orestes at the tomb, enters the house of fate, and only speaks this once, when the arm of Orestes falters, a grim, tragic awfulness, unparelleled in the Drama,—a very shadow of remorseless doom. Clytemnestra threatens a mother's angry Furies: but the dread of his father's shade sways his purpose to completion, and he slays her on the body of Ægisthus. [1]

In the succeeding choral ode, Vengeance and Justice are identified. [2]

> "Revenge, high heaven's daughter,
> Though known by Justice' name!"

Orestes declares his deed to be not an atrocity or even a murder, but the slaying of the proud oppressors of his country, the murderers of his father, the destroying angels of his princely house. Tyranny, impious slaughter, treason, in his double blow, are overthrown; yet the final twist in the knot of their fate had been given by their own wilful sin.

But suddenly he feels the horror of the deed to which he had been impelled. All the air becomes filled with the Furies of his mother, to his startled fancy the blood-avengers, the soul-hunters.

> "Grim-visaged, draped in gloomy dark array,
> With twisting snakes among their tangled hair!"

Hiding his face, he flies before them, seeking the shelter of Apollo's shrine, for peace, according to the promise of

---

[1] Not, of course, in the presence of the spectators.

[2] "Æschylus does not hesitate in such identifications. He does not seem to care whether the mother of Prometheus, for example, is called Themis, or Earth, or any other name. Names of the gods are of little account to him. πολλῶν ὀνομάτων μορφὴ ία."—PROMETH. 209-210.

the god; leaving the startled Chorus to murmur again to themselves the terrible tale of blood and feud that broods above the house; and to cry aloud their mingled blessing and their sorrow over him who flies, the victim of the gods, and yet also their chosen instrument, under that affliction of the Hamlet of every age, disjointed,—

> "The cursed spite
> That ever he was born to set it right!"

The last play of the Trilogy, "The Eumenides," or "Furies," reveals an Olympus divided over the action of Orestes,—the old heaven that was on the side of Fate, divided against the newer heaven that has looked on true humanity. One can feel old questions of family and feud being debated here in the poet's mind.

The Erinnyes or Furies, called from the point of view of ingratiation, "The Eumenides,"[1] are in Homeric usage the personification of a curse wrung out of the soul of some one deeply wronged, against the violator of his rights. All crimes against piety have their Furies.[2] There may be a Fury for every impassioned prayer broken out of the agony of a human heart. But with the certainty of doom whenever life's pathways are crimsoned with murder, these dread daughters of Night, with the blood-scent, like laughter in their nostrils, run the high fevers of the mad soul down. Even Delphi's altars cannot repel them from their chase, though they fall asleeping there, but only the reconciling

---

[1] As in the Highlands of Scotland, the fairies were called *an daoine sith*, "the people of peace," lest, listening invisible the while, they might hear what might offend them; but, by the Tragedian, named from the changed spirit evoked in them through Apollo's influence and Athene's decision in the case of Orestes.

[2] *E.g.* Against Parent, *cf.* "Iliad," 9. 453
Against Brother, *cf.* "Iliad," 15, 204
Against Hospitality, *cf.* "Odyssey," 17, 575.
Against Perjury, *cf.* "Iliad," 10, 257

The curses of an offended person become baleful in their power of summoning the Furies. See "Eumenides," l. 395, where the Furies call themselves Ἀραί or *curses*, from this originating source. They kept in check man's tendency to sin, performing the function of Conscience.

wisdom of Pallas Athene says to their passionate anger
" Peace! Be still."

Further, blood-pollution demands purification. [1] The
murderer with the fingermark of the curse upon his brow,
wandered the world a pariah, forsaken, until by means of
libations and sacrifice he was freed from the taint of blood:
thereafter he had to be tried before a competent court, and,
declared to have atoned fully for his guilt. The court which
stood above all others in this matter was the court of Areopagus, before which, by advice of Apollo, and under the
protection of Athene, the patroness of the city, Orestes
found his decree of liberation.

And here one sees a question of immediate political
interest enveloped in the play. Pericles and Ephialtes,
the Radical leaders, were intent on a root-and-branch reform
of the Court of Areopagus,[2] a reform which might obliterate
entirely this Athenian House of Lords, whose power was
unrestrained by any defined limitations. On the one hand
it was considered a dangerous weapon in the possession of
a privileged class: on the other it was esteemed as a sacred,
heaven-founded institution, whose roots were in the Councils
of the gods, and on whose maintenance, unsullied and undisturbed, depended the abiding greatness of the city.
Æschylus, the old Tory patriot, is of the latter opinion, in
contradiction to the popular cry of the moment, careless of
praise or blame. He sets the foundation of this Court as
a spiritual necessity for the liberation of the soul of Orestes,
by Pallas himself; and as a continuous reminder of the
constant care of heaven over the interests of Athens.

Again we find Æschylus in this Drama revivifying, with
a brave glory about it, the remembrance of the ancient

---

[1] By a law of Draco even an inanimate object, which has become an instrument of
death, was cast out beyond the boundary as a polluted thing.

[2] "καὶ τὴν μὲν ἐν Αρείῳ πάγῳ βουλὴν 'Εφιάλτης ἐκόλουσε καὶ Περικλῆς·   τὰ δὲ
δικαστήρια μισθοφόρα κατέστησε Περικλῆς."—Aristotle, " Pol." II. ix. 3.
See Müller's Dissertations on "The Eumenides." The Court of the Areopagus,
which dealt with homicides, received its name and functions from the first trial held
there, of Ares, for slaying Halirrhothius, son of Poseidon.

connection of Athens with Argos,[1] and using the legend of Orestes the Argive to make his countrymen welcome that coalition with Argos which was now a most desirable object, as a precaution, in view of the political struggle which was so soon to shake both Athens and Sparta in the terrible Peloponnesian War.

In this play the acme of fear and pity as the dramatic purpose is assuredly reached. The Chorus of fifty Furies, with the blood gouts dropping from their eyes, and their hair knotted and tangled with vipers, struck such absolute terror into the hearts of all beholders that in later representations, we are told their number was restricted, first to twenty, and then to twelve. Livy[2] tells us that the Romans themselves were once put to flight by the Gauls, dressed in the dire uniform of the Furies, and carrying blazing torches.

This drama, dealing with objects and scenes fraught with deepest awe for the Grecian mind, opens at the vestibule of the Temple of the Pythian Apollo, where the priestess addresses all the gods,

> "And lastly, thee, thou Jove supreme,
> Perfecting all things."

Then she enters the shrine, only to return affrighted, for there, she says, lies a man, abhorred by the just gods, bloodstained, a sword in one hand, and in the other an olive branch, and suppliant wreaths, while before him, fallen asleep in their horrid vigil, lie a troop of hideous female forms,

> "Wingless, in robes of night, hateful, abhorred,
> And as they sleep,
> Hoarse in their throats the harsh breath rattles deep."

Terrible indeed are those Furies, wakened by a man's sin or crime, relentlessly pursuing—agents of the punishment

---

[1] Except in "The Persians," all the extant Tragedies of Æschylus turn upon Argos. According to Aristotle ("Ath. Pol." ch. xvii. § 4), the friendship with Argos, which continued through long fluctuating periods of the history of Athens dated from the marriage of Pisistratus with an Argive woman.

[2] Livy, vii. 17.

of the gods—shadows of a soul on fire.   Themselves
declare,—

> " When, Fate drew the web of man's being together
>   She gave us our work,
> Saying, Loose on the impious, hell's black weather,
>   Till in shadows below, his dark spirit shall lurk.
> Even then no release can he know,—
> To the grim dreary shore we must go.
>   Children of Night, we pursue him,
>   With tortures and dread we undo him,
> And the chase of our blood-sprinkled feet drives his spirit to Woe."

The Priestess having proclaimed what awful forms are in
the temple, the scene opens, and Apollo is revealed, with
Orestes as suppliant before the shrine, the Furies still
sleeping.   The god promises him protection.

> " I will not leave thee.   To the very end,
> My watchful care shall guard thee and befriend.
> Distance cannot transport thee from my grace :
> But to thy foes I show no smiling face.
>   This horrid band !—see how the bonds of sleep
> Have bound them fast.   In vain their wrath shall sweep
> Across thy way.   Their home is deepest hell,
> Hated by men, and by the gods as well ! "

But the baffled hate of a mother's blood in murder slain,
stirs the very grave, and as they sleep, while Orestes flees
from the place, to Athens for purification and peace, the
ghost of Clytemnestra climbs the Charonic stair, stealing
upon the stage, with the ghastly death-wound still gaping
in her breast.   She chides the sleeping Furies—

> " What !—can sleep hold you yet,
>   While, like the leaping roe,
> He has escaped your net ? "

At her summons they awake, and scream their disappointment and their threats together, till Apollo orders them
away.

> " Hence—from my holy place !   My house abhors you.
> Go, where Revenge gouges, with hideous rage,
> The Victim's eyes, and rends the limbs apart,—

> Where slaughters please, and, in his horrid pain,
> The wretch, in torture, writhes upon the stake,
> Shrieking unheeded.   In such feasts of hate
> Your hearts, O hags unclean, find their delights ! "

Here Æschylus is shaking his poem free from the popular religious crudities.   The gods are just, and merciful, not fiends remorseless, revelling in the torments of a soul.

The Chorus remonstrate with the god, and elicit from him a hint of the defence he will make for Orestes.   They cry—

> " Thine the command that sent him forth to shed
> His mother's blood ! "

But he retorts—

> " Nay, but to avenge his father's cruel death."

The Chorus of Furies rush away crying,—

> " Lo ! here his trail ! leading us straight from the door,—
> Traitor, though tongueless, showing us where he went.
> Follow him ! as the hound, by drops of gore
> Traces the stricken deer, with wounds sore spent ! "

Then suddenly the scene changes from Delphi to the temple of Pallas on Areopagus, in Athens, with Orestes clinging, suppliant, at the shrine.   He calls upon the goddess ; and the terrible, haunting, wild things he has fled from, enter in.

> " Behold the hour,
> That gives thee to our power !
> Thy purple blood accurst
> Shall 'suage our thirst ;
> In the deep realms below.
> Thou, for thy murder's wounds shalt taste of woe,
> Learning the wage
> Of dark Impiety's unhallowed rage.[1]
> For in the shadows, Pluto, judge of men,
> Unswerving, weighs their meed to souls again ! "

---

[1] The special sins of Impiety punished in the lower world were those against parents and those of inhospitality.   *Cf.* "Æneid," vi. 608.

The goddess,[1] however, constitutes a court in the interests of absolute justice, while the Furies themselves acknowledge the integrity of her judgments. Orestes begins his story, but the goddess shrinks from herself giving a decision which may involve her land in a blood-feud with the Furies.

> " From noblest men,[2] whose souls are turned to truth,
> And justice, in this city, I will choose
> A solemn Court which shall through time abide."

Orestes makes his plea, telling of his kingly father, Agamemnon.

> " My mother, black of heart,
> Craftily murdered him. Then I returning
> From exile to my home, did hurl to death
> Her who had borne me. I deny it not.
> 'Twas vengeance due my father's outraged soul."

Now, above all things, the Athenian loved the excitements of the law: and this scene, with its familiar pleadings pro and con, with the life and happiness of a man hanging in the balance between heaven and hell, must have thrilled the audience with delight. This controversial passion was what swayed the later Tragedy in Euripides, till it swung it off the stage altogether.

The Furies, in their ode, protest against those upstart gods [3] with their new-fangled notions. Those deities of a later day, despised the privileges of the elder Titans, and awe shall soon be altogether removed, to the detriment of every sacred duty. The old Fate, stern, unreasoning, unbending, is fading off before man's growing sense of self, and in this declaration the poet strikes a strongly clanging note. The Titans symbolised rather the dark and mystic powers of Nature and of spirit; the later gods were rather of a world whose laws were systematised. The Furies represented the awakened conscience driven by vague fears, but

---

[1] The goddess, on her arrival, makes a reference to the dispute then proceeding between Athens and Mitylene regarding Sigeum, ll. 376-380.
[2] Rather "best-born." The Areopagus was an aristocracy, ll. 461-467.
[3] See p. 48 and chap. xvii.

in this play, giving way to Reason—herein, a marked advance.
The idea of evolution of deity is quite familiar in the Greek
mythology, and breaks out to the surface frequently in the
Tragic Choruses.

The Judges enter, and are seated among the spectators,
for the whole Athenian concourse is to share in fair-play to
this stranger suppliant at the Court of Athens.   Answering
his cross-examination by the Chorus, Orestes declares that
the murder of his mother was just punishment, demanded
by the gods, at his hand.

> "Her heart with twofold stain was deeply tarnished—
> My sire she murdered, when her lord she slew."

He pleads, too, the remarkable plea, not so strange to the
mind of the Greek, as it is repugnant to our age, that a man
is kin to his father, but not to his mother, a plea upheld by
Apollo, especially in the presence of Pallas, who according
to the myth, had known no woman-birth.[1]   This plea seems
to have had origin in Egyptian custom, or at any rate to have
been long located there.   The issue is then put to the
Court, but the Areopagus, so dear and precious to the
Athenians, has the memory of its lofty origin brought
forward strongly by the goddess.—

> "Hear me, ye men of Athens,—While this Court
> In bloody issues give their sentence first.
> Through time unborn, to Ægeus' host shall bide
> Its holy utterances revered, unshamed.
> This shall a rampart be around your rights,
> Keeping your laws secure, your state revered.
> No guard so noble any nation knows,—
> Free from the lure of bribes that blind the soul."

The pride of the Athenian in his ancient Constitution,
and in the venerable Court of the Areopagus, the defence
and glory of the State, was thus stirred to the deepest.   His
was a City whose most ancient institutions were established
by the very gods!   To him this was a gospel truth.   Here

---

[1] Diodorus, i. 80.

therefore, was he reminded strongly that he possessed above all other States, a tribunal incorruptible, and yet, at the same time, merciful, being just.

Pallas gives her casting-vote in favour of Orestes, thus establishing the principle, that, when the votes were equal, the verdict was acquittal. The casting vote in favour of the accused was, on this account, always called, " the pebble of Minerva "—*calculus Minervæ*. She says—

> " Unmothered I, a father's rights I guard.
> No woman, reddened with her husband's blood
> Wins grace from me."

The result is the acquittal of Orestes, who pledges the fealty of Argos to the Athenian State ;[1] a pledge which at the moment was actual fact, and not a mere poetic fiction, for Argos and Athens had politically joined hands, and the play seems, as we have seen, to have been intended to support and strengthen that alliance as against one with Sparta.

> " Homeward I go, and from my native State
> Never shall chief of ours against this land
> Lead war's proud spears. Ay, though my mouldering bones
> Lay in the grave, my ghost should intervene,
> Making the whole world frown on such a plan.
> Hail deity ! Hail, guardians of this State.
> Impregnable your walls, may Victory crown your spears ! "

The pride of the patriotic glory of the Athenian would here be kindled to enthusiasm. Yet the poet found more than politics and patriotism to teach, more than pride in the divine origin of his national institutions. He showed herein the potency of religion in hushing the soul's distractions,— the power of holy places to put a spell of peace around the struggling spirit. The very Furies, daughters of dark Revenge, shod with bloody purpose, fall asleep and are quiet,

---

[1] The alliance with Argos was made B.C. 459, just the year before the play was acted. As Müller has shown, this measure was brought about by the Party to whom Æschylus was politically opposed. The poet was above partisanship, and looked only to the good of the State. *Cf.* 1. 666.
τὸ μήτ' ἄναρχον μήτε δεσποτούμενον, κ.τ.λ.

at the holy shrine! And especially at Athens does the soul
that is wronged find support, comfort, calm and fair-play.[1]
The tangled threads of life's mysteries are put in heaven's
hands, and the gods are just. With heaven there is forgiveness, though with man, and with a man's own conscience,
that may be far enough away. Crime, with man, begets
crime, and only the mercy of the gods can cut the fatal cords
of doom above a race.

The Trilogy is the "Hamlet" of Æschylus. The shadow
at the Court, the infidelity to the living and the dead: and
the sad, terrible fate of the son, whose heaven-given lot it
is to bring justice ripely to pass, with the adjustment and
unification of tangled threads of purpose and fate, constitute
a soul-drama only equalled by that of the shadow-haunted
Court of Elsinore. It makes it a gaunt sequence of great
acts in the outworking of the tragic destinies of a great race.
Doom,—and is there any way out of it?—is the question for
the tempest-driven soul. Can a man escape the horror of
his heredity, his environment, and his duty? Yes, replies
the poet,—by facing duty, and trusting in the Highest, the
Unseen,—the Divinity that lives and works behind blind Fate.

The Trilogy reveals some distinct features. In the
"Agamemnon" you find a Tragedy of Freewill. It at the
same time embodies the sin and punishment of pride,[2] the
sin of indomitable ambition, stained with impiety. To the
poet it seems that ambition leads men astray by a sort of
divine infatuation, which whispers evil deeds, and emboldens
men to wrong: and its wage is ruin at the flood-tide of pro-
sperity. Masterly contrasts vivify the play—the splendour of
conquest, the magnificence of the palace, are painted with
powerful breadth in order to intensify the fall of the proud

---

[1] *Cf.* page 78.
[2] ὕβρις. The haughty heart is the constant provocation for the judgment of
heaven. In the Agamemnon Trilogy there are two powers of evil, namely, Ἄτη =
destruction, and πειθώ = persuasion, the self-persuasion of Pride and Vain-confidence
whereby a man justifies his Evil in his own sight, and so gets driven upon destruction.
See Prof. Butcher's "Aspects of the Great Genius," p. 109 *et sqq.*

vanquisher of nations, and the terrible black weight of ancestral guilt that drives him on, through glory, to disaster and despair. The character of Clytemnestra stands forth as one of the most cruel and subtle of the world's dramatic creations.

In the "Choephoræ" the footfall of Fate shakes the stage,—the murder of Clytemnestra is driven to fulfilment, partly by Fate, and partly by the piety of nature; partly by the duty of vindication of a father's honour, and partly through the agony of a sister's love. Yet the most terrible opposition of duties is revealed, in a man being called upon to avenge his father, but at the same time, also, to be guilty of the impiety of becoming his mother's murderer. The "Furies" represents a turmoil and conflict of the most sacred emotions and duties; finding pacification in the evolution of blessing from evil, of mercy out of cold and cruel revenge, all set against the background of the pride of the city dearest to the poet's soul, with its spirit-soothing, wrath-destroying institutions, touched by the calm of the gods.[1]

[1] Æschylean Tragedy is, in fact, the meeting-point in the region of Imagination, of Bacchic enthusiasm, of Epic Tradition, and of Orphic Pantheism, with the triumphant energy of Athenian civic life.—Prof. LEWIS CAMPBELL.

CHAPTER IX

SOPHOCLES AND THE ATREIDÆ

SOPHOCLES takes up in his " Electra," the Tragedy of the house of Atreus, but more from the human standpoint than Æschylus. Æschylus goes in behind the veil,[1] catches mystic clues of divine judgment, and gropes in the depths of the human conscience, in the shadows of the human heart, in the entanglements of the gods. Sophocles shows rather the working-out of a retribution by purely human means. Sophocles differs from Æschylus alike in his method and outlook.[2] Through him spoke all the culture of the Periclean age. Æschylus burned on the Altar of his own lyric fancy,—he was flame and light, his feeling flowed over as from a surcharged fountain, and Art was the slave of pure imagination. Sophocles was an artist, who drove both Imagination and Feeling on the curb, and made Art the dominating master of human passion. To him there are laws which have been begotten entirely apart from and transcending both the gods and men, eternal and changeless, and so the fates that overhang some human families have their springs in the moral action, manifested through pride of spirit, or dark · sin, rather than as inevitable and irresistible powers.

The heart of Electra hardened by horror and revulsion, till it is like a cold shining flint, remembers continually the cruel murder of Agamemnon by her mother, purely for the

[1] Æschylus was the poet of the gods: Sophocles the poet of the feelings: Euripides the poet of reality.—PALEY.
[2] See " Sophocles " in Prof. Butcher's " Aspects of the Greek Genius."

sake of her intrigue with Ægisthus, though ostensibly as a punishment for the sacrifice of Iphigeneia. She is absolutely merciless and unmoved, swerving not an inch from her resolute purpose of revenge. But she looks upon her fell purpose as an entirely just retribution. Analysing motives, and remembering the emotionalness of a woman's nature, one can see, displayed by Sophocles more clearly than in Æschylus, the tangled line of view along which Clytemnestra judged her own actions and feelings, especially when between her and her lord now lay the deep gulf of cleavage opened by her guilty love.

The play opens before the Palace of Ægisthus at Mycenæ and discloses the old slave to whom, after Agamemnon's murder, Orestes had been entrusted, speaking now with his ward, welcoming him back on his errand of vengeance, along with the mysterious Pylades, cousin of Orestes, and afterwards the husband of Electra.

> " It is the early morning ;
> Already the bright sun
> Awakes the birds to singing, and the night
> Fades with his stars into the broadening dawn."

Orestes tells how the Oracle had advised craft,—not open force, but guileful arts, and silent well-conducted fraud. He is not, as in " The Choephoræ " to be his own messenger. He instructs the pædagogue, since long absence has aged him, and made him practically unrecognisable, to learn the secret councils in the palace and to

> " Say, and confirm it with a solemn oath,
> Orestes is no more,—by a rude shock,
> Thrown from his chariot at the Pythian games."

Then with an urn in hand, they will go and tell the usurpers that they bear with them the ashes of Orestes.

> " What should deter me from the pious fraud ?
> .   .   .   The deed
> Which brings success and honour must be good,"—

a principle which is fraught with ethical danger,—the end
justifying the means! The voice of Electra is heard mourning within; but Orestes does not wait, being impelled to
attend to the duties of piety incumbent on him, at his
father's tomb.

> " These pious rites performed shall fire our souls,
>   And crown our bold attempt with fair success."

Duty helps duty, and a deed well-done becomes the effectual
step towards another.

When they depart Electra comes upon the stage, wailing
for her grievous life, the terrible burden of persecution she
has had to bear, and the ever-abiding sorrow for her
murdered father. She invokes heaven's help and pity.

> " Ye vengeful Furies, come and help my prayers.
>   O quickly bring Orestes to my need.
>   For 'neath oppression's woes I sink forlorn,
>   And can no longer bear the weight alone."

In vain the Chorus come and counsel her as to the fruitlessness of grief, since neither tears nor prayers can recall the
dead. In her emotion she feels, not only as though the
gods have become careless, but also as if Orestes were
forgetful of his duty, and of all she had borne for him.
The Chorus plead with her for submissiveness and patience.

> " Despair not, daughter: Jove is still in heaven,
>   The god who sees, and knows and governs all:
>   Time is a kind indulgent deity,
>   And he shall give thee succour for thy grief."

That time and the gods are always on the side of the just,
is a common comfort in all ages, but it demands strong,
patient faith to hold fast to it till it justify itself. The
Chorus cannot enter into the feelings of a King's daughter,
with the shame of her house continually before her eyes,
and her grief for her father ever in her heart, especially
when, yearly, the dance and song and solemn feast, instituted

by Clytemnestra, celebrate with rejoicing the tragedy of Agamemnon's death.

Now Chrysothemis, Electra's sister, enters, bearing offerings from Clytemnestra for the tomb of her murdered husband. The queen has been moved to this by fear of a dream, in which she has seen Agamemnon bearing the royal sceptre, whence a green branch seemed to spring, which shaded all Mycenæ. Chrysothemis, apparently of a softer nature, had chosen the quiet way of obedience, rather than Electra's method of resistance, and threatened revenge.[1] She advises her sister to follow a similar course for safety.

> " Meantime, with lowered sail, to bear the storm
> Befits us best."

But Electra refuses to listen to so pusillanimous a policy. She feels that she herself is in the better way, since her grief tortures her foes, and at the same time venerates the dead. She does not heed the warning that, on the return of Ægisthus, banishment and confinement are to be her lot. She will die rather than surrender her pious duty to her father. And now she herself sends offerings by the hands of Chrysothemis, to be laid upon her father's tomb.

The Chorus feel intensely the premonition of advancing fate, and hear as it were the whirr of the wheels in that old chariot race when Pelops won the wreath through treachery of Myrtilus the charioteer of Œnomaus—a treachery rewarded by Pelops with death, after he himself had gained his own desire.

> " Swift comes the fury speeding,
> The trampling hosts of her dread judgments leading,
> And the old curse of Pelops' perfidy
> Has never left his house from sorrow free ! "

The next scene is one of great power, when Electra and Clytemnestra are face to face,—a scene that stands almost on

---

[1] *Cf.* Ismene, sister of Antigone. One would be apt to imagine that the one model sat for both.

a par with the interview between Hamlet and his mother.
The guilty queen does not deny the crime, but cries —

> " Mine was the deed—the pride of it mine own !
> Thy sire I slew : yet Justice was behind me ;
> And thou, hadst thou been true, hadst borne thy part.
> He whom thou wailst forever,—cruel heart!—
> Heartless, among the Greeks, his daughter gave
> To bloody doom, to satisfy the gods.
> Why did he bring the guiltless down to death?
> For Greece? . . . for Menelaus? . . . or for Helen?
> What was thy father, but inhuman, base.
> Even thy sweet sister, murdered, could she speak
> Out of the grave, would join her words with mine ! "

Electra spurns the excuses, and declares the true reason
for the murder of her father. Not love of Iphigeneia, but
of Ægisthus,—the sin of adultery, had driven the arm of
Clytemnestra to the crime. And, further, she explains
that Iphigeneia's death was due, in expiation of an insult to
Artemis uttered by her father in the chase. Still more, she
rebukes the mouth of her that speaks so much about piety
and duty, yet lives in lustful union with Ægisthus, having
actually wedded the deadly foe of her murdered husband.[1]

This is a long and painful interview, and Electra's warning
to Clytemnestra to beware of her own doctrine, lest blood
for blood be the inexorable machinery of her own destiny, is
interrupted by the arrival of the old servant or pædagogue,
who announces himself a messenger, with dramatic brevity
intimating

> "Orestes is no more ! "

He tells his fabricated tale of Orestes, thrown from his
chariot at the Pythian games, and dragged, entangled in the
reins, to a terrible death. " Ah, in vain," says the messenger,
with words of double portent —

> " In vain strives man
> To circumvent the purpose of the gods ! "

---

[1] *Cf.* The Court of Elsinore and Hamlet's interview with his mother.

Clutching at this new hope, Clytemnestra in the sudden joy of her heart, after a make-believe regret, deepens her sin, exulting in the tidings.

> " Gone are my fears. Day had no rest for me,
> And night no slumbers. Constant dread of death
> Appalled me. Now my soul may dwell in peace ! "

But Electra summons Nemesis to hear—that dreadful goddess of retribution, always ready to punish impiety and human pride. Terrible was this deity, sometimes represented as winged, so swift was she to swoop upon the guilty, over sea and land. And when this Clytemnestra, the woman of the iron face, has taken the messenger within, Electra pours forth her grief.

> " Here will I lay me down, and end my life
> And sorrow both together. Life's one pang ;
> I have no wish to hold it in my heart." [1]

But Chrysothemis reappears, thrilled by the evidence, as it seems to her, of the return of Orestes, as revealed by libations and offerings which she has seen upon her father's tomb ; only to have her gladness dashed with the bitter tidings fresh with pain in the heart of sad Electra. The latter, lifted to the heights of tragic resolution, unfolds a scheme by which, now that death has apparently blasted their hopes, they themselves may wring revenge from the guilty queen and her paramour.

> " So shalt thou praises win,
> Both from our father slain, and from Orestes.
> Hearest thou not Fame's whisper of applause ?
> What voices shall combine to praise our faith,
> Saying, as on we move, Behold the twain,
> Who, to preserve their house, looked deep in death,
> Despising danger—sought revenge of blood,
> And held life lighter than a father's wrongs !
> So, where the people meet, our deed's approved.
> The memory of our name shall never die."

---

[1] The absolute *naturalness* of the characters of Clytemnestra and Electra stands out clearly here. The proud, brazen-hearted queen, not ashamed of her sin and her crime—the young pure soul of Electra, clinging, till despair shakes off her grip, to the hope of vengeance for her father's murder.

But Chrysothemis shrinking from the task, Electra declares that she herself will do the deed. Her proud, wounded spirit cannot bear this prudence of her sister.

> " Go thy way.   Henceforward
> I hold no commerce or communion with thee." [1]

Next on the scene enter Orestes, and Pylades, his silent tragic friend, asking the way to the palace, and displaying the urn, the make-believe tabernacle of her dead brother's ashes. A pathetically beautiful threnody is breathed by Electra over this sad memorial.

> " All, all, with thee is gone,
> Ah me, thy death, like devastating storm
> Hath borne down all.   My father is no more :
> And thou art gone ; and my sad footsteps, too,
> Move towards the shadows."

But Orestes discloses his identity, and she is restored to buoyant hope, in a recognition scene, deeply human, with touching beauty, haunting the dark hate of her heart for Clytemnestra.

> " Now that I see thy face,
> My heart could weep for ever."

Meanwhile, within, Clytemnestra prepares the funeral banquet for the anniversary celebration, and Orestes, with his silent witness, enters. Then the terrified cries of the queen are heard, pleading with her son.

> " Ah, hapless me !   Ægisthus, where art thou ?
> Pity thy mother.   O my son, my son !
> O, I am slain ! "

One is reminded of such historic episodes as the murder of Agrippina, in that cry; while the ecstasy of vengeance in Electra's

> " Again—-again !   Smite, if thine arm be able ! "

exceeds, in the deepening of the tragic horribleness of a

---

[1] The tragic choice of Electra lies between mere worldly prudence and loyalty to the dead.

soul estranged from natural relationships, anything I know.
The cup of the curse is brimming over.

> " O wretched race !   Thy fate, that dogged thy steps,
> This day completes it ! "

Ægisthus now returns, full of triumphant joy at the news
that has been conveyed to him.   He asks,

> " Shall we behold the dead ? "

Electra answers,

> " Ay, but it is not beautiful to see."

Nevertheless, in pride uplifted, Ægisthus cries, as he
approaches,

> " Silence, I say.   Wide let the gates be thrown,
> That Argos and Mycenæ view the sight,
> Seeing the hopes that fed their treason up,
> Withered for aye, that fear may make them wise."

The scene falls apart, in obedience to his call, and the
corpse of the newly-slain is disclosed, but shrouded and
veiled.   Ægisthus, deeming it to be the body of Orestes,
and little knowing how truly he is made to speak, says—

> " O happy sight !
> O god supreme—without thy sovereign will
> This had not been.   May no dire judgment fall
> Upon me for my words.   Lift up the veil ! "

But Electra answers,

> " Nay.   Lift the veil thyself ! "

He commands them to call Clytemnestra.

> " She is near thee,"

replies the stern daughter of the slain.

He removes the veil—a scene worth imagining, in its
thrill of awe upon the spectators, the terrible irony of it
flooding him, and all who behold it.   Suddenly Orestes
faces him, as he stands thunder-struck, and orders him

within—the signal for death. Ægisthus, with a fine touch of scorn, impudently brave, with the courage of desperation, and discovery, says,

> "But why go in ?   If Justice guide thy deed,
> Let daylight clothe it."

Orestes, however, finds it more appropriate that he should die in the fatal place where Agamemnon fell,—a subterfuge necessitated by the Greek dramatic convention. The play, therefore, ends with their departure within for death ; and the cry of the Chorus,

> "O line of Atreus, through how many woes
> Hast thou at last found freedom, crowned with good
> From this day's doings ! "

Now, in this treatment of the tragic story, we are in quite a different field from that of Æschylus. He had to hew to shape the blocks he found in the old quarry of Homer ; but Sophocles came upon the stage when the myth had become a flexible instrument in the poet's hand, and when it was possible to widen the scope of the Drama by enlarging the Chorus, and adding a third actor.[1]

The story of the tragic line is seized at the central point ; and flung into dramatic form. A trilogy subject is reduced into one single play of complex interest. The absolute fatality of the oracle is displayed. The murder is a god-demanded act of retribution, the evasion of which means dishonour, alike to the dead hero, and the whole race. The attempted palliations of her crime by Clytemnestra are not considered at all. The Furies, whose dread hate hunting down the miserable soul, shook Æschylus's audience, are absent.[2] There is no moment's pause in the progress of the

---

[1] It was much more difficult after Thespis, Phrynichus, and Chœrilus to advance Tragedy to such a degree of greatness as Æschylus did, than for one who wrote after Æschylus to arrive at the completeness of Sophocles.—SCHOLIA.

[2] There is not even a hint that a son who slays his mother is liable to the attention of the Furies. Sophocles was at the Homeric standpoint, having resolved to limit his view by the epic horizon.—JEBB.

Tragedy from the outset to the end of horror. It is, all through, the drama of a mother's murder, atoning for her husband's death, and filling up the cup of suffering of the race, teaching the absolute doom-necessity of unswerving, emotionless justice. The tragic ironical contrast is the secret of its power. Electra wails within, despairing, but Orestes whom she can no longer hope to see, is at the very gate. Ægisthus rejoices, expecting to see the face of the dead he hates, and is smote in the heart by the vision of the dead he loves.

The poet also emphasises the relationship between Electra and Orestes by depicting the old retainer to whom she had, on Agamemnon's murder, committed the care of the child Orestes, for preservation against the day of full revenge.

The contrast of human piteousness with absolute un-swerving hate, in Electra, demands the largest possible creation of sympathetic interest to draw the pity of the spectators towards her terribly embittered utterance. She is strung to breaking point. We see only the victim of a shocking reaction, impelled and possessed by a dominating ideal. The apparently iron hardness of this woman's heart, however, melts in the recognition scene, when Orestes is declared before her, and the love for her brother rehumanises her.

Sophocles makes the return of Orestes the doomsday of impiety and tyranny that are based on cruel murder. It is the deepening of the awe of heaven's decree against bloody and selfish crime, and at the same time it is retribu-tion, with restitution of the disordered balance of the universe.

The Clytemnestra of Sophocles is not the tragedy-queen of Æschylus, but a weak woman, dominated by a base passion, and paying all its price. Nor is she painted with such maternal touches as in Euripides's later play. Ægisthus, on the other hand, is entirely cruel, vain and despicable, all the while ignorant of the shadow that has its hand upon his shoulder.

Sophocles is more of an artist than Æschylus, and is content to grip the human interests, rather than to walk behind the veil, seeking for solutions in the mysterious shadows, where the heart fails, and the spirit shrinks for fear.[1] Orestes achieves the purpose of his life as the instrument of the outraged gods. He is the sword of divinest justice ; and there, in the acknowledgment of the unswerving decree of the gods, the matter is resolved.

Æschylus showed innocence suffering for guilt; and even the standards of the moral system reeling beneath the difficulty of determining issues when both sides seemed to be in the right. Sophocles, however, puts rather the human action in the foreground, moving to the impulse of unseen laws divine, beyond man's explanation, though still binding him to their sway.

You have no longer the warrior-bard, whose huge creations move in " the light that never was on sea or land," but at one step you are in the presence of the cultured artist, with a real plot, and human characterisations. The blind Destiny, whose jealousy of the power and pride of men toppled the great to destruction—Nemesis, men named her (and they knew that they could never woo her from her work !)—a necessity higher in power than even Jove himself—this was now out-dated by the age of Sophocles; so rapidly men and their opinions grow when they begin, as the Greeks had, to move about the wider world, with open eyes. They became rationalistic questioners of the tremendous creed of their fathers. To them man is no longer a captive bound hand and foot, and flung into a dungeon which the gods call life, although, in view of the futility of human effort, such a thing can only be as a hell. Men begin to

---

[1] Divine Agency is the leading idea of Æschylus in working out human destiny. Man's own agency pulling the divine cords, is alike Shakespeare's and Sophocles's. Æschylus concentrated on divine action, while Sophocles looked into the heart.

give themselves some credit for their own evils, as well as
for their own good; and Destiny becomes rather Retribution.[1]
Our sins do become

> "instruments to scourge us."

Sophocles shows us how it is

> " Passion surging past control
> That plays the god to each man's soul."

We drag the roof upon us, when we smash the supporting
columns; and we must not curse the gods for what ourselves
have done; nor, till the full tune is sounded up to its last
chord can the melody begin again unjarred.

[1] The supremacy of Justice—or rather of Equity—is in Æschylus the "far-off
divine event towards which the whole Creation moves," but in Sophocles it is a
fixed decree, which is from everlasting, and fulfils itself regardless of human happiness or suffering.—Prof. LEWIS CAMPBELL.

CHAPTER X

EURIPIDES AND HIS AGE

EURIPIDES dealt in his own way with the Agamemnon myth, in his tragedies of "Electra," "Orestes," "Iphigeneia in Aulis," and "Iphigeneia in Tauris." He approached these ancient legends by the way of an age whose mental and political developments had altered the point of view. The period in which Euripides lived and wrote was that of Pericles and Alcibiades, Thucydides, Aristophanes, and Phidias—the full sun-burst time of Grecian history, as concentrated in the life of Athens. He was the friend and probably a disciple of Anaxagoras,[1] and he was also the friend and favourite tragic poet of Socrates. He was thus knee-deep and heart-deep in the thought of the school that was engaged in the conflict between the old orthodoxy and common-sense. A new policy had been instituted by Pericles, who, although aristocrat of the aristocrats, became the Liberal leader against the old conservatism of Cimon, whose policy he overthrew. This meant a period of keen discussion of all points of possible issue in regard to religious and political rights; for the suffrage secured by Cleisthenes for the Athenians, had practically thrown everything into the open market-place. The trend to centralisation at Athens ruined the old charm of country life; the question of the emancipation of woman was unsettled and not a little unsettling through the example of Pericles and Aspasia; while, through all the new windows that had been opened

---

[1] Fined and banished from the State, for free-thinking, on the instigation of Cleon. *Cf.* Laertius, " Vit. Anaxagoras," ii. 14, Plutarch, " Vit. Pericl.," c. 32.

by foreign travel and intercourse, strange lights began to fall athwart the old mythologies, the ideas of the national gods, and theories of ethical relations. It was in the poet's home that Protagoras is said to have read the work which brought him under the charge of atheism. No wonder, then, of course, that the poet's free treatment of the myths and of the gods involved him in suspicion. Yet atheist he was not; for the only atheist in his works is the Cyclops, whose ignorant brutality seems a rebuke on all his tribe.

But though his plays reflected thus remarkably the spirit of his times he was only successful in gaining a first prize on four occasions, and, for the first time, only in his fortieth year. He was not a flatterer of his times, nor did the conservatism of a radical populace approve of his free handling of the stories of their gods. Besides, the age does not always recognise itself in drama; or if it do, it seldom feels flattered by the recognition; so, late in life, he had to remove to the Court of the Macedonian king Archelaus. His times were "out of joint." Tradition makes him sit in the Isle of Salamis, his birth-isle, composing his plays, in view of the changing sea, with its myriad moods reflecting the changeful complexion of his own soul, with its doubts, its search for the abiding amidst fluctuating uncertainties,—its hopeless, faithless quest for hope and faith. His attitude was, by nature, a pensive, gentle agnosticism.

The kind of criticism which quarrels with a dramatic poet for the maxims put in the mouths of his creations is unjust. For example, to condemn Euripides, as many have done, because of such a line as, in the "Hippolytus,"

"My tongue has sworn it, but my heart is free,"

is as unfair as it would be to condemn Sophocles for teaching duplicity, treachery, and murder in his "Electra" or "Philoctetes," or to carp at Shakespeare for the words which he puts in the mouth of Iago; or even Milton for the speeches in hell.

Hippolytus, indeed, dies rather than break the very oath he speaks of; and the whole matter has its origin in the dramatic clothing of the tragic creations in the word and deed appropriate to the character they embody and typify. For the Drama in Euripides's time had become a thing of plot and action rather than of situation and character. A spirit of change was abroad even here. The use of scenes in perspective was being tried by Agatharchus the painter; and, often, one feels that Euripides has created a lyrical intermezzo rather than a play; for his choral odes, however beautiful they be, are rather interludes than integral parts of the drama in which they are set.

A very striking characteristic of the plays of Euripides is the introduction of the prologue, which tells the whole story at the offset; and the continual extrication from difficult dilemmas, by the intervention of the gods. Thus, Iphigeneia is, by divine magic, saved from the sacrificial knife; again, by the intervention of Pallas, she is allowed to escape with Orestes and Pylades; and when Orestes, in frenzy, to repay Menelaus for a slight, has Helen under his very sword, she also is snatched, very mysteriously, away. He seems to create a dramatic situation of over-mastering difficulties, shows a soul entangled in the wiles of the gods; and then, in a half-petulant mood, and with a dash of scorn, drags in the gods to pull apart the difficulties which themselves have made. It is a slap in the face of popular superstition. He cannot endure the popular gods, except as rude masks of the divine and spiritual, whom yet he cannot fully grasp and know.[1]

The conventions of the stage were doubtless beginning to gall both poet and audience, but it is remarkable, that this only occurred when the greatest phase of the Drama was declining. Novelty was demanded by the times, and the

---

[1] He wonders that men can put their trust in beings to whom every crime is attributed by the very mythology whereby their existence is declared.—PALEY, *cf.* chap. xvi.

poet had to meet the demand. Such an attempt destroyed the inevitableness of his work, and Drama suffered. For, as was well shown by Aristotle, what is said to have happened in the past, however strange it may be, is accepted as possible. But the effort after reality gave way to the demand for illusion and surprise. Cheapness and tawdry trick, trap-door and mirror-work, so to speak, sapped the great, giant majesty of true Drama. Euripides had fallen on such a time; and, in consequence, a composite of truth and artificialism, he has been one of the most severely criticised of poets. Yet, sometimes, the condemnation of him, for his form, for his use of prologues, and for his agnostic teaching, is overdone, and somewhat unfair, like setting modern war-methods against the methods of the Mutiny for comparison and measure.

A poet is not rigidly bound and chained.[1] He is, as much as anything, almost a vehicle, and instrument of Vision and Passion struck into utterance by the pain or triumph of his times.

The criticism which says he shall always pour his molten utterance into the same old bottles, does not know the material it criticises. Euripides, in his "Alcestis," the only satyric drama left, mingled humour with tragedy, and was condemned, but his faults arose from the fact that his age had advanced. He felt, besides, that the old satyric play was too much of a shock after the tragedy preceding. Philosophy like that of Anaxagoras, and methods like those of Socrates, were knocking at the door of things, as the young mind of the Press in later days cross-examined the dogmatic Pulpit, and awoke a new voice within it.

The old Tragedy of Æschylus loomed heavy on that day. So Euripides really went back beyond it to the archaic field,[2] when Humour and Horror stalked alternately; and who

---

[1] It is, besides, unfair to put any man's utterances in parallel columns. "The foolish and the dead alone do not change their opinions."—LOWELL.
[2] *Cf.* Aristophanes, "Frogs," 909.

knows but that Drama is the truer to real life itself where the ridiculous walks at funerals, and sits sometimes by deathbeds?

Euripides, in reality, obeyed the maxim of Aristotle [1] in taking the old myth, with its complications, looking at the characters as purely human, and then making his drama answer the question as to what men and women would do and should do under the circumstances presented by the story. Sometimes, of course, he could not resist, in this way, attacks upon received principles, assaults upon accepted evils, and not infrequently upon accepted individuals, thus making Tragedy invade the realm of Comedy and Invective; and often awakening the suspicion of a laugh or a sneer at things which had grown to be considered sacred. [2]

Even his prologues did not matter nearly so much as the modern critic sometimes thinks. The explanation might be needed sorely, as Euripides took liberties with the ancient stereotyped myth, and this would shock his hearers, with surprise, away from the real action and motive of his play unless prepared for it in the way he adopted. The very objection that the audience knew what to expect is no real objection, for they knew the myths which were the foundation of the Drama quite clearly already. The quick Greek mind would then be able to follow and appreciate without questioning. Æschylus had dealt with the big questions of the heroes and gods, and the relation of man to these. [3] But men had begun to perceive that they were as good as their gods were represented to be, at least in the popular theology. Art broke them away from mere religion, though art was religious itself in its origin. Sophocles dealt with humanity, its outlook, and its remedies. Poetry, particularly, in Euripides and Sophocles, departed from the stories of the gods as persons, and devoted itself to the setting, develop-

---

[1] " Poetics," 17.

[2] He is especially impatient of soothsayers and necromancers.

[3] Where Æschylus tried to scare, to strike, to impress the Imagination, Euripides strove to meet, to humanise, to enlist the affections.—PALEY.

ments, and resolution, of moral problems in human
surroundings.[1]

The Attic world had taken rapid strides. History had
been keeping step with it. Its intellect had been growing,
and growing inquisitive, and rather sceptical. Euripides
cannot believe in blind Destiny; so, his characters are
frequently creatures of a blinder Chance.[2] And the oracles
of the gods are to him often mere provocatives to sin,
punishment for which, by the very gods themselves, is a
shameless anomaly. The introspective attitude is sure to
come in all progress, and especially in the progress of a mind
like the Grecian. The poet is the product of his time,—the
ages' gold and dross together get welded into the harp. The
chords are restrung as they wear through, and they inevitably
get the cry of the new era into their voice.

Traces of the Athenian love of gossip referred to in the
Acts of the Apostles as a characteristic of the people, are
found in the tales about this tragic poet.[3] His love of
solitude could only be interpreted in some evil fashion by the
company-loving Greek; and his name became identified with
much that was churlish and grim. And yet, how true and
tender—thoughtful of the slave, in whose mouth he puts
clearest wisdom, in whose heart the deepest faithfulness;
and gentle in his delineations of womanhood, which he
adorns with highest moral graces and dignified power of
character! A man above his time, was this.

> " Euripides the human,
>   With his droppings of warm tears."

---

[1] Euripides was a sympathiser with humanity as a fact, but a despiser of polytheism
as an invention.—PALEY.

[2] In a fragment he says—

$$\pi o\lambda\lambda\acute{a}\kappa\iota\ \mu o\iota\ \pi\rho a\pi\acute{\iota}\delta\omega\nu\ \delta\iota\tilde{\eta}\lambda\theta\epsilon\ \phi\rho o\nu\tau\grave{\iota}s$$
$$\epsilon\emph{\i}\tau\epsilon\ \tau\acute{\upsilon}\chi a\ \tau\iota s\ \epsilon\emph{\i}\tau\epsilon\ \delta a\acute{\iota}\mu\omega\nu\ \tau\grave{a}\ \beta\rho\acute{o}\tau\epsilon\iota a\ \kappa\rho a\acute{\iota}\nu\epsilon\iota\cdot$$

Cf. also " Hecuba," 491, and " Ion.," 1512.

[3] He was before his time, whole ages,—in the attitude of his mind toward slaves and
slavery especially. See " Medea," 54, and " Orestes." 869: where he recognises the
sympathy of slaves, with the misfortunes of their masters, and their gratitude for
kindness in times past. See Professor Butcher's, " Aspects of Greek Genius," p. 167.

Aristophanes, of course, was unrelenting in his dislike,[1] and even death could not stay the keen whip of his satire; and in this the comic writer had the advantage over the other, whom he hated as a rigid "old light" would hate any "highest critic," for the dead had no retort.

Euripides, on his part, took up the position that the tragic poet was not the slave of the people's whim; and he did not fear to defend, in face of the mob, a sentiment to which they had objected, by declaring to them, "It is my business to teach you,—not yours to teach." He heeded no rebuff; and the day of his consolation came to him in due time; for, when in 413 B.C. the Athenian host which had been sent to Syracuse was swept away,—ships and men together,—in her hour of deepest misery, Athens heard that any of the prisoners who could recite portions of the dramas of Euripides were taken from the dungeons and tended with kindly care, and partial freedom. In less than fifty years after his death, his name stood on the topmost line of tragic poets.

Of course, when he appeared a fierce light beat upon him, as on all new poets. Æschylus had just died. Sophocles was passing. And, as in our own days, when we remember the echoes of the great who have gone, leaving none to fill their places, men were wondering who next was fittest to strike the great poetic note in succession to those whom death had silenced. Yet the younger was the stronger influence, affecting even his rivals in the contest, unconsciously—as for example, in "Philoctetes," even Sophocles himself revealing the yeast of Euripides working in his art.

---

[1] The sting of the comic poet is keen in the "Acharniars," where Dicæopolis sneering at Euripidean artifices in costume, begs the poet for the loan of

"A suit of tatters from a cast-off Tragedy."

Again, rather meanly, casting the poet's mother in his teeth, he wishes—

"May you prosper, like your noble mother."

And he begs—

"A little bundle of leaves to line my basket—
A single lettuce from your mother's stall!"

Perhaps a little jealousy would account for much, as it is apparent from the "Clouds," 1364, that Euripides was the fashion among the poets of his time. So far from his mother Kleito being a coster, she was probably even of noble birth.

CHAPTER XI

In the "Electra" of Euripides we find the subject of Æschylus's "Choephoræ" dealt with; but here we see how far apart this poet stood from those who had gone before him in the same track. Often it seems, indeed, as if his work were an open criticism of the older methods, and every deviation from these is carefully and specifically defended.

In this play, instead of the highborn maid appealing to our sympathy at the palace gates, we have her in a harrowing position of degradation, which had been thrust upon her by the vindictive oppression of Ægisthus and Clytemnestra. Of course history supports the feasibleness of such a scheme, for in 1648 a somewhat similar degradation was proposed for the Princess Elizabeth, Charles the First's daughter, whom it was designed to appentice to a buttonmaker,—a scheme which she evaded by dying in Carisbrooke, where she was confined along with her hapless father.

The peasant Auturgus to whom Electra is formally married, though he has respected her virgin state, is of good enough blood; and he is depicted as one of Nature's gentlemen. One is here forcibly reminded of some of the aspersions cast upon Euripides himself on account of his birth. Of his father, Mnesarchus, not much is known; but the rancour of the poet's many enemies made little enough of him, and added to their venom, the circumstance that his mother Kleito was a herb-woman or fruit-hawker. The Athenian attached great importance to good birth; but perhaps even more to the opportunity of a laugh at any price, so long as themselves did not pay it.[1] We can find in Euripides, often, such references as let us see how such things hurt him, when he speaks, as he does here, of the true nobility of heart which makes a gentleman.

Auturgus, in the prologue, enumerates the stages of the story of the Tragedy of Agamemnon and the Warriors of Troy, and touches with pity, on the humiliations of Electra. She herself now enters on the scene, under the shadow of

" Sable night, nurse of the golden stars."

She bears a vase in which she is to carry water from the river,

" Urged by no stern necessity,
But that the very gods may see the wrongs
Laid on me by Ægisthus; and to pour
To listening heaven my sorrows for my sire."

When Auturgus gently protests against her taking this labour upon herself, she reminds him of his great forbearing kindness to her, and her own duty to attempt to lighten his arduous life, of which he is not a little proud, as he remembers the lazy excuses of the much-devout. For he holds that

" No lazy fool, though prating of the gods,
Can win life's needs without life's sacrifice
To daily labour."

Next Orestes and Pylades come upon the stage, having poured libations, and paid memorial rites at the tomb of Agamemnon. And now, as

" Morning opes her shining eyes,"

they retire from the public path, to wait till some passing ploughman, or female slave may give them tidings of the whereabouts of Electra, whom they seek. Even while they are speaking she appears, carrying the water from the well.

[1] See page 86n.

In a very touching ode she sings of all her sorrows, and the
sorrows of her line,

> " As some poor swan that cries
>   Among the river reeds its mournful song
> For its lost sire that in the meshes dies ! "

The Chorus ask her to join them in a festival at Argos,
as all the virgins are speeding to Hera's shrine ; but she
replies,

> " Nay, not on festal joy my heart is set.
> The charm of golden chains my thoughts forget,
> Nor heed the gladsome glance ;
> Nor can I beat a merry foot in mazy circling dance.
> Weeping I spend my day,
> And in unsolaced griefs my life must pine away."

Orestes breaks in upon her lamentation as if with a
message from her brother ; and the interview is depicted
with a human-hearted pathetic naturalness truly worthy " sad
Electra's poet."   Recovering from her sudden fear of outrage
or assault, she makes no secret of her confidence in the
revenge which her brother, if he ever do return, will execute
upon Agamemnon's murderers.   One cannot help feeling
that out of the depths of the disappointed heart of the poet
himself comes an utterance like this—

> " Those who've looked into knowledge, learn pity ;
> And yet the bitterest pain is child of knowledge,
> Too much knowing."

She tells of the neglect of her father's tomb, and of the
vulgar insulting pride of Ægisthus, who risks the anger
both of the dead, and of the gods,[1] when

> " Mad with wine,
> That noble hero, now my mother's lord,
> With insult shames the grave where sleeps the dust
> Of Agamemnon ; taunting with his scorn
> The helpless dead, and crying, ' Where's thy son ?
> Vaunted Orestes, where ? He guards thee well ! ' "

---

[1] To pelt a tomb with stones, as Electra had heard that Ægisthus had actually
done, was accounted an irreparable insult and impiety.

Auturgus, her husband, now welcomes the strangers; and here again the radicalism of the poet speaks, through Orestes, opinions of true gentle-manhood.

> " Nature no mark sets on a true man's state
>   To tell the generous mind.   I've seen a knave
> Shaming a noble line ; while some I've seen
> Making the commonest blood a bounteous thing.
> I've seen a rich man's heart an empty house,
> While in a poor man's dwelt a kingly soul,
> What then our guide ?   Wealth ?   'Tis a fickle dream.
> Or poverty ?   Nay, oft it fathers crime.
> Or courage ?   But the same spear suits the hand
> Of valiant and of coward.   Here's this man,
> Not marked by lineage, of a common stock,
> Yet gentle, for he hath a gentle heart.
> The true nobility of noble deed,
> And noble word, alone makes gentlemen."

This is a new doctrine on the Attic Stage—a dangerous doctrine it might seem to some, whose only right to honourable seats was that their fathers had sat in them.

In the house, the aged servant, who had carried off Orestes, in infancy, to a place of safety,[1] at the critical juncture of his father's murder, tells of the signs and traces of some friendly presence having been at the king's tomb. The scene, for various reasons, is worth reproducing.

> " Methinks thy brother secretly has come
>   To pay due honour to his father's grave,
> Neglected.   See these locks,—compare thine own,
> For one sire's children like each other are.

> ELECTRA.

> Thy words are all unwise.   Thou shouldst not think
> With coward steps of stealth my brother comes
> Fearing Ægisthus. . . . Then, how weak a clue !
> His hair a man's, roughened by manly toils ;
> Mine soft as is a woman's, combed and curled ;
> And many are like-moulded, each to each,
> Who knew not common sire, nor kindred blood.

---

[1] Stesichorus and Pindar make Orestes rescued from the wiles of Clytemnestra by the nurse Arsinoë.   Pyth. Od. xi.

SLAVE.

Measure his footprint, then.   Put thine in his,
See whether his be not the same as thine.

ELECTRA.

How could the hard rock yield and keep the shape
Of his tread passing on it ?   And besides,
What brother has a foot the same in size
As any sister's ?   Larger 'tis, by far !

SLAVE.

Hast thou no token, if thy brother comes,
Would guide thee—nothing woven in thy loom—
The robe he wore, when snatched from death that day—

ELECTRA.

Old man, thou dreamest.   A babe myself was I
When poor Orestes' life was saved by flight.
And, even had such been his, a man's growth leaves
The garment of his childhood far behind.
Clothes grow not daily with a body's growth ! "

You are here looking, with Euripides softly laughing, at
the old conventions, which so long had satisfied.   This is a
bit of criticism ; and at the same time, the poet's apology
for the lifting of the dramatic incident into the domain of
common sense.   It is a slightly sneering reflection on the
treatment of the same episode in " The Choephoræ " of
Æschylus,[1] and of course, and more truly, a rebuke of the
popular traditional demands made upon the poet.   Little
objection was popularly felt to the hero circumventing his
foe by craft.   Euripides, however, feels that the tragic hero
should be above a mean trick; and he pours all his scorn
into the mould of Electra's words which refuse to admit that
her brother could possibly come like a sneak, to the completion of his whole life's dream and duty.

The old servant who saved Orestes seeks to question the
strangers about his ward, but the old eyes remember signs

---

[1] " Choeph." 218 et seqq.

and marks which make him recognise the man who stands before him, and Electra, at length, sees how truly it is her brother that has returned.

The plot they fix upon is a very simple artifice. Orestes has just got to have himself invited to share in the sacrifice which Ægisthus is directing, and then there will be ample room and easy opportunity for fulfilling destiny. This also is of a piece with what has gone before. Instead of taking the murderers in the palace, where guards would be about, and the scheme have risk of miscarriage, how much more natural is the country-place, and the confusion of a festival of the gods! The plan is carried out in its perfect simplicity; and Ægisthus having been slain, the Chorus tell Electra how the hope of her heart has been realised.

> " Now lightly lead the measure,
>   For the task is done.
> And the harvest of thy waiting hopes
>   Is fully won."

They return with the corpse of Ægisthus, and Electra, not without fear of provoking Nemesis, apostrophises the dead.

> " Long have I wondered how I'd speak to thee !
> Each dawn began anew my untold tale
> Of all my wrongs to fling into thy face,—
> Curse of my life and all my sorrowing line !
>   Wretch ! Time has shown thy sin in its true plight,
> Though little didst thou reck the wage it cost.
> Fool, who could dream, because the start seemed fair,
> That man could flee where Justice could not follow ! "

And now the tremendous climax of horror in the retributive task of Orestes, the murder of his mother, has to be faced. Orestes shrinks shudderingly from it; argues within himself, that the oracles have spoken with a voice of fiends and not of gods. Nerved by Electra, however, he enters the house, Clytemnestra having been summoned thither on the simple pretext that Electra has just given birth to a child. The Queen, with the shadow of doom above her, speedily appears, and in her speech with her daughter, some trace of a hunger for reconciliation may be found. The human motherhood of the harrowed soul speaks in her haste.[1] She pleads the unfaithfulness of Agamemnon, and his cruel sacrifice of Iphigeneia, as justification enough, alike for her own unfaithfulness and crime. The scene is full of the argumentative thrust and parry, reflecting the spirit of the Law-Court debates, so true to the Grecian heart.[2] She is enticed into entering the house, and there, at the hand of her son, she meets her doom. The humanness of agonising repentance with which Orestes and Electra, after the terrible event, bewail the awful fate which has thrust this matricide upon them, moves even through the cold print yet.

> " O earth, and Jove All-seeing—lo ! this deed !
> Dark deed of horrid blood ! . . . .
> Alas, thy doom,
> My mother ! What thou'st borne at children's hands !
> Ah, Phœbus ! this is thine—this ghastly deed ! "

He then recognises that in this fearful deed there is found atonement for their wrongs; but, suddenly, his agony deepens into despair like Cain's, and he cries—

> " Where shall I run ?
> What city shall receive me ?
> What house that fears the gods
> Shall open its doors to me,—
> Unclean, polluted with my mother's blood ? "

In the description by Orestes, of his tragic act, we feel very strikingly the influence of sculpture on the Drama. The tradition of the art-education of Euripides peeps over the scene. Even such a group as his words depict, might be standing in imperishable marble somewhere above Mediterrean shores.

> " My hands within her locks I twined and twisted,
> And, with my robe before my eyes, I slew her."

---

[1] There is a piteousness also in a certain penitence which she expresses for her past which has alienated her daughter from her.

[2] And especially dear, sometime over-dear, to the heart of the poet, under the influence of the Sophistic which he had imbibed from his philosophic friends.

And, now, as so often the case, the gods [1] appear overhead
to extricate affairs from the pressing impasse, and to declare
the position.   This episode very strikingly reveals the whole
spirit of Ancient Tragedy.   Man being a puppet of necessity
and the gods, he is continually being driven from one dilemma
to another, till he scarce can tell on which hand duty lies ;
for the gods admit that it is a just retribution that has fallen
on Clytemnestra, while on the contrary, in Orestes her son
the act itself has been unholy ; and, as for the command
of Phœbus, in obedience to which Orestes acted, Castor
shakes his head—and says

> " Wise though Apollo be, to thee he gave
>   An answer, not in wisdom."

There is here, undoubtedly, a sneer at the popular religion,
the superstition of the oracles, and the uncertainty of the
religious utterance in regard to the gods.

Orestes is sent to Athens, the city of Reason, and of
the heaven-founded Areopagus ; which had its origin first
of all in deciding the blood-guiltiness of Mars.   In this
Euripides follows his predecessors : but the spirit of the
trial is his own.[2]   Here you find the atrocious deed laid
without a moment's hesitation at the feet of Apollo.   Orestes
is but a blind creature of Fate driven before a god's decree.
The question as to why the gods, who declare their sympathy,
did not avert this trouble, is answered by the assertion that dire
necessity and the oracle, even though the oracle be unwise,
are unavoidable, and cannot ever be unfulfilled or disobeyed.
This is the secret of the intense tragicness of the life of
the human soul in the Drama.   Think what it means to
Orestes—the unpleasant consequence of a blood-stained

---

[1] Castor and Pollux also appear at the close of the " Helena " and with wonderful
fitness, for they are, of course, brothers, both of Helen and Clytemnestra.

[2] The account of the trial is told by Orestes himself in " Iphigeneia in Tauris," 945
et seqq. Æschylus represented the trial of Orestes as the first that had taken place
at the Court of Areopagus, and as instituting that Court, deriving the name from
the sacrifice of the Amazons to Mars. Euripides simply hints at the divine origin
of that important factor in the life of the State, in order to support its claim upon
the cities. See also page 67n.

soul, a harder exile, and, what is specially in discord with
the Grecian mind, submission to the dictates of a foreign
court. Castor feels the power of Orestes' pleading, and
declares above it all that Heaven pities him ; [1] which is
indeed a huge advance on the theological standpoint of
Æschylus's "Prometheus." Then the Chorus sum up the
lesson.

> " There is no certain bliss
> In a changeful world like this;
> Nor can a mortal man be counted blest,
> Till, undisturbed by woe, we see him sink to rest."

---

[1] 1329. " Know that from us and all the hosts of heaven
Nought but deep ruth for all his griefs to mortal man is given ! "

CHAPTER XII

EURIPIDES AND THE ATREIDÆ

"IPHIGENEIA IN AULIS." "ORESTES." "IPHIGENEIA IN TAURIS"

WE find many of the most characteristic touches of Euripides in his treatment of the Agamemnon episode as preserved in the three Tragedies which we will now consider. The lyric beauty, the unconventional conventionalities of the poet, the passion and scorn all finding voice strangely on the stage that Æschylus had shadowed with the doom-driven race on whom lay the curse of the gods.

In "Iphigeneia in Aulis" the story of the Atreidan Tragedy is retold,[1] but here again with a fearless freedom in the handling of the myth. The fleet of the Greeks lies bound by opposing winds at Aulis, and the oracle has declared that only by the sacrifice of Iphigeneia, Agamemnon's daughter, can Diana be appeased. If this demand is acceded to, the ships will reach the Phrygian shore, and Troy will be taken. So, on pretence of giving his daughter in marriage to Achilles, Agamemnon sends for her, though torn by love of his child, and agonised by the thought of what a sacrifice it means to part thus with her.[2] Love of his country, the hunger for martial glory, and the awe of the gods prevailed over his natural affections.

[1] The subject is from the "Cypria," an Introduction to the action of the "Iliad." The play is said to have been exhibited by the son of Euripides, or, according to some, his nephew, after the poet's death. It probably, therefore, bears traces of the hand of its producer. Scholia on Aristophanes' "Frogs," 67.

Bœckh attempted to prove the authorship of the younger Euripides throughout. Monk (Cambridge, 1857) satisfactorily repelled the attempt.

[2] He had vowed that he would sacrifice to Artemis the most beautiful object the year of Iphigeneia's birth should produce.

The cares and pain of soul of the great king are well depicted in the night-scene with which the drama opens.

" Agamemnon

The birds are hushed ; the waters of the deep
Are sleeping, and the winds are quietly laid
In silence on the bosom of the straits.

Slave

Why then unrested stays my sovereign lord ?
All here in Aulis is unbroken quiet ;
The watch not yet upon the walls is stirring.
Let us go in.

Agamemnon

Old man, I envy thee,
And every soul that lives a life secure,
Free from the world, and followed not by fame.
But never those to life's high places raised !

Slave

Yet such we deem the happy, glory-crowned !

Agamemnon

Still is that glory danger ; for Ambition,
Far-off a pleasant dream, becomes, at hand,
A bitter thing of sorrow. . . ."

The old sad refrain of the Greek fear of dignity and achieved greatness breaks out here in the complaint of a distracted heart. The pinnacle of human success is insecure, between the blasting lightnings of the gods and the hatred and envy of men. The distracted monarch tells at length the tale of the fleet's necessity and the dictate of the god ; and, having now repented his obedience to the oracle, he sends the messenger post-haste to Argos, cancelling his previous instructions.

" Rest not on the banks,
By shady fountains, nor thine eyelids yield

> To soothing sleep.
> Watch at the Cross-roads where the ways divide ;
> That, in thy speed, the car which bears my daughter
> Even now, upon her coming, 'scape thee not."

The messenger, however, is intercepted by Menelaus,[1] who, wresting the letter from him, confronts Agamemnon, charging him with treason to the Greeks, and as having, through folly, failed as leader of the host.

> "Wisdom must be the key
> To leadership.   Each wise man is a king."

But now the arrival of Clytemnestra and Iphigeneia is intimated, and Agamemnon feels the tightened chains of fate about his heart.

> " Alack,—unhappy me !   What can I say,
> And how begin ?   Lo, how grim destiny
> Has bound me fast.   My cunning falls to nought,
> Before the simple skill of circumstance.
> Happy the poor unknown—their hearts can speak,
> But pride seals up the sorrows of a king,
> Slave to his subjects, though in golden chains !
> Shame keeps my tears from falling ; yet, to weep not,
> Makes me ashamed, in this my woeful lot." [2]

Compelled thus to refuse the altered mood of Menelaus, he can only blame the gods and face the ordeal.

The poet presents a very human Clytemnestra, all agog with a mother's keen anxiety over her daughter's nuptials, and she refuses to return home meantime.   Meeting Achilles, she discovers that the tale of his having sought Iphigeneia's hand was all a wily subterfuge of her husband ; and then, further, both have revealed to them, by a servant of Agamemnon, the design to sacrifice Iphigeneia to appease Diana's wrath.   The queen throws all her hopes upon

---

[1] Euripides' dislike of the people of Sparta makes him continually paint Menelaus in an unfavourable light.   His duplicity, and, here, his meanness, stand out very clearly, for, of course, the Trojan War arose from his domestic affairs.

[2] Evidently quoted by St Jerome, as shown by Voss, in the Latin translation of Ennius.

Achilles, and the hero's heart is touched. He will try to help her, no matter what the oracle has said.

> " The prophet? What's a seer
> But one whom luck leads till on truth he stumble,
> Led blindfold through a thousand groping lies."

In vain she pleads with Agamemnon the hardships it must mean to her.

> " 'Tis winning Helen back again to Greece,
> Buying a wicked woman's life with blood
> Of innocent beauty—paying as the price
> For what we hate, our dearest and our best."

Anon she cries of what her grief and pain shall be, when in her halls of Argos, once again, she dwells without Iphigeneia.

> " Think—when I look around to see my child,
> And see but empty places ! All alone,
> Weeping, I'll wail for her, and through my tears
> Cry, Child, thy father slew thee. This the gift
> He gave his house from Troy ! "

Beautifully, too, Iphigeneia pleads—

> " O sweet it is to see the light o' the sun.
> What the grave holds is night and nothingness.
> O mad is he whose heart desires to die,
> For life's worst ill is sweeter than Death can give ! "

And now, Agamemnon himself is torn between two terrible alternatives.

> " For me, to do is dire ; yet not to do
> Is dreadful to me, since I fear the gods."

Iphigeneia, at last, impelled at once by pity for Achilles and by pride of fatherland, yields herself to the terrible sacrifice.[1]

> " If heaven must have me, take me.—I am free.
> For Greece, and for the sails of Greece, I die.
> Let Greece win victory through my flowing blood.
> Her triumphs shall eternalise my name."

---

[1] *Cf.* Macaria in the " Heracleidæ " ; Polyxena in the " Hecuba "; and Menœceus in the " Phœnissæ."

At the last moment, however, she is snatched away, and a hind is seen struggling under the knife, a prodigy of substitution which seems to have arisen in later versions of the myth, when it became a thought intolerable that the gods should demand such sacrifices. Æschylus in his "Agamemnon," and Sophocles in his "Electra," had both made her die upon the altar, at Aulis, under the knife, as Jephthah's daughter is supposed to have died in Holy Writ, while something like the same substitution appears in the sacrificial moment of Isaac under the hand of Abraham. The "Iliad" itself, remarkably, does not refer either to the sacrifice or substitution, and, instead, presents her at Argos, being offered to Achilles by Agamemnon ten years later than the episode of the dramas is supposed to have occurred. The above version, however, was just what would appeal to the very human heart of Euripides, and it also fell in with the stage-artifice necessity of his romantico-dramatic tendencies.

The character-painting is very masterly and clear, especially the beautiful Iphigeneia. Aristotle,[1] it is true, quotes her against Euripides, as an instance of inconsistency in art, because at first she begs her life and then surrenders it gladly—a criticism most blind, artificial, and narrow. It is indeed, on the other hand, a transcript from the soul of a king's daughter, at first so loath to leave the world she loves, and then, kindled with thought of fatherland and pride of race, standing up straight, in virgin purity, to die.[2]

But the tide of doom presses on to the flood, and the poet takes up, in the "Orestes,"[3] the judgment of Clytemnestra for her revenge upon her cruel lord, after his

[1] "Poetics," chap. xxviii.

[2] It is also a mark of the humanness of the conception of Euripides, for nothing deepens the tragic pathos of the scene so much as this fair young girl, willing to turn from the world and die for the sake of others. The chivalry of Achilles, the meanness of Menelaus, and craft in conflict with paternal love in Agamemnon, all live and move in the play.

[3] The "Orestes" was the most generally read in post-Attic times, and more quotations are taken from it than from all the plays of Æschylus and Sophocles together.

return, with the dire consequences which that judgment
entailed upon its instrument.

In this play, inspired by " The Furies " of Æschylus, we
have, in the madness of the protagonist, a strong representation of a soul driven to actual distraction as a consequence
of his obedience to his destiny.[1]   In it we find the conception
of Æschylus, but touched again by the human tenderness
so characteristic of Euripides.   The play is a remarkably
composite production.   The introduction of Menelaus, and
the change of character from the Homeric representation of
him, is not only unnecessary—it is really poor art, and does
not help the play one whit.   The appeal to the Assembly of
Argos is one of the characteristically Euripidean artifices
which continually show his plays as set in a period and
environment really neither past not present, as never at all
possibly existent, a distorted view of reality, sometimes seen
through tears.   The later stage of the play with its scream
for blood reduces the tragedy to the realm of melodramatic
burlesque, though Euripides certainly never meant it for
such.[2]

The scene opens at the Royal Palace of Argos, when
Electra, watching by the bed of her brother, declares that
miserable man is but a repository for all that is distressful in
the stores of angry heaven, and, in a long prologue, she
reiterates the scheme of the terrible story of the house of
Atreus.   It is the day of the doom of the matricides, who,
having been forbidden shelter or fellowship by the State,
are to be condemned to die, either by stoning or by the
avenging sword.   Their hope is in Menelaus, their father's
brother, who has arrived from Troy.   But Helen enters—
Helen from whom so much of all this woe has had its
origin ; and she explains that she does not consider herself
polluted by speaking with Electra, as she imputes the whole
blame for this blood-tragedy not on the poor instruments

[1] The " Electra " is separately considered, as it has always stood by itself.
[2] Müller calls the "Orestes" a strange mixture of old legends and modern opinions.

who suffer, but on the crime-originating gods. And she
herself knows what it is to have suffered at the hands of the
divinities. She sends libations and offerings to the tomb of
her sister, the murdered Clytemnestra, by the hands of
Hermione, with the prayer to the dead to be propitious—

> "To me, to thee, my lord, and these poor twain
> Whom Phœbus has so darkly led astray."

Meanwhile Orestes sleeps ; and the Chorus wail—

> "Alas ! his wretched lot,
> With woes relentless given
> To miserable man by cruel heaven ! "

Suddenly he wakes, with a beautiful apostrophe—

> "O blissful sleep,—thou Saviour of our pain !
> How tenderly thou comest in our need,
> Giving forgetfulness to mortal woe ! "

But anon, the recollection of his deed of retribution shakes
him in a spasm like those which, later, shook Macbeth—

> "Ah, mother ! in thy mercy, loose them not
> To torture me.   Their eyeballs glare in blood,
> And in their hair the hissing snakes are curled."

In wild madness he spurns even the faithful Electra, who
suggests that they are but "coinage of the brain." Then in
a lucid space he shudderingly says—

> "The blame is heaven's,
> Who whipped me on to this most impious deed ! "

Nor can he believe that even Agamemnon, for all his wrongs,
would have commanded such a crime, since it could not recall
the dead, and yet would give the avenger a cup of bitter
pain to drink. As he himself admits to Menelaus,[1]
Conscience, the conscious guilt of horrid deeds, is his
disease.

Tyndareus approaches—father of Clytemnestra and of

---

[1] Menelaus, according to the "Odyssey," Book iii. 309, returned on the day
Ægisthus was buried.

Helen; and the scorn of popular religion echoes in the greeting of Menelaus to him as he comes—

> "Hail, aged rival of the loves of Jove!"

Tyndareus argues against the Vendetta. He pleads the law of banishment as embodying a better scheme of settlement than the continual opening of the floodgates of revenge, so persistently detrimental to the equanimity of the State. But Orestes again shews, in a long speech, the anomalous position in which he has been placed :—

> "I slew my mother,—such, indeed, my crime :
> Yet 'tis no crime, my father's death avenging . . .
>   Greece owes me thanks !   Should wives their husbands slay,
> And then, with womanish tears, divert stern Justice,
> Weeping till Judgment's hand forgets to chide,
> How easy for the state to swim in blood!"

Was he not hedged in by two dire necessities? he asks.

> "Had I, by silence, sanctioned all her crimes,
> How would the dead, in rage, have left his grave
> To hound me with his Furies through the world?"

But, get the proper culprits, he cries. We are puppets of the gods. Bring in the master-players to the judgment.

> "Arrest the god, whose word we must obey.
> He slew my mother, with his dire command.
> His is the sin, not mine."

He argues with Menelaus and Tyndareus; but his boldness only estranges them. To the former, he flings the angry reminder that it was for his outraged honour that Agamemnon left his house, and for his sake sacrificed the beautiful Iphigeneia, so stirring against himself the whole weight of subsequent disaster.

Pylades, now himself an exile, because he had assisted Orestes in his crime, enters, and claims his right to share the obloquy and suffering of his friend; and together they go to brave the Council of Argos and defend their cause. The Chorus, as they pass, raise their voice against them.

The issue of the Council and its whole progress are reported, in the full mode of the prologue, by a messenger. Evidently drawing from life,[1] he says—

> "Another rose,
> A brave man—little known.   The market-place
> Where idlers thronged, had little charm for him.
> He said Orestes should be crowned by Greece,
> For showing to Ægisthus and his kind
> That fireside purity should be esteemed
> And guarded as an ever holy thing."

One wonders, who was this?   And did the audience look at one another, and recognise the picture?   All the eager interest of Athenian law-courts vibrates through this scene.

The doom, however, mercilessly goes against Orestes, and a frenzy of despair seizes both him and Pylades, as they resolve, in revenge for the treachery of Menelaus, to slay Helen.   Orestes will have blood and vengeance.   Alone he will not die, but, in his fall, drag punishment on his foes. Thereupon ensues the most melodramatic, burlesque, swash-buckling scene, in which Helen is miraculously abstracted from beneath the very sword of the madman; the whole account being again, like a special editor's latest telegram, gone over in full, by an escaped Phrygian slave.   Menelaus and Orestes have a retort-and-repartee conflict; and, just at the critical moment, when Menelaus is calling the Greeks to arms, and Orestes has ordered Electra to fire the house, Apollo enters "from the machine," and orders Orestes to one year's exile.   Thereafter he must go to Athens and the Areopagus.

> "There yield thyself to trial before the Three
> Dread Furies, for the blood that thou hast slain;
> With heaven as arbiters, your cause shall stand
> Approved, and justified before the world."

He arranges all the weddings, smoothes away the wrath, and everybody seems "happy ever after."

---

[1] This sturdy and independent figure is in striking contrast to the demagogue, moulded on Cleophon, who has just spoken. Paley identifies him as a type of the agriculturist whom Euripides constantly sets apart as the stay of the nation.

The latter part of the play is quite unworthy of any master-hand, and almost drops into the realm of farce. The opening, however, is as tender and fresh as anything ever written out of the experience of human sorrow. The play is an impeachment of the gods for their making man the plaything of their whim, pouring punishment and agonies upon the blind instruments of their crude predestination.

The miraculous escape of Iphigeneia from death at her father's hand supplies material for the play of "Iphigeneia in Tauris." The period is twenty years after the sacrifice at Aulis, when Iphigeneia was translated miraculously to the altar of Diana at Balaclava in the Crimea, and Thoas, King of the Tauric region, appointed her priestess of his temple, where it was the custom that every Grecian who should be cast upon the shore must be sacrificed to the goddess of the place.

The inhabitants of Taurica were particularly attached to the worship of Diana, or of some earlier savage deity to whom they had transferred her name; and they cruelly offered on the altar all strangers [1] that were shipwrecked on their coast. In Aricia her shrine was served by a priest who always sacrificed his predecessor; and the Lacedæmonians annually offered human victims at her altar, till the time of Lycurgus, who changed this custom, substituting flagellation for it.

Iphigeneia, in a long prologue, narrates the story of her trials and her recent vision :—

> " In sleep I seemed to be again in Argos,
> Argos, dear home my innocent childhood knew.
> Sudden, earth shook. I rose and sped without,
> And saw our palace, shattered, fall to ruins,

---

[1] The poet, for dramatic purposes, particularises these as Grecian strangers. Evidently a form of devil-worship is here transferred in name to Diana. Ovid described this Tauric temple of Artemis, and Müller fixes the first seat of this bloody rite in the Pelasgic Lemnos, where Stephanos of Byzantium records that virgins were sacrificed to her. The principal seat of this worship in Hellas was at Brauron in Attica, where the Tauric image of the goddess was shown. See Ovid, "Fasti," iii. 260 *et seqq.*

> All save one pillar; and as I looked thereon
> It changed to somewhat human; and, remembering
> Unconsciously, my awful office here,
> I found me sprinkling it for sacrifice,
> Mine eyes all blind with tears."

This she interprets as signifying that Orestes, her brother, is dead.

While she is speaking, Orestes and Pylades draw near, having been sent on a quest to steal the image of Diana from the Tauric shrine. Orestes again bewails the inconvenient attentions of Apollo, and his awkward influence on his life.

> "Why plagu'st thou me, Apollo?   Since the hour
> My red hands slew my mother, fury-driven,
> Outcast and vagrant o'er the world I flee.
> What is thy cure?   That from this cruel coast
> I bear Diana's image, which, from heaven,
> The popular tongue declares, in this place fell,
> To gentle Athens, when, my toil completed,
> Then shall my sorrows likewise have an end."

Pylades, in answer to his complaint and question, again, as in Æschylus, declares that, before all else, the god must be obeyed; but, meanwhile, they must hide in some sea-cave till darkening night comes down. Iphigeneia's ode has beautiful descriptive power, production of a poet who had lain near the sea-places, watching the drift of Nature. She addresses the dwellers—

> "Nigh this unkindest sea,
> Rending the rocks with wild impetuous rage."

She proclaims her vision to the Chorus of captive Grecian women who are now attendants on the temple-services; and she proceeds to prepare libations for the dead, wailing her forlorn condition. Suddenly a messenger from the shore comes speedily on the scene, and tells how two strangers had been discovered in an ocean-cave, one of whom, suddenly convulsed with madness, had rushed among their flocks, and only after a severe struggle had they been able to overcome them and carry them to the king, who had sent them on to the altar of horrid sacrifice served by her. Her heart, now that Orestes seems to her dead, is hardened and relentless; but she refuses to blame this evil on the gods. She cannot believe heaven to be unjust or cruel, and all the old tales are unworthy of belief, inventions of a cruel age, to cover with excuse their own wanton cruelty.

The very fine choral ode that follows asks—

> " Ah, who are they that sail
>   O'er waters rude,
> To this barbaric shore
>   With blood imbrued?
>
> Is it for love of gold?
>   Ah, hope of gain
> Can draw men to their doom
>   Across the main.
>
> O that the breeze might bring
>   Helen of Troy-town here,
> Her whose proud beauty brought
>   To us such woe and fear.
>
> Or might some Grecian come
>   Across the sea,
> And, from our bonds and shame,
>   Now set us free.
>
> O to see home again—
>   The sedgy streams,—
> The joy of meetings given,
>   Only to us in dreams."

Orestes and Pylades are led in upon the scene, but Orestes refuses to disclose his name. His name is "Wretched!" He is "Tristram"; but at length he reveals Argos as his home. Inquiry elicits all the Agamemnon-story, and the confusion of the issues of the gods. Orestes tells how Agamemnon was murdered by a woman's hand, and how Clytemnestra the queen has been slain by her son to avenge her father's death. She approves of the deed, though she calls it "ill, but righteous, and yet justly done." With her interest deeply stirred in the two young men, she proposes that Orestes shall be sacrificed, but Pylades shall bear for her a letter to Argos.

Her interest in Agamemnon and his fate strikes Orestes as remarkable. It does not, however, seem strange to Pylades that the fate of kings like Agamemnon and the rest of the great Trojan host should evoke such inquiry as Iphigeneia's. Men like these live in the public eye, and the rumour of them floats about the world.

And now ensues a contest of friendship between the two noble youths, as to which shall die for the other. Orestes demands that Pylades go free on his errand.[1] As for himself,

> "Though the god cheated me, and drove me far
> In misery from Greece to hide his lies,
> That here to death I'd stumble, 'tis my meed
> To die—because these hands my mother slew."

Then comes the dénouement, and by a method not uncommon on the stage. Lest the letter be dropped or mislaid, or if, by dark mischance unforeseen, it be lost at sea, she tells what message it contains for her friends at Argos.

> "This letter bear to Agamemnon's son,
> Orestes; say to him his sister lives,
> Iphigeneia, who at Aulis, once
> On cruel altar of the gods was bound,
> And saw the keen blade flash above her breast."

Orestes is amazed. He cries, as if blinded with wonder.

> "Where shall I find her, dead, returned to life?"

But she proceeds with the message.

> "I who now speak am she. But let me on.
> Say to him, 'Come, my brother, bear me hence
> Out of this place of blood, these shores unkind.
> Take me again to Argos, ere I die."

---

[1] A scenic passage often imitated. *Cf.* Cicero, "De Amicitia," c. 7.

Pylades, with a laugh, exclaims—

> "No long delay I need to do my vow
> Full justice. Lo, Orestes, here I bring
> Iphigeneia's letter to thy hands."

After a most touching recognition scene,[1] Orestes enters into particulars of his trial at the Areopagus, from which, though freed from the doom of blood, he had been sent on this final quest to secure and bear the image which fell from heaven and fix it in Attica. A hasty scheme is devised whereby both Iphigeneia and the idol shall be borne away. She fears the tyrant whom she meantime serves, but she will pretend to cleanse Orestes, unclean from his mother's blood, and the image polluted by his touch, in the sea-waves, preparatory to his sacrifice, and so, securing privacy for this ordeal, manipulate flight from the horrid bondage she now serves in.

The Chorus of captives, pledged to aid the escape, break at the same time into a song of regretful exile :—

> "O bird that, 'mong the rocky reefs,
>   Wailest thy bosom's griefs,
>   O'er thy lost mate,[2]—
> We join with thee our melancholy lay,
> Thinking of home beloved and far away,
>   And our sad fate.
>
> Ah, sore our hearts with pain and fear,
>   When, 'neath the unpitying spear,
>   Our band they bore
> Across the sundering, never-resting waves,
> Far from our home, and from our people's graves,
>   To this rude shore.
>
> Swift will the eager shipmen carry thee,
> And soon, afar from us, thou shalt be free
>   Upon the foam ;
> O could we follow the westward-speeding ray,
> And catch once more, before our closing day,
>   One gleam of home ! "

---

[1] This is one of the most famous scenes in antiquity. Ovid gives it briefly in "Epistles," ex Pont. ii. 73-92. A fresco representing it was discovered in Herculaneum.

[2] The halcyon or kingfisher. See Virgil, "Georgics," iii. 38 ; Ovid, "Heroides," xviii. 81 ; also a parody of this passage in Aristoph., "Frogs," 1309.

King Thoas now enters, and the plot upon his credulousness at once succeeds. He agrees to what she, as priestess, proposes, and she begs to have the prisoners chained; while, lest the city be polluted by even the sight of the blood-stained captives, she has a notice sent abroad that all abide within doors, the king himself remaining veiled before the shrine. But soon a messenger breaks in from the direction of the sea, and, thundering at the temple gate, tells the king how, waiting long where she had set them, they had been prompted, by suspicion, to follow Iphigeneia, and they beheld

> " A ship of Hellas, with its flashing oars,
> And half-a-hundred seamen at the thwarts . . .
> Free from their chains the strangers stood astern,—
> The anchor's weighed—some hauled the cables in,
> And tried to push the vessel to the main,"—

and how Orestes rescued his sister from their grasp and carried her through the waves. The tide, however, swept back the ship, and the people are invoked, summoned, and exhorted to pursue and capture the fugitives, by this time at their mercy, stranded on the shore. And now, again, as so often, just at the height of the tragic difficulty, Artemis steps upon the scene and vindicates the commanding dignity of Athens; tells how Poseidon, calmed at her behest, bears the flying ship upon his tides; while she commands Orestes, though distant on the deep, to hear her voice, to build a temple for the image at Halæ, and institute a rite com-memorative of his deliverance. This doubtless, in Grecian fashion, explained the origin of some symbolical sacrifice already existing there.

And now all is solved. The old sorrows of the race are laid to rest. The captive maidens of the Chorus are sent home, and the anger of the king miraculously calmed. The gods are seen to be just and pitiful, and submission to the will of Heaven is a constant, solemn duty, incumbent on mankind.[1]

---

[1] The mechanism of the play is similar to that of the " Helena."

CHAPTER XIII

THE MYTH-CYCLE OF THE LABDACIDÆ

In the treatment of the myth-cycle of the Labdacidæ we again see the old haunting fears of life and judgment, the power of the spoken word, the danger of cross-examining the will of heaven, and the duty of watching carefully against the impious trespass of the soul through anger, ambition, or lust. Further, it smites, like iron upon iron, the resounding truth that moral action cannot be isolated. The wireless telegraphy of conduct sends the ethical message on through the generations after the deed. In the moral world no man's folly or sin falls dead at his feet.[1] This was the background of Tragedy for the Greek. For the interest of horror, nothing could surpass this terrible, old-world child of gloom.

Laius of Thebes, having, in a moment of impious abandonment, broken the wall of restraint built by the gods around moral relationships, had, as his punishment, this doom hung over his head—that he should either die childless or be slain by the hand of his child. Thinking to evade this judgment, he had the child whom his wife Jocasta bore to him handed over to a servant to be put to death. The heart of this emissary was moved, however, to leave the babe, whose feet had been pierced, to die of exposure on Mount Cithæron. Found in this terrible state by a shepherd of Polybus, King of Corinth, he was carried to Court, where

---

[1] The apparent lack of poetic justice, in consequence of which deficiency the innocent are involved in the disasters of the guilty, arises from the fact of the idea of sacrifice being ever present in Greek tragedy, and atonement being demanded for sin.—WORSFOLD.

the queen, who was childless, nursed him tenderly, and adopted him as her son. He became known as Œdipus,[1] in consequence of the ordeal he had endured. His wit and attainments of mind made him the object of envious admiration with his fellows, who at last, in order to mortify him and satisfy their spite, cast aspersions on his birth. This at once set insatiable curiosity running through his brain, and, notwithstanding the assurances of his foster-mother, being subject to as morbid an imagination as Macbeth, he consulted an oracle, which warned him that he should be the murderer of his father and the husband of his mother. Knowing only Corinth as his home, he fled on in fear, till in a narrow road he met an imperious personage in a chariot with his armour-bearer, whose curt command to clear out of the way Œdipus resented, and, in the scuffle, the proud unknown was killed.[2] Ignorant of the name, rank, or personality of the man he had murdered, Œdipus pressed on, attracted to Thebes by the rumour of the Sphinx, which Juno had sent to harass that city and vicinity. The issue of a successful answer to the enigmas of this monster would mean her death, and the release of the country from her oppression; so Creon, who had succeeded Laius on the Theban throne, offered the crown, and the hand of Jocasta, as reward to the man who, by discomfiting this cruel oppressor of the State, might prove himself the redeemer and restorer of his country. Where all failed, Œdipus, with his fateful luck, succeeded, and the monster, in chagrin, dashed her head against a rock and died.

But now the cords of Destiny draw closer. Œdipus won the promised reward, ascended the throne of Thebes, wedded Jocasta, and had by her two sons, Eteocles and Polynices, with two daughters, Ismene and Antigone.[3] And then,

---

[1] *I.e.* Swelled-foot = Proudfoot.

[2] *Cf.* the murder of the unknown son by his father in Arnold's "Sohrab and Rustum."

[3] The marriage of Œdipus and Jocasta was not an original part of the legend, but was a very early addition to the groundwork. The "Iliad" only once glances at the story of Œdipus (Bk. xxiii. l. 679). Pausanias makes the four children born to

again, the blight of the curse and the hungry demand of mysterious Justice entered his life. Plague devastated the territories and the city, and the oracle declared that it could cease only when the murderer of Laius was brought to justice. Indefatigable in his inquiries, the king unravelled the whole sad tale, till the final knot was disentangled by the very slave who had exposed him on the mountains long ago, and he was proved at last to be murderer and incest-guilty. In his agony of grief and shame he tore out his eyes, and, Jocasta having destroyed herself, he was, on the terrible disclosure, banished by his own sons, whom he cursed to strife and division. He retired to Colonus; but the web of destiny had still some bloody threads to weave. The sins of the fathers cast shadow over their children. His sons Eteocles and Polynices agreed to share the kingship and to reign alternately each for a year. Eteocles ascended the throne first,[1] but, at the end of his stipulated period refused to implement his bargain, whereupon Polynices, incensed at such perfidy, retired to Argos for aid, and receiving the daughter of King Adrastus as his wife, schemed unfraternal war against Thebes, thus precipitating upon all concerned fulfilment of the ancient curse.

Œdipus to have been by a second wife, named Euryganeia. Pindar (*Ol.* 2, 42) makes the sons destroyed in direct retribution for the parricide, and apart altogether from any reference to the curse of Œdipus.

[1] Being, according to popular tradition, the elder, but Sophocles reverses the popular order.

CHAPTER XIV

SOPHOCLES AND ŒDIPUS

THREE dramas of Sophocles are woven around this old sad tale.[1]

The opening scene of " Œdipus the King " reveals a band of suppliants, old and young, led by the priest of Jupiter into the wise monarch's presence. Nearly sixteen years have passed since his conquest of the Sphinx had freed Thebes from that monster's tyranny, and he had won Jocasta as his queen, and the crown of Laius as his reward. Two sons and two daughters had Jocasta borne to him, but now the cloud of disaster has settled over Thebes—plague, blight, and ruin. They appeal to his wisdom for light to show them some way of escape, else his kingship shall soon be only over a desolation.

> " O king, remember,
> A king's best treasure is a peopled realm."

He tells them of his anxieties about their griefs, and how he has enlisted higher wisdom in their needs, having sent Creon, Jocasta's brother, to Apollo's shrine at Delphi. But, while they speak, Creon is seen advancing, crowned with laurel, in token of good tidings. The oracle has revealed the only remedy for the evils of Thebes—the murderer of King Laius must be driven forth. So the king gathers the citizens together and invites information. He puts his own ban upon the murderer.

> " Give him no shelter, speak to him no word,
> Share neither prayer nor rite with such as he ;

---

[1] See, especially, *Sophocles*, in Prof. Butcher's " Some Aspects of the Greek Genius."

114

Your doors keep fast against him, and your hearts;
For I the king am ally of the gods,
And while I reign these words of mine hold fast.
Ill may the murderer wear his evil life
Unblest, uncared-for, whether on his heart
Alone the guilt lies, or with others shared.
And, if within my house the shadow creep,
Or, having crept, abides, may my own curse,
Thus spoken before heaven, rest on me;
So may the sorrows of our land find peace."

The Chorus, in response, declare that none of the guilt lies upon them—their hands are clean.

While they debate, the blind prophet Teiresias is brought to elucidate, if it may be, the oracle just received, and the king appeals to him for help—

"Since man's most noble task
Is to give help to man in grievous need."

But the prophet refuses to speak.

"Easier shall I bear
My burden to the finish:
So, too, shalt thou bear thine
By silence aided.
What must be, cometh,
Maugre our speech or silence."

The king,[1] losing his self-control and forgetting respect for the prophet, hurls threats and angry epithets on Teiresias, who at length is goaded out of his silence to retort—

"So, since thou speakest thus, I charge thee hold
To thy decree, and speak to me no more.
Nor to another, since thou art thyself
The foul defiler of this suffering land."

And when Œdipus cries—

"Where do you look for help to escape your due
For such bold treason?"

the prophet very finely and bravely, with high passion, answers—

---

[1] *Cf.* Lear's character, chap. 25.

> " No runaway road I need, since truth itself
> Is my embattled strength, and holds me safe.
> Thou art the man upon whose hand the stain
> That drags across the state this curse of heaven,
> Those long years, now is lying. Nay, I am blind,
> But oh, how blind art thou, who open-eyed
> Livest in shame, incestuous, unbeholding
> The horror of the sin in which thou art." [1]

Like another Cassandra's, however, the truths which the prophet has been goaded into revealing, fall unbelieved upon the king's ears. He suspects that this is but the outcome of a treasonable plot of Creon.

> " Creon the trusty—he who was my friend,—
> Oh what an envy clings to wealth and state,
> Since such a man I loved and leaned upon
> Must creep into a treason, drawing to him
> This charlatan, to thrust me from my throne ! "

But the prophet refuses to admit either the domination of Œdipus or the alleged patronage and co-operation of Creon.

> " Apollo is my master whom I serve,
> Not Œdipus—nor Creon ; and I see
> With my blind eyes what from thy sight is veiled,—
> Thou that hast sight, yet seest not what thou art,
> What shadow is behind thee, nor what shame
> Thou dwellest with ; nor with what headlong haste,
> Driven by the curse of mother and of sire,
> And their dread Furies, blinded shalt thou fly,
> Seeing, in bitter blindness, what thine eyes,
> Now filled with sight, refuse to look upon."

Then, ere he goes, with the scorn of the king flung at him, he leaves his riddle for the king to solve—

> " Him whom thou seekst I see,
> Here in our town, born in our midst, yet seeming
> A stranger and sojourner, proud and rich,
> But soon flung forth a pilgrim,—soon to be

---

[1] With Sophocles, Fate is just the unknown and incalculable, because unseen element of human life. It is this blindness of soul in Œdipus that inveigles him in tragic horror.

Poor, blind and homeless, seeking a far-off land,
Feeling his way with blind-man's staff before him,
Unclean—curst in his children—parricide,
Adulterer, and incestuous. Think of that,
And, when the dread hour comes, tell me thy thought
Of what's the worth of prophecy. Farewell."

The Chorus is perplexed. Certainly the doom once spoken
at earth's central shrine lives, flitting, like a shadow, step
for step with the man accursed; but Œdipus the king has
always seemed most fortunate and wise of men, and they
refuse to see in him the terrible criminal, guilty of the dark
crimes hinted at by the blind prophet.[1]

Creon now comes, indignantly repudiating the charges and
insinuations made against him. But Œdipus, infatuated and
like a man blinded by the gods, enters and assails him with
rebukes. He will not listen to defence or denial, nor tolerate
arguments. In vain Creon pleads—

" Shall I resign
My friendship and my peaceful walk with men,
For envies and unrest born with a crown? . . .
To fling away a friend,
Rashly, on weak suspicion's flimsy test,
Is found a treason 'gainst your own heart's life.
But time that tries all troths shall surely show
The light about a true man ere he die."

The king, however, will not be satisfied even with banishment. He threatens such punishment as shall serve for an
example to others.

" Nay, I will have thy death, that, o'er thy corse,
Envy be pilloried, and Treason warned."

At this stage, Jocasta for the first time intervenes upon
their quarrel, and with the aid of the appealing Chorus she
separates them, though the king is still stubbornly convinced
that the charge against him comes indirectly from Creon.

1 See Prof. Butcher's " Aspects of the Greek Genius," p. 105.

He tells Jocasta the allegation; but she
They are impossible, she says—

> "No man of mortal birth
> Can share the will of heaven"—

and in proof of her incredulity, tells ho
husband, had been warned that he shou
hands:—

> "But when the child was born just three
> Laius the king, maiming its helpless feet
> Sent it abroad to die in trackless wastes
> Of lonely hills. True, Laius fell,
> Yet slain by strangers, where three cross
> And so the Oracle was fruitless wind!

The inquisitive mind of Œdipus has a t
started; and his fears, awakened by the
of the murder of Laius, thus thrown ou
clear answers. He asks—

> "What was he like, and of what age was

and she replies—

> "Tall, somewhat like thyself, of kingly fo
> With age, like silver, lightly, here and t
> Shining among his locks."

Further questioning, prompted by fatefu
him that he has probably cursed himse
already, ignorantly, under the ban of heav
of his father. Yet his only hope is that whe
the sole survivor of the wayside skirmis
the rumour that the crime was the act of a
shall be confirmed, and he be found innoc
thing, his conflict sixteen years ago havin
by himself alone against his insulters.
life-story as he knows it, and she comfor
out that, even though he slew Laius, th
fault, he being, as it seems, the son of Po

Poor, blind and homeless, seeking a far-off land,
Feeling his way with blind-man's staff before him,
Unclean—curst in his children—parricide,
Adulterer, and incestuous. Think of that,
And, when the dread hour comes, tell me thy thought
Of what's the worth of prophecy. Farewell."

The Chorus is perplexed. Certainly the doom once spoken at earth's central shrine lives, flitting, like a shadow, step for step with the man accursed; but Œdipus the king has always seemed most fortunate and wise of men, and they refuse to see in him the terrible criminal, guilty of the dark crimes hinted at by the blind prophet.[1]

Creon now comes, indignantly repudiating the charges and insinuations made against him. But Œdipus, infatuated and like a man blinded by the gods, enters and assails him with rebukes. He will not listen to defence or denial, nor tolerate arguments. In vain Creon pleads—

" Shall I resign
My friendship and my peaceful walk with men,
For envies and unrest born with a crown ? . . .
To fling away a friend,
Rashly, on weak suspicion's flimsy test,
Is found a treason 'gainst your own heart's life.
But time that tries all troths shall surely show
The light about a true man ere he die."

The king, however, will not be satisfied even with banishment. He threatens such punishment as shall serve for an example to others.

" Nay, I will have thy death, that, o'er thy corse,
Envy be pilloried, and Treason warned."

At this stage, Jocasta for the first time intervenes upon their quarrel, and with the aid of the appealing Chorus she separates them, though the king is still stubbornly convinced that the charge against him comes indirectly from Creon.

[1] See Prof. Butcher's " Aspects of the Greek Genius," p. 105.

He tells Jocasta the allegation; but she sneers at oracles.
They are impossible, she says—

> "No man of mortal birth
> Can share the will of heaven"—

and in proof of her incredulity, tells how Laius, her former
husband, had been warned that he should die by his son's
hands:—

> "But when the child was born just three brief days,
> Laius the king, maiming its helpless feet,
> Sent it abroad to die in trackless wastes
> Of lonely hills.   True, Laius fell,
> Yet slain by strangers, where three cross-roads met;
> And so the Oracle was fruitless wind!"

The inquisitive mind of Œdipus has a thousand suspicions
started; and his fears, awakened by the hint of the locality
of the murder of Laius, thus thrown out casually, demand
clear answers.   He asks—

> "What was he like, and of what age was he?"

and she replies—

> "Tall, somewhat like thyself, of kingly form;
> With age, like silver, lightly, here and there,
> Shining among his locks."

Further questioning, prompted by fateful dread, convinces
him that he has probably cursed himself, though he was
already, ignorantly, under the ban of heaven as the murderer
of his father.   Yet his only hope is that when the old shepherd,
the sole survivor of the wayside skirmish, shall have come,
the rumour that the crime was the act of a band of marauders
shall be confirmed, and he be found innocent of this dreadful
thing, his conflict sixteen years ago having been experienced
by himself alone against his insulters.   He tells Jocasta his
life-story as he knows it, and she comforts him by pointing
out that, even though he slew Laius, the oracle is still at
fault, he being, as it seems, the son of Polybus of Corinth.

Meantime the Chorus reiterate the old dogma of the retribution of the gods :—

> "Pride breeds the tyrant; but when pride
> Climbs to its highest, then the gods' just wrath
> Hurls it to doom, deserving, lamed and lost.
> The gods are just; and whoso dares profane
> Life's sanctities, must pay the ill-starred price.
> What if the oracles no more be true?
> What if the issue fly the prophet's word,
> And the old tales be nought but laughter-crowned,
> And the old worship of the gods go by?"

Jocasta herself is going to seek Apollo's shrine; for Œdipus is now ready to believe everything, if only it be dire enough; and all begin to fear, as when men see the man at the helm afraid in stormy seas.

Just then enters the messenger from Corinth announcing the death of Polybus and the accession of Œdipus. Jocasta turns at once from her pious intention, and, with reiterated scorn, cries—

> "Speed, tell the king,—his destiny is free.
> Ha! oracles of gods, where stand ye now?"[1]

Œdipus joins with her, though less scornfully, in discounting the value of prophecy; for here is Polybus his father dead, by no man's blame, far less by his. Still, not quite free from superstitious faith, he shrinks from going to Corinth, lest by some stroke of the irony of fate he be driven to fulfil the other part of the prophecy. But, thinking to liberate him from all his fears by the simple truth, the messenger tells him that, after all he, was only an adopted child of the Corinthian Court—nothing whatever in blood either to Polybus or his queen. Then all the miserable horror of the tale leaks out—nay, bursts in a flood upon the wretched king, now that this one withholding stone

---

[1] All through, Jocasta has an attitude of impious sneering at the gods, which is a feature, apparently, of her character, and certain to drag its punishment upon her. Œdipus also has been guilty, not only of sneering at the art of the prophet, but has cast upon this messenger of heaven the imputation that he is merely a mercenary charlatan.

is pulled away. Whence, then, his origin? He begs. And he hears how he was a foundling, an adopted child, got from a shepherd of Laius by this man, in Cithæron's winding glens; and all the truth blindingly, agonisingly blazes upon Jocasta's soul. The king, however, does not see it yet. He only sees that he is of lowly origin, elevated by his own excelling genius; and, caught by the glamour of intellectual questioning of clues, he never for a moment wonders why Jocasta his queen has rushed away from his side.

The Chorus, too, proud of their king, find in the story only some hint of a divine mark upon his birth.

> " What god, in the quiet green glens,
> Gave thee thy life?
> Was it the great god Pan,
> Wandering the whispering woodlands lone, remote?
> Was it Apollo,—for he dearly loves
> The pastoral uplands?
> Or what fair maid,
> Near Helicon's sweet fountain brought thee forth,
> For love of Bacchus, the beautiful, the wise,
> The soft-eyed god who laughs among the hills?"

But soon the whole terror of doom stands out revealed, when the old shepherd and the man from Corinth are brought face to face; and, bit by bit, the ragged-edged story is broken out of his silence, cutting the listening heart; and, drop by drop, the double bitterness of Doom is squeezed into the life of Œdipus. Nothing can exceed the sad beauty of the Choral cry then :—

> " Ah, me, ye flickering shadows,—
> Ye human generations, how ye pass;
> Who shall win happiness, or grasp
> Aught but the semblance of it, ere he die?
>
> Thy fate, O hapless king,
> Silences me; nor shall I ever call
> A mortal blest.

He saved our land,
He won the meed of wisdom,
And he reigned, our king.

Ah me, I wail,
For from thy life new life to me was given,
And from thy life now gloom and death are mine."

So, the queen dead by her own hand, and the king self-blinded, all the woe of the household-curse falls in a stream at once, and he comes forth seeking exile.

" Oh dark, unutterably dark,
And dark my fate,
Smote by Apollo,—
Wherefore should I see
That could see nothing sweet !
O lead me hence, accurst,
Lost, most abhorred of heaven. . . .

O that my soul had died,
Long since in the mountain's solitary waste.
Blind would I rather go
Hence, where the dead await me :
And so these sightless eyes
Should not behold my father whom I slew.

Say, were my children fair,
My city good to look on ?—Did I see
The faces of the people whom I loved,
I, the unholy, worthless of the gods ?
Hide me beyond the land,
Or in the sad sea's waves
Bury me, deep, unseen ! "

He is led in by Creon, and the dread spectacle closes with the sob of each beholder's heart, expressing the true meaning of Tragedy.[1]

" Lo ! this is he, the wise,
The glory of our Thebes,
Envied by all our folks for his good fortune ;

---

[1] This is the great lesson for ever being driven into the heart of the Greek audience —the uncertainty of life, honours, riches, the fickleness of human happiness.

Therefore, until the final day is past,
Till the soul takes its last step o'er life's border,
Say not a man is happy,
Free from pain."

But the problem of this great agony, that seems to have come without seeking, finds no explanation thus far. Searching, therefore, for a solution, Sophocles takes up again the thread of the life of Œdipus,[1] the scene opening at Colonus near Athens, in front of a grove sacred to the Furies.

Years have elapsed since the dénouement of horror and frenzy was reached in Thebes. Œdipus had remained a while in Thebes after the first agony; but, at last, at the instigation of Creon,[2] the Thebans expelled him from the city, his sons in no way attempting to stay the decree of banishment. Cruel as the daughters of Lear, the ambition-hardened sons of Œdipus shut their eyes to duty; but Antigone, the Cordelia of Greek Tragedy, goes forth into the uncertain world with her father, as his attendant and guide, Ismene, meanwhile, remaining in Thebes in his interest. With her he left, in that city, his curse upon his unkindly sons, to work their ruin. These, at first, on his expulsion were inclined to let their claims to the kingship fall aside, but later they began a feud over the crown rights; and Eteocles, the elder brother, succeeded in averting these from Polynices, who was driven into exile. He went, as we saw, to Argos, and for policy's sake married the daughter of Adrastus the king; and, now, supported by an army of the Argives, led by six noted heroes of that race, he is preparing to march against Thebes to vindicate his claims by arms. The pity and fear of the audience are at once awakened by the spectacle of this monarch fallen from his high estate, and led like a blind beggar, by the hand into a strange country.

---

[1] Perhaps twenty years elapsed between these dramas.
[2] Creon's character throughout this play is represented in quite a different aspect. He is here a heartless and hypocritical villain.—JEBB.

" Whither have we come, O daughter mine ?
Who will this day with poor gifts entertain
The wandering outcast King, blind Œdipus ?
Little my needs, and little do I crave,
Yet less than that my little I receive ;
But it contents me, for my weary pain
Has taught me patience—to be still and suffer."

He has found peace out of storm, and, in the dust, humility.
They sit down to wait for a chance of learning where they
are. A stranger enters and warns them that they have
trespassed on holy ground, sacred to the dread Furies,
daughters of Earth and Night. But the king exclaims—

" Then never will I leave this hallowed land,
For 'tis the watchword of my fate ! "

While the stranger goes off for advice, Œdipus prays to the
awful deities to whom the grove is dedicated, and tells how,
long ago—

" Phœbus, when he declared presage of grief
To me and mine, spake of a land of rest,
Where I should find my shelter and my grave,
With blessing for the land that gave me peace,
And woe for those who drove me harshly from them ;
Even a land where dwelt the holy shrine
Of these dread deities, so feared by men ;
And how the signs and warnings out of heaven
Should be revealed in thunders, or in earthquake,
Or in the flashing lightnings of high Jove.
Hear, goddesses,—give me my final goal ;
Hear, Athens, honoured over earthly towns,
Pity this woeful spectre of a king ! "

The Chorus of elders enter in eager search, while Œdipus
and Antigone hide themselves to listen, and conjecture what
kind of reception they may have given to them. At length
he goes forward, and has to be led, " with dark steps," to a
place where piety can speak to him free from fear. Forced
by the Elders to reveal his name, he is received with shouts
of horror. They veil their eyes from the polluting vision,
and order him out of the land, lest evil come by his foul

presence. Antigone pleads with them for her father, asking
their pity for " his unpurposed deeds," which, through no
fault of his, brought such a freight of agony upon him.
This is an important keynote of the teaching of Sophocles,
in regard to this great mystery of the providential dispensa-
tion of pain.

Œdipus puts forward the plea on which the Athenians
were most proud of their city as the shelter of the stranger,
and the helper of the weak and distressed. Why should
they fear?

> " 'Tis but my name ye dread.   My life has been
> In suffering more than deeds.   My feet walked blindly.
> Not in my nature evil, I knew nothing.
> Nor will your mercy pass all unrewarded,
> Since, even with my sorrows, here I come,
> Bearing a mystic blessing."

Meanwhile they wait the arrival of Theseus, the king of
the territory, and, while they wait, they see Ismene approaching. She tells him about his sons. His curse is working.
It is their dark hour. He is moved by the affectionate
fidelity of his girls, shining out like sunlight against the
gloomy impiety of his sons.

> " One, gentle from her womanhood hath been
> My guide in lonely wanderings, through wild woods
> And desert places, beat by wind and rain,
> And in the heat of fiery noons unsheltered,
> Bare and by hunger tried, yet ever true.
> And thou, with watchful heart, when I was driven
> From thankless Thebes, hast been my listening angel,
> Bearing to me all oracles the gods
> Have given to men about my hapless fate."

She tells, now, the miserable flight of his wretched sons,
and especially does she bear tidings of an oracle which
declares that Thebes will prosper if the king's grave be in
Theban soil, while, if it be in Attica, Athens will prevail
against Thebes. So now the gods uplift him, whom,
previously, they had whelmed in bitter ruin. This knowledge

embitters him the more against his sons, who in his weakness had preferred the kingdom for themselves, when one word from them would have saved him from poverty and exile.

> "They have sold me for a throne and sceptred sway,
> They shall win ruin, bloodshed, death, for wage."

On the instruction of the Chorus, Ismene goes to perform purifying rites at the shrine, while he unfolds his story to them.

Theseus, now entering, kindly recognises who he is, and asks what his suit is, for he himself has tasted exile, and he knows how fickle is man's fortune, and what a risk To-morrow always holds. Œdipus states his request—life's last boon, a grave to Attica. But why? Would not his sons bear him away to Thebes. No, the old king replies, and states the reason. He wishes to bless Attica, beloved by gods and men.

> "The gods alone are proof,
> Against Time's changes, sorrow, pain, and death.
> All else must alter—faith dies, doubts prevail,
> Strength perishes and friendships pass away.
> What though the sun of peace to-day is shining
> 'Twixt thee and Thebes, some day the gloom of war
> Shall cloud the light, and battling spears drink blood.
> Then shall it not be found an empty deed,
> Without reward from heaven, to shelter me,
> Unless the gods deceive me."

Theseus agrees, and leaves him in the protecting care of the Chorus and citizens.

The Chorus [1] sings one of its finest odes, in praise of the land.

> "Here to our fair Colonus,
> Fairest of all earth's homes,
> Stranger, thy steps are come,
> Where constant throbs the mourning nightingale,
> Hid in the covert of our deep green glades,
> Among the wine-dark ivy, and the woods
> Sheltered from storming winds.

---

[1] The Chorus display reverence for the gods and compassion for human suffering, the two great virtues attributed to Athens by her poets.

> Here the narcissus blooms,
> Clustering in beauty ;
> Here the sweet crocus blows,
> Beauteously golden.
> Here the unslumbering streams
> Of still Cephissus murmur,—
> Streams unpolluted, blessing our bounteous land
> Here our strong pride stands fast
> 'Stablisht by strength of our steeds,
> And the mastering might of the sea."

This ode, according to tradition, was to be the touchstone of the old age of Sophocles.[1] His son Iophon had, in a misguided moment, brought an action against his father, as being imbecile and unfit to manage his estates. Sophocles, then in his ninetieth year, came into Court, leaning on his grandchild's shoulder—like the figure of his own Œdipus ; and his only defence was, to recite this ode, which gave him the victory he deserved.

Creon, with the band of followers, now comes upon the scene. At first, with gentle words, he pleads with Œdipus to return.

> " Bid adieu to this kindly state,
> And come,—thy people call thee, and thine own
> Sure first can claim thy piety,—for Thebes,
> The city of thy race, nursed thee of old."

But Œdipus will not listen.

> " Why shouldst thou try to take me in the toils,
> Wrapping hard, cruel thoughts in gentle words,
> Like swords in velvet scabbards ?   Dost thou know
> This kindness, when I need it not, is vain.
> If, when my heart was hungry for it once,
> It had been offered, well : but now my spirit
> Finds peace and gentleness.   I need thee not.
>
> Not for myself thou seekst me, but that Thebes,
> With me at hand, may win heaven's victory.

---

1 Cicero gave his authority for the story. *Vide* " Cato Major seu de Senectute," 7, 22. Plutarch identifies the part of the play.   From an anonymous life it would seem that this scene in court provided a theme for a contemporary comedy.

> Not for thy city that ; but this, my curse,
> Ever abiding in her.   And my sons
> This be their heritage,—within my realm,
> Room for them both to die."

Creon, then, with scornful laughter, declares that Ismene
has been already seized; and now he will remove Antigone
with him.   They seize Antigone, and Creon threatens the
removal of Œdipus also, approaching him to fulfil his
purpose ; when Theseus appears, and, hearing what has
happened, sends a band to intercept at the cross-roads the
captors of Ismene.   He turns indignantly to Creon then.

> "Thou hast disgraced my crown, my race, my realm,
> Thrusting aside our justice, pride, humanity,
> As if we had been slaves, and I were nought ;
> Spoiling the gods whose suppliants thou hast snatched.
> Hand back thy captives, or a prisoner thou
> Thyself here lingerest.   Now my soul has spoken,
> Not empty threatenings, lip-deep, meaningless."

Creon sneers, as justification for seizing Œdipus, that he
is outcast, polluted, and polluting ; but the old king
himself protests.

> " O shameless soul,—these horrors have I borne
> Never by mine own choice.   The gods so willed,
> Angered of old against my hapless race.
> Take me and try me by myself alone,
> I have no sin.   Was it my fault my sire,
> Shadowed by doom divine, to die by me,
> As yet unborn, should be marked out by heaven ?
> I knew not whom I slew.   Blind was the deed.
>
> Wouldst thou hold inquest if thy murderer came
> Before thee now,—' Art thou my sire or son ?'
> Or rather face the fight and do thy best ? "

They all go forth, Creon with them, to recapture the
captives, while the Chorus sings of the conflict.

> " O to be where the foemen, turned at bay,
> Join in the battle-clang ! . . ."

But anon, the maidens return, escorted by Theseus, who intimates that a man, a kinsman of Œdipus, had cast himself supplicant at the altar of Poseidon, and desired speech with the outcast king. Œdipus recognises that it is his son Polynices, and only after Antigone's entreaty allows him to be brought.

A fine ode, expressing wondrously the melancholy of human life and hope, fills in the scene.

> " Fool is the man
>   Who lightly prays,
>   For lengthened days,
> Nor is contented with life's briefest span.
>
> For what long life lays up
> Within its cup
> Is less of joy than pain :
> And, as for life's delights, thou know'st how vain :
> Till the deliverer come,
> And joy sinks dumb,
> Sans wedding song, or harp-strings' throbbing,
> And all is past,
> Ending both laugh and sobbing,—
> Even death at last.
>
> Not to be born is best,[1]
> Or, when life comes, to speed
> The swiftest ways that lead
> To silent rest.
> For youth goes by,
> And all its follies die.
> What cometh next ?
> Suffering and grief,
> Envy and strife ; nor, when the soul is vexed,
> Finds it relief :
> And then, old age, infirm, without a friend,—
> Who would not see its long pains have an end ?
>
> Yet strange is life's poor wage,
> Look not at me alone ; behold the King,

---

[1] Cf. " Theognis of Megara "—

> " Best never to have seen the light.
>   Next best by far to die."

πάντων μὲν μὴ φῦναι ἐπιχθονίοισιν ἄριστον . . .

> Like a grey crag facing the northern rage,
> On which the wide winds bring,
> Sweeping against him, desolate woe on woe,
> Till to the deep, forlorn, forgot, he go ! ''

Polynices enters. Distraught with the contending forces of his own ambition, the tortures of exile, and his father's curse, he cries—

> " Why art thou silent ?   Turn not away, my father !
> Why art thou angry ?   Hast thou no word for me ? ''

He tells of his strife with his brother, his exile, his hardship, his enterprise of war now pending against Thebes, and he begs his father's presence as voucher of victory.   But the answer of the king is pitiless and dire :—

> " No gleam of gladness shall my words give thee,
> That, when both throne and crown were thine in Thebes,
> Didst drive thy father, homeless, to the world.
> To thee I owe my wandering days of hunger,
> Begging my bread from strangers ; now no son
> Art thou of mine, forgetting sonship then.
> Fate looks upon thee sternly ; yet more stern
> Her eyes will frown if thou 'gainst Thebes will go.
> Never will victory crown thee ; death for thee,
> And for thy brother, at her gates abides.
>
> Disfathered by thyself, accurst by me,
> Go—ne'er to vanquish, but, by kindred hand,
> To die.   My curse shall fight for me
> Against thy banners and thy marshalled spears.'' [1]

Stunned and saddened, the outcast son, bowed down by doom, yet rises to a brave despair, sets his face to his fate, and bids farewell to his sisters, asking only one thing from their hands.

> " May the great gods make bright
> The path you tread in, if ye do by me
> The last sad deed of piety when I'm dead.
> Farewell,—ye look upon my face no more.'' [2]

Somehow, our pity marches off the stage to death with him ;

[1] *Cf.* " Lear."   [2] *Cf.* " Eteocles," p. 135.

yet, to the Greek, the wrong of impiety must be atoned for by the sinner himself—and here, not in the mystery of another world.

Now thunder is heard, and Œdipus recognises in it the sign foretold. Three times the sound rings forth. When Theseus is brought he is told how Œdipus will reveal the place where he must die, now that the summons of the gods has come; but that place must be secret, unrevealed forevermore, save to his heir, and so through all the line succeeding

> " But thus for thee 'twill a sure defence,
> Better than shields, against thy foemen's spears.
>
> For the gods are slow, though sure, in visitation,
> When men scorn godliness and turn to wrath.
>
> Farewell, and when your land is blest, remember
> Me, whose dead dust has blest thee evermore."

And so he goes, unaided and unled, as if inspired, followed by his daughter and Theseus. The story of his marvellous death is told by a messenger—how, lingering over farewell with his daughter, a voice, from heaven reiterated, called—

> " Œdipus, why delay we now to go?
> Too long thou tarriest."

They all withdrew, and, when they looked again, the king could not be seen, but only Theseus stood, with his hand before his face, as though some sudden glory blinded him. Surely no cry of a daughter's love was ever lovelier than Antigone's as she returned.

> " Now is it strange that sorrow past should seem
> As it were gladness lost. For that which knew
> No sweetness, yet was sweet when shared with him ! "

while the Chorus comfort her with—

> " Nay, since a blessed end the gods have given him,
> Lament no more. He hath the common doom
> Escaped; so easy is it for ill fortune
> To lay men by the heels."

The play ends with the entrance of Theseus, who promises to send to Thebes, and try to save the brothers from the dreadful bloodshed of their feud.

No imitation of this master-play has ever even touched the spirit of it, with its deep spell of human sorrow, chastening, and then its peace, when pain is drawn, by the voice of heaven, beyond earth's "hoarse disputes."

CHAPTER XV

THE CHILDREN OF THE KING

ÆSCHYLUS: "SEVEN AGAINST THEBES." SOPHOCLES: "ANTIGONE."
EURIPIDES: "PHŒNICIAN WOMEN" AND "SUPPLIANTS."

NATURALLY the family of this doom-chased king takes up
the interest of the Tragic writers. We hear, of course,
above the closing music of the blind man's parting, the
hurtling din of battle beating around Thebes, and all the
woe born of unbrotherly feud breaks loose upon the world.

From Æschylus, the oldest of our poets, we have still
preserved the "Seven against Thebes."[1] This is one of
four tragedies which he wrote on the subject of the woes
and sufferings of the House of Laius, King of Thebes.[2] He
grasps the threads of the story at the point where the sons
of Œdipus are on the threshold of fratricidal strife.

The opening scene is in Thebes, before the principal
temple, within hearing of the clash of war. The Chorus
consists of a band of distracted Theban ladies.

The play is vivid, and picturesque in detail; the shields of
the champions are described in minute heraldic phrase, as
symbolical of the character and intent of those who bore
them to the fray, while artistic contrast is strongly and
strikingly secured by means of the distress and horror of the
Chorus, in the midst of the dreadful din of warfare, the
shouting of conflict, and the ardour of the heroes. One

---

[1] B.C. 467.
[2] It is believed that an epic of Thebes, attributed to Homer, enjoyed a popularity
almost as great as that of Troy. Herodotus (iv. 32) refers to the "Epigoni" as being,
in his time, attributed to Homer.

feels intensely the warrior-poet's intonations as the speeches flow.

> " People of Cadmus's City, the man at the helm
> Of the state, weary steering, no drowsiness ever must know,
> But must wake and be watchful to tell how the winds and the
>   sea-currents go ;
> For all good is the gift of the gods, but if ruin o'erwhelm,
> Then the king gets the blame, when the blasts of dismay
>   o'er the trembling towns blow ! "

In words that must have thrilled his hearers, proud of their bravery in the past, he tells them—

> " 'Tis only right you arm yourselves to guard
> Your city and the altars of your gods,—
> Ah, may their honour still unsullied be !—
> Your children and your country too, whose soil
> Nursed you and fed you, clothed you, held you up,
> That for this service proud ye might be strong
> To lift in her defence the fearless shield."

A messenger enters, telling how he has seen the seven champions from Argos sacrificing to Bellona, and dedicating themselves to battle.

> " Each iron spirit glowing from the fire
> Of courage, as the lion's soul glares red,
> Watchful for fight—determined."

The Chorus of women on their way to supplicate the gods now cry aloud their fears.

> " Yonder they come. The cloud of dust suspended,
> Marching above them, marks their progress plain."

They are rebuked in imperious scorn by Eteocles. This is not a time for crying on Phœbus, or Artemis, or to bewail the crash of war, and all the risk of things.

> " What aid is this ye lend ? . . .
> O far from me in good or evil fortune
> Be woman's aid. For now, Fear gazing for you,
> Our foes are magnified, and your wild cryings
> Turn our brave men to cowards, and urge their flight."

The audience would fully approve of this rebuke to these women, for feminine interference in manly works was resented by the Greek.   Some very fine descriptive lines break out from the soul of a man who has known and tasted what he sings of.

> " What ? when the labouring ship scarce rides the surges,
>   Think ye the pilot should forsake the helm ? "

Or, when the Chorus, in answer, say—

> " I flew to clasp the gods, when at our gates
>   The sharp sleet of the arrow-showers drove snell "—

one knows that the Poet has heard the " on-ding " of the rain of death somewhere.

Even here a little sarcasm at the cost of the gods breaks from Eteocles, as he feels himself hemmed in by external war and internal fear, and abandoned by all hope of help from heaven.

> " Ha,—like the rats, the gods
>   Prepare to scuttle from a sinking ship ! "

while he emphasises the duty of work as the accompaniment of prayer—

> " Cry to the gods—'tis well ; but let your care
>   Be ever on the watch amid your prayer."

The Chorus beautifully excuse their womanly tremors, by pleading that they are,

> " As the dove in her nest,
>   All trembling with fear,
>   Believing each breath
>   That rustles the leaf
>   Is the portent of grief—
>   A snake from the woodlands, with death
>   For her loved, drawing near."

And they proceed to depict the horrors of a vanquished town, the blazing roof-tree, the heroes slain, the women outraged and led captive, the greedy victors loaded with spoil, heedlessly dropping treasures as they speed along in their hasty rapine, and even the gods, homeless, hurled from their shrines by the invaders.

When the soldier who, in the very spirit of the ancient epic, describes the war-panoply of the seven champions that are approaching,[1] comes to Polynices, the tragic impiety of the unbrotherly warfare strikes Eteocles, and the terrible cause of it—the anger of the gods, and unavoidable ruinous consequence of sin, wrings from his heart the cry—

> " O terrible heaven's hate ! Unhappy sons
> Of Œdipus, your doom deserves our tears ;
> Now stamps the father's curse its imprint deep
> In vengeance on you." [2]

Impiety, plunging the country in the disaster of war, deepens the gloom of the play. In vain the Chorus beg Eteocles not to go forth, pleading—

> " What expiation can obliterate
> The stain of brother's blood by brother shed ? "

But he will not listen to their pleading, for his heart is darkened and maddened with injured pride, and with anger against his brother. He replies to their remonstrances—

> " Well should it be if man could bear defeat
> Unshamed : but what shall linger o'er the brave
> Save gladness of true fame for duty done ;
> While to the coward, Fame holds no crown like that,
> For all his labours. . . .
>   Nay, since the gods now drive me,
> Onward I rush.   Sink all the race of Laius,
> Hated by heaven, whelmed in this hurricane
> Of ruining fate, headlong to deepest hell ! " [3]

---

[1] Euripides has a slight snigger at the longwindedness of the soldier in the " Phœnissæ," 751.

[2] His curse is a living thing. Œdipus curses his sons and they slay each other ; he curses Creon, and his wife and son commit suicide, while he himself has the crowning misery of outliving all, in an old age of fruitless sorrow for the evils of self-will and tyranny uncontrolled.

[3] A regular Macbeth, he will die, curse or no curse, at least " with harness on his back." He challenges the curse, and it enters into the arena in response.

The Chorus foresee the horror upon which he is rushing, the murder of brother by brother. They speak in vain of " unpermitted blood " whose fruit is sorrow, bringing a deeper curse to the land and deepening the shadow on the house of Laius. But he feels his father's curse, a stern, relentless fury, driving him on, waving the bloody sword that parts his kingdom.

> " She the abhorred,
> Who Fate's brood brings,
> The curse-fulfilment, that, in fury blind,
> Lap up the blood of Kings "—

reminding the hearer of the old dark tale of terror that lies like a mist of shame about the feet of Thebes. The inevitableness, the living efficacy of a spoken word, is shown in the terrible fulfilment of the curse of Œdipus on his sons.[1]

> Hate, quickened with woe,
> By the deep pain of the dead,
> Is wakened by curses old
> Of the heart that long is cold,
> And Murder, uncontrolled,
> As the shuttles go to and fro,
> Stains sudden the woof deep-red."

Soon a soldier comes disclosing how heaven has saved the city, and how Phœbus at the seventh gate has repaid on the sons of Œdipus the old sad sin of Laius—how brother has fallen by the hand of brother, how the impious struggle about a kingdom has only won for each the limit of a tomb, and—

> " their father's curse,
> Fatally cruel, sweeps them both away ! "

The awful horror of the deed is laid back at the door of Laius, the bitter stream tracked to the black source of the race. The two dead warriors are brought out upon the stage, and Ismene and Antigone enter, lamenting above their brothers slain, bewailing the sorrows of their race.

[1] See pp. 148 and 166n.

And now the tragic interest is intensified by the proclamation of the purpose of the Theban state, that—

> " Eteocles shall have an honoured grave,
> For, shielding native land, he gave his life "—

while, of Polynices—

> " In death the anger of his country's gods
> Whose shrines he scorned, leading an alien host
> To take and storm the town, pursues him still.
> This his reward—to lie dishonoured, outcast,
> Food for the vultures, robbed of every rite
> Wherewith men's sorrowing love reveres the dead."

The horrible deprivation of interment—the refusal of burial or even of a handful of dust thrown over the dead, was harrowing, especially to the spirit of the Greek. It conveyed a slight to the gods of the underworld, and a wrong to the shade of him whose corpse had been uninterred, for it was doomed to wander homeless by the banks of Styx. To the human heart nothing was ever more precious than to secure due burial for their loved ones. The dramas with this motif caught, thus, the very strongest sympathetic interest of the people. It meant all the difference between the eternal rest and the eternal disquiet of the soul. The indignant heart of Antigone gives expression to the feeling of outraged national religion.

> " Let cowards listen.   If none other dare
> To give him burial.   I myself will go,
> Not fearing, in my love, to scorn the state.
> Nature has laws that surely bind together
> The children of one mother's bitter sorrows,
> And the same stricken father's blinding pain.
>   Though I be but a woman, I will go,
> Make his tomb ready—with these very hands
> Dig up the dust and bear it in my bosom,
> Till with the pitiful earth his corse I cover."

Vainly the Chorus, torn now between sympathy with the love of a sister determined to fulfil the last pious duties in death, and condemnation of the impiety of unfraternal and unpatriotic rage, exclaim—

> "Many shall wail thy ruin, while, for him
> No eye shall drop the tear, nor share his pain.
> Untended save by thy heart's lonely sorrow,
> Into the shades he sinks."

while the second semi-Chorus declare—

> "Do the state what it will, we will go,
> Share his funeral rites and help her in her woe.
> All the world feels the pain of a sweet spirit's sorrowing fate,
> And love is above all the laws of a pitiless state."

Eteocles, the first tragic hero whose portrait is elaborated by Æschylus, moves our sympathy by his devoted, passionate patriotism and by his unmoved resolution under the very shadow of approaching doom. When Polynices draws near, he cannot restrain his rage, and stands forth defiant of the very fate he knows awaits him, in whose hand is the paternal curse like a sharp-edged sword.

Now, in this harrowing play of the entanglement of souls with the destiny of their house, we find Æschylus emphasising his interpretation of suffering. The popular idea was, of course, that suffering was the result of the mere whim of the gods falling, in haphazard, spiteful hate, upon a soul's progression. Nay, said Æschylus, the curse does not fall causelessly. At the back of blind Fate there is an intelligent arbiter; and though suffering, it is true, comes from the gods, it is the inevitable offspring of sin. No matter how long ago, or how far away, down through the blood steals the dark stream of doom from the mills of God, and the sin is, at last, atoned for, sorely and surely. Impiety, the breach of natural laws, not only shocks humanity but unbalances the spiritual universe; and the conservation of justice demands retribution in order to secure the necessary readjustment. Sure as the acorn growing in the bosom of the dust, the punishment of sin grows in the garden of human conduct. [1]

He also emphasises the eternal weight of words. Words are the double-barbed arrows of the soul, and unseen agents seem to lie in wait, and carry them to fulfilment. Especially potent was the idea of a father's curse, just as strong as, with the Hebrews, was the idea of a father's blessing; and here we see it, in all its uncontrollable, indomitable destiny, in unfraternal hate, wherein, according to tradition, even in the funeral pile, the dust of the very dead leapt wide apart, refusing to mingle.

Sophocles, in "Antigone," [2] follows the thread of the fortunes of the Tragedy-haunted family of Œdipus, during the attack on Thebes, by Polynices, in his campaign against his brother.

This play has had a long line of popularity from the days of the Athenian theatre till modern times. Mendelssohn's music has brought the sorrows of this ancient house before those who otherwise should never have heard of them, and deepened interest all the more. Nor is the secret far to seek. This fearless pure soul of womanhood who faced death for the unwritten law of duty, stands up in dominating beauty over all ages, proclaiming the great secret of abiding love.

> "No law man-made can ever cast aside [3]
> The laws of nature, and of nature's lord,—
> Not in the dying pages of a book
> Writ in dim characters that Time can bleach;
> Dateless, not Yesterday nor our To-day
> Saw their beginning. No man knows their fount
> Whence first they flowed. This, only, man can know,
> That ere Time was, they won their mystic power
> Which shall be theirs, when Time shall cease to be."

---

[1] The play was said to have been politically on the side of Aristides as against Themistocles.

[2] The order of composition of the plays was "Antigone," "Œdipus Tyrannus," and "Œdipus Coloneus." The legend was of Attic origin.

[3] Here, as in his "Ajax" and "Œdipus," Sophocles gets hold of the notion of unwritten law. With him right is always supreme.

The assault has ended in disaster for the invaders.   At each of the six gates of the city one of the renowned Argive champions has been slain, and, at the seventh, the two brothers have met, and they have both fallen by each other's hand.   Under the cover of the darkness the Argive army has fled.   Creon, now King of Thebes, has issued a decree that Eteocles shall be interred with honour, while the corpse of Polynices shall be left lying, dishonoured and unburied, for the birds and the dogs a prey.

The scene is before the Royal Palace, the morning after the flight of the defeated Argive warriors from the gates of Thebes.   Antigone speaks to her sister Ismene.[1]

> " What sorrows in the heritage of pain
> Bequeathed by Œdipus, remain for us
> Unrealised, untasted, from the gods,—
> Dishonour, ruin, shame, and agony.
> Have they not been ingredients of our cup?
> And now this new decree, that rings through Thebes,
> Threatens our friends the doom that falls on foes."

She tells the disgrace that has been put on Polynices, and tries to get her sister to aid her in defying the edict, and burying their brother's corpse.   She is absorbed in her own duty, and cannot see save along the clear narrow track before her.   Ismene, not from lack of love for her dead brother, but from greater softness of nature, shrinks from the ordeal.[2] She feels—

> " 'Tis never woman's part to strive with men ;
> Nor, since the strong compel, to disobey,
> But to obey even in things more bitter."

Antigone looks wider, and with a deeper thought, pathetically piercing beyond the veil.

[1] Neither Antigone nor Ismene are mentioned by Homer, Hesiod, or Pindar, nor does Pindar seem to know the legend of refusal of burial, for he speaks of the seven pyres for the seven divisions of the Argive army.   Ion of Chios, a contemporary of Sophocles, speaks of the sisters being burned in the Theban temple of Hera by Laodamas, son of Eteocles, when Thebes was taken, evidently not knowing the legend of Antigone's deed.

[2] Ismene and Chrysothemis are Greek Tragic types, as seen both in "Antigone" and "Electra."

" Nay, I will never force thee.   I myself
Will lay his dust in dust.   It were not ill
To die for such a deed.   Then should I rest,
Loved evermore by him for whose sweet love
I gave my life.   For life's brief day goes by ;
So swift, so brief it is.   The dead Beyond
Is evermore,—my love lives longer there." [1]

They retire, and the Chorus join in an ode of gladness over
the recent victory, when Creon enters to proclaim his policy.

" The gods have laid their hands on us at last,
Steadying the ship of state, erstwhile so tost
By storming billows.   Now by kinship's tie
I hold the throne of Thebes. . . . False is the man,
Unworthy of regard, who holds a friend
Dearer than fatherland.   No foe of Thebes
Shall be a friend of mine, or share my heart.
Such is my charter ; so my just decree,
Flinging my kinsman's corpse to shame abroad,
Because against our gates with arms he came,
Holds fast in Thebes ; the wage of disregard
Is death.   The other, for he fought for us,
Finds, with all worthy honours, rest revered."

Even while the proclamation goes forth, a guard enters in
haste, a vulgar semi-clown, to tell reluctantly, for he fears
the wrath of Creon, how some one, unknown and unseen, has
given the corpse burial.

" Not shut within the tomb, but lightly strewn
With reverent dust, as by some pious hand
Dreading a dead man's curse."

Such a brief rite was reckoned sufficient to evade the
pollution of being left unburied.[2]   Creon gives way to anger,
and alleges treason, with suspicion of bribery ; but he warns
them of a wage for such a work.

The Chorus express in chaste verse the wonder and
power of man, but hint at the peril of interference with

[1] Here, as so often, Sophocles looks round the corner of To-day, and sees the
importance of what lies behind its brief shadow.
[2] Cf. Hor. "Odes," i. 28 : "Licebit injecto ter pulvere curras."

the laws of a land, and with inscrutable but invincible justice.

> " Wonders are many, but none
> Can exceed the wonder of man,—
> Tracking the trackless waters
> Of the wan seas, riven by storm.
> Boring a path through the threatening surges
> That break in wrath overhead. . . .
> Winning with wit in his meshes of skill
> The birds and the beasts of the forest,
> And the brood of the ocean deeps. . . .
> Thought, winged swift as the wind,
> And speech, he has bound in his chains,
> Master and Monarch of all. . . .
> Only death can he never enslave.
> But cross-roads wait for his cunning,—
> Now to good his skill leads him, anon
> His feet are entangled in ill.
> If he honour the laws of the land,
> Standing fast by the justice of heaven,
> Nor skulk with the shadow of sin,
> His city in certitude bides ;
> But citiless, homeless is he,
> Who takes evil to dwell in his heart."

The guard enters, leading Antigone captive, caught burying her brother. He had watched near the dead, but a whirlwind had swept the dust from the corpse when Antigone had returned, and again she began to cover it where it lay. He describes to Creon how she faced the task—

> " Crying aloud,
> With a bitter sharp cry, like a bird
> When it looks on its sorrows around,
> In a desolate nest."

She avows the deed. It was man's edict that she broke, but there were laws of heaven behind and above it, justifying her, dateless in origin ; and no man's law can abrogate these forever.

> " Have I not known I'd die since first I saw
> The sun, though ne'er were uttered thy decree ?
> And if before my time death grip me fast,
> 'Tis but to sleep the sooner ! "

Creon summons Ismene on suspicion of complicity, and she comes to claim her share in the offence.

> " Lo, here Ismene comes with weeping heart ;
>   A cloud above her brow o'ershades her face,
>   And breaks in rain of tears upon her cheeks."

Antigone, however, denies Ismene's claim. She will not drag another down with her. Untouched by the pathos of her love or by the knowledge that she is affianced to his son Hæmon, he orders her within, as one already dead, while the Chorus mourn over the deathlessness of a curse.[1]

> " The sorrows are heaped upon sorrows,
>   Even on the griefs of the dead.   And the living can find
>   Wheresoever they turn, no open way of escape.
>   Now even the light that flickered awhile with hope
>   Over the last dying root of the house of the curse,
>   Is quenched by the folly of speech,
>   And the madness that blindeth the heart.
>   Ah, nothing that's vast
>   Curseless and painless can enter the life of the world.
>   For, to him whom heaven urges hellward,
>   The blindness of heaven shall come,
>   And evil seem good to his soul."

Hæmon, moved by his deep love for Antigone, now pleads with his father for clemency, supporting his plea by the statement that the whisper of the city approves of the sisterly deed. But the two strong wills clash like swords till sparks fly from them, kindling a fire that even tears can never quench. Creon's pride is hurt, and his son's argument whips him up to scorn and anger, till he orders that Antigone be brought in, that she may die in the very presence of her lover, who rushes from the scene, exclaiming—

> " Now come what will, thou seest my face no more ! "

Here the poet treads very close upon the verge of a parting scene of passion between lovers, more nearly than anywhere

---

[1] The position of the Chorus of Theban elders is very striking, for at first they support Creon, holding that the self-will of Antigone has wrought her ruin ; but they are changed by Teiresias and turn against the king.

else in the Greek Drama. The later dramatists would not have let this opportunity go. Yet, even in the scene with Creon, Hæmon pleads rather justice and the opinion of the world than his own love for Antigone.

Creon now discloses the doom he has designed for his prisoner. She is to be immured in a rocky vault to starve to death, unless, may-be, the gods find for her a way of escape, or till she learn at last, though late, that it is lost labour to revere the dead.

The Chorus bewail the infatuation of love :—

> " O love, that never lost the victory,
> Whose throne is set on a soft maiden's face,
> Thou hast thy field of conquest everywhere.
> Wealth is made waste by thee,
> The vast sea cannot fright thee from its surge ;
> The squalor of the desert, and its huts
> Cannot dismay thee.
> Gods and men alike are at thy bidding,
> And whom thou masterest is surely mad.
>
> The just thou blindest,
> Kinsfolk thou sunderest ;
> Eternal as undying things art thou. . . ."

While they sing, Antigone passes on the way to her living death, and as she goes she sighs—

> " No song is mine
> Of the revellers at the bridal ;
> For the silent Lord of the gloomy Lake
> Of Death weds me."

At Creon's imperious command she is led away [1]—

> " Dreeing the weird of the impious,
> For piety's sweet sake."

---

[1] Nowhere else has the poetry of the ancient world embodied so lofty or so beautiful an ideal of woman's love and devotion. The Macaria of Euripides resigns her life to save the race of the Heracleidæ; his Iphigeneia, to prosper the course of the Greek fleet; his Alcestis, to save the life of her husband, but all by compulsion to begin with. Antigone is crucified between Conscience and Tyranny, giving her life for love and duty.

In this the Chorus see hints and shadows of Fate. They see the black night of the father's sin far away behind to-day, carrying its own sting with it.

> " Nought shall deliverance bring from doom,
>   Nor wealth, nor war,
>   Nor battlemented cities,
>   Nor dark, sea-beaten ships."

But swiftly the feet of judgment seek the door of Creon himself. Teiresias, the blind prophet—the Elijah whose presence is a portent of woe to cruel kings, enters, with his message. He shows Creon how his impious cruelty, denying burial to the dead,[1] has poisoned the altar-sacrifices, all the birds of omen having been polluted by the unholy food; and the anger of the gods has been stirred against the sacrilegious deed. Scorned again, as previously by Œdipus he had been, he tells the secret of his soul.

> " Thine own shalt thou receive
>   Dead for the dead, for that thy pride has thrust
>   The living into graves, yet kept the dead unburied ;
>   For thee the Furies wait, and heaven repays
>   Thy coin to thee, in sorrow and in pain,
>   Wailing within thy house ; and, in all states
>   Whose dead have e'er been outraged, hate of thee."

Creon, disturbed and crushed with awe, suddenly, like the passionate soul he is, repents and speeds to liberate the living, and to give burial to the dead. But a messenger appears, hotfoot with bitter tidings.

> " No life's estate in certainty is 'stablished,
>   Creon, once blest and blessing, has lost all,
>   And when all joy is past, a man is dead.
>   Wrath is but vanity, and kingly state
>   A shadow of a mist if peace be flown."

He tells the culmination of distress that has fallen on the

---

[1] No greater injury could be done to one's foes than to refuse burial. Lysander omitted to bury the Athenians who fell at Ægospotami, and it was remembered as a stain on his character for centuries.— JEBB.

house of Creon,[1] how, when they reached the cave, they found the stone-built entrance broken open, and, in the gloom, Antigone hanging dead; and Hæmon, who had meant to deliver her—

> " Clasping her to his heart,
> Wailing the loss of her, to him most dear,—
> His father's crime, and his own ill-starred love."

But as his father entered, the frenzied youth struck at him with his sword, then turned its edge upon himself, and died. A tomb in Verona became likewise a college of enlightenment, too late, when human feud and pride drove love to death.

Meantime Eurydice the Queen has heard the story, and, in grief, retired, and when the king returns he finds himself heirless and wifeless, and understands his madness.[2]

> " O let my last day come,—the sweetest gift
> The gods can give me. Let me not behold
> The light of a To-morrow. . . .
> > Lead me hence,
> Cursed by my pride and folly—crushed and slain."

The agony of self-will, blinded prejudice, and desolating pride, with all the wage it wins from injured heaven, brood above this play. It needs no voice from heaven, no " god from the machine," to whisper brokenly across that silenced crowd the warning that there are laws unwritten, yet recorded in the human breast, which even kings dare never transgress lightly and think to escape retribution.

Euripides deals with the same episode of the old sad story in the " Phœnician Women," [3] wherein is displayed at once the poet's defects in dramatic construction, and his unique

[1] Creon held, and perhaps rightly, so far—that no subject must presume to decide what edicts to obey or disobey ; but he puts upon Polynices a punishment which outrages humanity and religion alike.

[2] Why are both Creon and Antigone punished? Hegel says, " In the view of the Eternal Justice both were wrong because they were one-sided, but at the same time both were right." Is it not rather to teach that human law must yield to the divine ?—JEBB.

[3] It has been suggested that this was written to compete with the " Seven against Thebes" of Æschylus, especially in view of the disparaging references to that play contained herein.

power of pathetic and picturesque beauty. It stands, of course, in dangerous contrast with Æschylus's "Seven against Thebes," and the "Antigone" of Sophocles. Jocasta, the Queen, in a long prologue, tells the tale over again, and we see with what freedom Euripides handles the myth.[1]

Thebes is besieged by Polynices, but Œdipus is meanwhile in confinement in the city, and Jocasta endeavours to reconcile her sons. She makes appeal to Jove.

> "O Jove, who dwell'st in glory of heaven on high,
> Surely if justice be with thee,
> Thou wilt not thus, eternally,
> Give endless pain on our stricken souls to lie."

The famous and masterly scene of Antigone on the walls[2] is perhaps one of the most imaginatively touching pictures that the poet has created. Though it be suggested by Helen on the walls of Troy, it is here the master's own. The description of the plain, one blaze of bronze, makes the whole panoply of war live before us.

A truce is declared in order that the brothers may discuss their quarrel. Polynices states his case moderately, but firmly, while Eteocles, in his own way, pleads the right of possession and the title of might. He begins by asserting a principle which thrusts all reconciliation out of the bounds of possibility.

> "If all the earth were agreed
> Wherein consist wisdom and honour,
> 'Twere easy to settle up strife :
> Yet honour and justice are nought
> But a name in this world of men ;
> And, for me, I would climb to the stars,
> Or follow the sun in its flight,
> To win me that chiefest of glories—
> The power of a king and his crown.
> So I have it, and hold what I have,
> Nor e'er to another will yield."

---

[1] *E.g.*, Œdipus is still living and confined to the palace. Jocasta also is alive.

[2] A. W. von Schlegel, and many who follow him, are very absurd in condemning this scene, when we remember what a place in the public eye this woman has to fill. She, the strongest woman in the city, is most aptly set in this post of vision.

There is a breath of Elizabethan passion in this passage.
This man, like Percy Hotspur, would—

> " Pluck bright honour from the pale-faced moon,
> Or dive into the bottom of the deep,
> Where fathom-line could never touch the ground,
> And pluck up drowned honour by the locks. . . .
> So he that doth redeem her thence might wear
> Without co-rival, all her dignities."

Jocasta cries out against ambition, that curse of the gods.

> " No justice she knows. . . .
> Through homes and through cities she goes ;
> Black ruin and grief grow behind her ;
> And mad they who seek her and find her ! " [1]

She points out that—

> " Man is but steward of heaven ;
> For a while the gods' gifts are but given ;
> Poor comfort are they in his pain,
> For soon they're demanded again."

Eteocles, however, is blinded and irreconcilable, and he turns
to his brother with—

> " As for thee, hence or die."

Thus is he guilty of a breach of the laws that govern both
the family and the state ; and he further darkens the outlook
of doom by his curse—

> " Let hell's black ruin reel our house to doom."

The Chorus sing some beautiful odes, dealing with the
history of Thebes.   The blind prophet Teiresias is brought
and reveals how the gods demand a sacrifice of Menœceus,
Creon's son, who, evading his father's scheme to save him,
immolates himself, and so secures the victory for Thebes.
And then the storm of battle rages; the two brothers
decide upon single combat, and Polynices is mortally stricken.
But in his dying effort he kills his brother, and Jocasta,

---

[1] *Cf.* Wolsey's speech in King Henry VIII., " Herodotus," iii. 53.

too late to prevent the deed, slays herself beside them. And now Antigone's tragedy claims her. Amid her lamentations, Œdipus gropes through his blindness in upon the scene, as if from a living grave into the light of day once more, to learn how well the gods have wrought fulfilment for his curses. All whose lives have touched his have been accurst, and now, on the king himself, the burden falls.

> " And who will be my guide,
> And, moving by my side,
> Lead me where'er I go?
> For sure the gods have now filled up my cup of woe! "

Creon, as in Sophocles, refuses burial to Polynices, and banishes Œdipus, but Antigone scorns the dictates of the tyrant, and chooses to share her father's homeless state rather than abide in Thebes. So the king stands up before the people—

> " Behold me. Œdipus am I,
> Whose wisdom made the proud Sphinx die.
> Now grief and exile to me given,
> I drift before the doom of heaven."

The " Suppliants " of Euripides is a sequel to the preceding drama which we have discussed. Adrastus of Argos, the solitary survivor of the Seven who had marched against Thebes, has taken refuge at Eleusis on the Attic border, and Theseus, though reluctantly, espouses the cause of the slain,[1] whom Creon's persistent refusal has so deeply outraged. It is rather a combination of pathos and music than a play—episodic rather than dramatic, dealing with the recovery of the corpses of those heroes whom Polynices had led to death before Thebes.

The duty of pious burial, like a haunting echo of the wars, comes in again. Theseus says—

> " What fear ye? that the dead within their graves
> Will undermine your country, or, in gloom,
> Deep in the womb of earth beget a race
> From whom shall spring avengers of their wrongs? "

[1] Prevailed upon by his mother, who is sacrificing at Eleusis at the same time.

His pleading and the firm courage of his demands win what he seeks for the dead heroes of Argos, and the city swears eternal fealty to Athens [1] for her help in time of need and pain.

The main purpose here seems to have been the praise of Athens, reflected from the praises of Theseus. Indeed this play, in its emphatic enunciation of the duty of Argos to hold to an alliance with Athens, really becomes a sort of political pamphlet; and in the debate between the herald of Thebes and the Athenian king regarding kingship, democracy, and policy of state-government, one almost feels as if Euripides were using the drama as a leading article on the Peloponnesian War.

[1] Hermann and Boeckh, confirmed by Thucydides (v. 44), assign the play to the year of the treaty between Argos and Athens. Müller ("Greek Literature," p. 371) says it is very likely the poet had in mind the dispute between the Athenians and the Bœotians after Delium (Thuc. iv. 98), when the latter refused to give up the bodies of their dead enemies, B.C. 421.

CHAPTER XVI

THE MYTH OF HERCULES

EURIPIDES : " ALCESTIS " AND " HERCULES FURENS." SOPHOCLES : " TRACHINIÆ."
EURIPIDES : " HERACLEIDÆ "

THE myth of Hercules, the great strong giant bound, in necessity of the gods, to countless labours, gave a theme to the Tragedians.

Euripides in his " Alcestis "[1] gives us a glimpse of the hero, rude, roystering, and convivial, yet eager to be benefactor to all who have been generous and kind to him. Here we see him " harrying hell " for the sake of the sorrows of men !

Only an artificial view of Comedy can look upon this as other in spirit than tragic. It is one of the most pathetic of all the works of " Euripides the Human." It is a lifting up of the curtain that hides the sorrows of a princely house. We forget the purple of Admetus in the anguish of the man.

Euripides is strong in depicting his half-burlesque, gross yet kindly-hearted giant, whose nature touches both the earthly and divine.[2]

---

[1] 439 B.C. Euripides got the second prize with his Tetralogy, of which " Alcestis " was the closing play. Sophocles got the first prize. Hence the " Alcestis " is the earliest of the surviving plays of Euripides.

[2] A sort of Falstaff among the demi-gods ! *Cf.* Aristophanes' " Peace," translated by Rogers—

> " A Hercules needy, and seedy and greedy—
> A vagabond sturdy and stout."

On a Greek vase found in Sicily, the demi-god is represented drunk, lying outside a closed door, from above which an old woman is pouring water upon him. To elevate a figure like that into tragic interest involved a characteristic of genius strikingly Euripidean.

Admetus of Pherai is threatened with death, but is permitted by the Fates to escape, if only he can find a substitute. This concession, as is explained in the prologue, has been secured by Apollo, in remembrance of the piety and kindness of Admetus, when the god was compelled to serve in Pherai as a shepherd, in expiation of his having slain the Cyclops. With a little touch of satire the god explains how Admetus had gone as suppliant among his friends, but had found them all, and even his aged father and mother, too tenaciously fond of life to surrender it for the sake of another. Only his wife was found willing to say farewell to life and the light of the sun ; and now she is in the house, gasping out her being, for love of him.

> " To-day is the day of her doom,
>   And she passes away from her life ;
>   And Death, the old shadowy priest,
>   Comes sharp and sure as the hour
>   That steals over the dial of Time,
>   Nor can be turned back by a prayer."

A controversy between Apollo and Death ensues, in which, for the benefit of the audience, the former throws out the hint of a deliverer. The Chorus, now, questioning and groping, wonder at the stillness of the palace—wonder if Alcestis is dead, and then break forth—

> " Surely the true of heart
>   Must weep,
>   To see the good depart
>   Into the house of Sleep,
>   Sudden enveloped in gloom,
>   Sent to the tomb.
>
>   Who shall bring us again
>   · Our loved, our lost ?
>   To whom of the gods or men
>   Shall we wail what our sorrow has cost ?
>   Only Apollo's son, the kindly and true,
>   Whom, for his raising the dead, alas, Jove's thunderbolt
>   slew."

The wife now tells how she is dying, and how she had prepared herself for death for the sake of him she loved, asking only the blessing of heaven on her boy and girl.

> " Let them not die, like me,
>   Before their time,
> But let them a full life's happiness see,
>   Here in their native clime."

It had been better for Admetus to have submitted to fate, for—

> " Dying, he had died but once for all,
> Now through this grief he knows a thousand deaths."

Alcestis, in her husband's arms, is carried forth to look her last on the sun.   She cries—

> " The two-oared skiff I see,
>   And Charon, ferryman of Fate,
> With hand on pole, is calling me,—
>   ' Come, hasten.   Wherefore should'st thou wait ? ' "

She lays the blame of their sorrows at the feet of some un-known god.   Admetus hears her last request, and reassures her.

> " Fear not, thou that alone hast held my heart,
> And still shalt hold it.   True my heart shall be.
> My life shall be one long dark year of sorrow ;
> My rooms no more shall ring with revelry,
> Nor trembling harp-string sound, nor Libyan flute,
> Nor voice of song uplifted from my soul."

And so she dies, with farewells to her children, while the Chorus bewail her going.

> " Tell Death's dark ferryman that ne'er
> Hath he crossed the stream with a soul so fair,
> Peerless amongst all woman-kind.
>   Oh, oft, on the seven-stringed mountain-shell,
>   Of thee shall the sons of the Muses tell,
> For earth can never thine equal find."

Hercules, on his way to fetch the chariot steeds of Thracian Diomedes, now enters, all ignorant of what terrible experi-

ence has just racked the house of Admetus.   The Chorus
warn him what a task is his.   Meanwhile, Admetus comes,
and gives him welcome greeting, staving off with ambiguous
phrases the questions of the hero, and insisting upon his
accepting the hospitality of the house, though Hercules is
loath to intrude upon a most apparent grief.   The disgrace of
having rejected a stranger is, however, intolerable to
Admetus, and the Chorus, having remonstrated with him,
break into a beautiful ode of praise.

> " O house of kindness, always open-doored,
>   Where Phœbus deigned to dwell, within thy walls,
> When in the shepherd life, across the downs,
>   He sang sweet madrigals.
>
> And spotted lynxes couched among his sheep
>   To listen to his song,
> And from the pine-wood's crested steep
>   Came down the forest throng.
>
> O home of hospitality untold,
>   The wanderer who thy threshold haps to win,
> Finds wide the gate, though love be lying cold,
>   And freely enters in."

While the corpse is being carried out to burial, the father of
Admetus comes with offerings for the gentle dead, but he is
received by his son with rebuke and railing, called a coward,
and unkind, because, though so old, he had not offered to
die for his son's sake.

> " Go,—for no burial shall my hands give thee,
>   I being dead for aught thou'st done for me."

But the father defended himself with spirit.   It is neither a
custom in Greece, nor a law of the land, that fathers should
die for their children.

> " And weary's the while, I trow,
>   In the place of the dead below,
>   And though life be incomplete,
>   Even its brevity's sweet."

While it would seem to him that Admetus was himself the coward, glad to dodge behind his wife for shelter from the terrible shafts of Death. So, after bitterest reproaches, they go out to bear the dead to her rest.

An attendant enters with his complaint. Never has he waited upon so shameless a guest! He has invaded a house which he must have seen to be a house of mourning, and has drunk deeply of the strong wine-cup, crowned himself with myrtle, and shocked and grieved all hearts with his convivial choruses. Hercules now rallies the attendant for his sombre face—

> " Come, learn from me,
> Death is the common fate of men,
>   None knows if he may see to-morrow's light,
> For Fortune's lot is not within our ken,
>   And who of man can master it aright ?
> Then, don't you see,
> Fill up the cup and drink,
> Nor sadly think ;
> Count but this hour thine own,
> Let fortune have the rest, so swift 'tis flown.
> Come, fill the cup of wine,
> And let the tide divine
> Waft thee from gloom where gleams of gladness shine."

Roused by the pain such conduct wakens, the servant reveals suddenly the terrible grief that has enfolded the house in its shadow, and the great human generosity of the demi-god is stirred in the breast of Hercules. He will repay the self-denying kindness of Admetus with such a gift as seldom comes to men.

> " I will rush, I will ambuscade death,
> And redeem this sweet wife from his cruel embrace ;
> Yea, follow, if need be, far down to the sunless abodes,
> And lead her again to the lover for whom she gave life,
> The kindly, the true."

So he departs on his errand of grace. Admetus enters, and mourns, nor will he be comforted.

> " Happier far than the living
> Are those that are dead,

> For sorrow no more can pursue them ;
> Her labours are ended,
> But forever endureth the pride of her name."

The Chorus plead that he must submit to Necessity, which guides even the gods, without whose aid Jove himself cannot bring his will inevitably to pass.

> " Much have I followed the tracks of the Muses,
> Moved 'mong the stars, and my hand laid on wonders,
> But never have found, 'mid the strong things, a stronger
> Than heaven's Needs-must-be. . . .
> So weep no more,
> Nor keep thy sorrows burning ;
> Thy tears can win from the silent shore
> For thy loved one no returning.
>
> Yet, not as the grave where common ashes lie
> Shall be her tomb, who dared for love to die,
> She shall have honours like the gods of bliss,
> And pilgrims, passing, tearful-eyed, say this,—
> Here slumbers she who died her lord to save.
> Hail, blessed soul, unmastered by the grave ! "

But, now, Hercules re-enters with a lady, veiled ; and in a clever scene of remonstrance and persuasion, she is recognised as the one whom they have been mourning, dragged from death's clutch by the all-conquering arm of the grateful but penitent guest.[1]

There is here, of course, a twofold reward for a twofold hospitality. The kind generosity of Admetus to Apollo, when the god was outcast and suffering, finds its meed in his liberation from death ; while the self-denying goodness of the host in the midst of his great grief is rewarded by the invasion of the kingdom of the dead and the restoration of his lost loved one. The Chorus sum up the further lesson.

---

[1] The Greek Tragedies may end happily, because they purpose to call forth sympathy with ideal sorrow, and to infix and deepen the truths of human experience. It is a σπουδαία μίμησις.

> " Many the shapes of Fortune ;
>   Not one of them ever reject,
> For the gods delude us,
> Of hopes denude us,
>   Yet give to us oft what we never expect.
> And, though, often perplexed, our spirits are blind,
> Yet heaven through the darkness a way can find."

The play may seem in parts grotesque ; but the lessons it teaches are among the highest ; and it is of little enough account what kind of vessel is used, if the wine that is in it be drink of the gods.

In the play of " Hercules Furens " Euripides finds the material of his thought in the toils and sorrows of the hero under the exacting tyrannies of Eurystheus.[1] He has been sent down into Hades—

> " To drag from hell the hound of triple shape ; [2]
> And from the shades his steps return no more."

Lycus the king, who, having slain Creon of Thebes, has now usurped the throne, intends to slay Megara, the wife of Hercules, and their children, with Amphytrion, the father of Hercules—

> " For the dread lest they,
> Crown to man's state, one day claim man's full title—
> A ripe revenge."

So the play opens with these, sitting, suppliant, at the altar of Jove ; and, in dialogue between Amphytrion and Megara, the situation is unfolded. She and the children have no escape from doom.

> " How, as a bird,
> Gathering under her wings the young ones round her,
> Have I watched over these. By turns they seek me,
> Saying, " Where is our father ? When shall he come back ?

---

[1] Paley says of the poet in this play—" He seems to have aimed not only at the grandiloquent and Æschylean style of diction more than was his wont, but also at the Æschylean ἔκπληξις or terror, in addition to that πάθος or feeling, of which he is in a peculiar sense the great tragic master."

[2] The last of his twelve labours. See p. 159.

> And, just when a fresh excuse to my lips is rising,
> Sudden the door creaks, and they leap to welcome
> Him who returns from Death's dark night no more."

Amphytrion does not suffer himself to abandon hope so utterly as she does.

> "Who knows what sudden breeze,[1]
> Filling our sails, unlooked-for, may uplift
> Our bark from these close straits in which we struggle?
> Wear-out our griefs by craft.   Exhaust disaster,—
> Hang on to storms until they veer to calm.
> 'Tis the brave heart that holds the hand of Hope;
> The caitiff is the comrade of Despair."

The Chorus of Theban aged men, sympathising with Amphytrion, as an old companion in arms, can only utter "sobbed-forth dirges," feeling that—

> "The old misfortunes never tire,
>   The race pursuing;
>   But, Greece, 'tis thy undoing
> When children such as these from thy fair fields expire."

Lycus enters, with blustering insolence—

> "How long do you intend to spin life out?
> What hope upholds you?   He'll return no more.
> Who now in Hades lies forever vanquished."

One would fancy that a state discussion had been going on as to advantages of archery in warfare, by the argument which ensues as to the wisdom or courage of such a method of fight.[2]   Iolaus's retorts are straight as a shaft themselves.

> "Nay, you are wise
> To fear the sons of brave men,—you a coward;
> Yet bleeding us will heal not your disease.
> Rule if you will, only let us depart,
> For who can tell what wave will swamp your ship
> Should the wind shift to Judgment?"

---

[1] See p. 397.

[2] *Cf.* Ajax, 1220.—The Greek looked on the bow as barbarous and cowardly,— slaying at a safe distance; and Lycus's sneers at the bow of Hercules are Greek sneers.   On this principle Menelaus is taunted by Peleus in "Andromache" as never even having been wounded by an arrow—not even a far-flung missile could find him!

Lycus orders trees to be felled, and timber gathered, to make a pile, on which this race he hates may be consumed. The Chorus will not be cowed by his threats. They represent the old faith and the old blood.[1] Their hero is not dead beyond recall. But Megara has no hope of such a wonder as his return after this long silence, though her despair is threaded upon a proud resignation.

> " My lord would never love
> To have his children saved because they feared
> To face what he himself ne'er turned from, dreading.
> Dost thou expect my long-lost lord's return—
> To come again from Death's great gloomy halls
> Where long his shade has with the shades been dwelling?
> Alas, who of the chiefs of Greece returned,
> That went away from us, the long road seeking?
> What shall we look for?   Exile?   Nay, the doors
> Even of friendship close on guests like these.
> Death waits us all,—life's most sure certainty.
> So let us die together."

She wins permission from the king to dress herself and the children, for the sacrifice, in funereal garb; while Amphytrion openly rebukes Jove, as a god who, having first betrayed the wife of another, neglects his offspring, a typically daring Euripideanism.

> " Justice thou neither knowest,
> Nor to defend thy friends.   If god thou art,
> Wisdom and justice are not known by thee."

The Chorus sing an Ode of the labours of Hercules,[2] bewail-

---

[1] They call upon Thebes to rise against him.   Only old age keeps themselves from taking up arms to fight his tyranny.

[2] 1. The capture of the Nemean lion.
  2. Defeat of the Centaurs.
  3. Slaying the stag with the golden horns.
  4. Taming the horses of Diomede.
  5. Slaying Cycnus.
  6. Bringing the golden apples from the Hesperides.
  7. Clearing the seas from monsters.
  8. Supporting the heavens, in place of Atlas.
  9. Victory over the Amazons.
  10. Slaying the Hydra.
  11. Defeat of the tri-bodied Geryon.
  12. The descent into hell for Cerberus
Later writers differ in the order of the labours.

ing the absence of the hero, and their own inability, through age, to help the unfortunate, who now re-enter on their way to the place of execution.   Megara is wailing, but Amphytrion appeals to heaven, yet in his appeal acknowledges the brevity of life and the happiness and glory of men, a topic ever a favourite with " sad Electra's poet." [1]

> " Little the bliss life offers ; make the hours
> Vessels of sweetness.   Lo, our fleeting hopes
> Time ne'er considers, speeding on rapid wings
> After his own pursuits.   Ah, look on me,
> How, through brave deeds, I clothed myself with glory ;
> Now fortune in one day strips all from me,
> And, like a feather, lightly sets it sailing
> Through the vast void of Nothingness and Night."

Suddenly, intercepting them in the way of death, Hercules himself appears, having returned from hell to save them. He elicits the story of the violence of Lycus, his pride and cruelty, and the false friendships that had turned away from his children in their adversity.   He explains his long delay bringing back Theseus to Athens from the shades.   Tenderly he takes his children—

> " As a great ship takes little boats in tow,"

and, expressing deepest love for them, enters the house. Lycus again appears, and, ironically induced by Amphytrion, goes to lead Megara and the children forth at once to execution.   Amphytrion exults—

> " He goes ; but the path of his feet
> Is beset with the sword.
> He will fall on his murderous purpose—
> The villain abhorred.
> I will in, for, to see one I hate
> As I hate him, depart,
>   Makes my spirit elate—
> Floods joy o'er my heart."

---

[1] *Cf.* the dirge of " Œdipus at Colonus," 1211.

The vengeance of Hercules is heard within, and the Chorus answer the cries of Lycus, reminding him of his blasphemy and pride.

> " There's a good starting note
> For a heart-stirring tune ;
> But 'tis only the prelude,—
> All the music comes soon.
> Now, tyrant, the morn
> Thou ne'er dreamedst to see,
> Opes the door of thy scorn,
> And its one look slays thee.
>
> Now the rout and the riot,
> The revenge of the strong,
> In the palace is quiet,
> Let us raise our glad song,
> To the gods who from hell sent our saviour along."

But in the midst of their thanksgiving they see above the palace the fiend of Madness,[1] sent by the spite of Juno to distract the victorious Hercules, and make him by his own hand perpetrate the crime his return had thwarted, so learning the bitter revelation of the vanity of life's triumphs, the indomitable power of the gods, and the punishment of murder. In fierce frenzy, blinded by strange delusions, he slays his children and his wife. The terrible tragedy of his fury is told to the mourning Chorus in vivid narrative by a messenger, and how, just as he was about to kill his father, Pallas intervened and cast him in a deep slumber, headlong where he fell. And now he lies within, bound with strong cords to the pillars of his house. The scene falls apart, and he is discovered, prostrate, sleeping. Suddenly he wakes to wonderment at finding himself bound,

> " Like a hulk disabled, dragged across the bar,
> Into some harbour."

But, when the full horror of his frenzy and its fruit have been disclosed to him, he longs for death.[2]

---

[1] Lyssa. Euripides borrows her from Æschylus's Ξάντριαι.
[2] In a passage between Theseus and Hercules, suicide, which was considered at the

> " A leap from some high crag, or the sharp blade
>   Of some bright sword deep in my bosom plunged."

Theseus approaches, announcing his arrival with a band of Athenian youths to aid Hercules in the overthrow of Lycus.[1]   He finds Hercules in the scene of his terrible sorrow, transfixed with grief, and angry at heaven.

> " The stony-hearted gods, self-willed and cruel,
>   I do defy."

He narrates the constant persecutions he endured from Juno, and now, outcast, through his unwitting impiety, murderer of his children and his wife, earth, air and sea shall spurn him.

> " Who can pray
>   To such a goddess, torn by meanest spite,
>   And jealousies of Jove in his amours ? "

Theseus tries to comfort him by pointing out that, if the old tales be true, even the gods do not escape misfortune, and he reveals the scandals and intrigues of Olympus.

> " Have not the gods
>   Made lawless weddings, even in their high heaven—
>   Flung into chains their sires to win heaven's crown.
>   Lo, dwell they not in bliss, and lightly bear
>   The load of all their crimes?"

And he invites him to go to Athens, the universal home of all distrest and persecuted souls.[2]

I fancy the voice of the poet, in protest against the old mythology, speaks through Hercules when his hero says,

> " I cannot hold the faith that gods are chained,
>   Nor that their hearts rejoice in rites unclean,
>   Nor that one bears a rule above the rest—

---

time a brave and noble thing, is condemned as commonplace, and the very reverse of its popular estimate.   In this opposition to the ideas of his day the poet was followed by Plato in " Phædo," and Aristotle in his " Ethics."

[1] He owed his restoration from Hades, of course, to Hercules.

[2] A flattery of Athens reminding it of its mythological connection with him who was the representative of strength, chivalry, and invincibleness.   Athens was not alone in its openness to such flattery.

> By some false bard of old these tales were spun
> Into a web of lies.   Not like a coward
> Shall I flee life.   I'll bravely wait for death,
> With you I'll go, to your kind city, now."

The number of sea-metaphors in this play is very striking and makes clearly live before our imagination the old legend of this poet lingering in the sea-girt Salamis watching what passed before his pensive eye, and weaving all things into his anguished thought about the problems of the gods.

The tragedy of the death of Hercules is narrated in the "Trachiniæ" of Sophocles.   Deianeira, the daughter of King Œneus at Pleuron in Ætolia, was wooed by a river-god Achelous ;[1] but, as she tells the story in a prologue of much beauty,

> " At last to my joy, my glorious hero came,
> O'erthrew my foe and made my spirit free.
> How went the battle ask me not, for there
> My soul with fear sat swooning, lest my face,
> Heaven had made fair, should bring me deathless grief."

She narrates the constant care the strenuous life of her lord caused her, and how she and her children are dwelling in exile even now, owing to the murder of Iphitus by Hercules. She is torn by anxiety over his long silence, and she discloses all her grief to the nurse who is beside her.   On the advice of this woman,

> " A slave, who hath spoken in the spirit of the free,"

she sends her son Hyllus to seek his father.   The Chorus of maidens reiterate their questioning of the Sun-god,

> " Tell me, O thou, whom Night
> Leads forth in glorious light,
> When her starry glowing crown
> In the dawn she layeth down ;
> Thou that beholdest all,

---

[1] In " Andromache," 167, and "Bacchæ," 625, *Achelous* is used for water generally. *Cf.* Virgil—

> *Pocula inventis Acheloïa miscuit uvis.*

He is the King of Rivers, and eldest son of Oceanus and Tithys.

Tell us what fates befall
Our hero,—where is he ?
Dwelling in what strange land afar ?
Or threading the straits of the sea ? ' '

They try to comfort Deianeira's anxieties by reminding her how life and hope continually drift and change ; but she will not be comforted ; [1] for, when he went away, it was with a shadow of doom hanging over him, talking of death and its chances, and not of brave conquest as of old. For he knew that in fifteen months death was to draw near him, while, if he escaped the crossing of the threads of doom at that period, he was to live henceforward a life of peace. And now the anxious time is quite at hand.

While she speaks, a messenger enters, telling that in the meadows a herald is proclaiming the approaching return of her lord. Followed by captive maidens, among whom is Iolê, the herald brings his tidings,—how he had left Hercules in Eubœa alive and well, with spoils from the city of Eurytus, upon whom he had wrought a splendid revenge. Deianeira addresses Iolê, but can elicit no reply. The herald says,

" Not a word has she uttered, borne down by the load of her sorrow,
   Bitterly wailing in grief, since she left her wind-swept home."

When the herald and the captives have gone away, the messenger, with an officiousness fraught with mischief, discloses another side of the story, which the herald has kept in the dark, and which this man feels should be told to his mistress—how the war had been waged by Hercules, not for revenge after all, but for love of this weeping maid, the daughter of the king. The herald, returning, asks for messages to his master ; and, when pressed, admits at last, though reluctantly, the truth of the story that has just been told.

Deianeira's heart is wrung with pain to think that Hercules

---

[1] The charm of Deianeira can no more be described than the perfume of a flower. . . . One of the most delicately beautiful creations in literature.—JEBB.
Seneca's Deianeira is a virulent Tragedy-queen breathing revengefulness.

has sent to her roof this war-won paramour; and, in her
yearning, she bethinks her of a charm to bind his love to
herself forever. And the secret of it lies close at hand:
for when, after she had wedded Hercules, they were on
their way to their home, they were to be borne across the
stream Evenus by the centaur Nessus,[1] who, for hire,
was wont, in his arms, to convey passengers over the deep
pools. While he was carrying her he wantonly insulted
her, and Hercules with an arrow mortally wounded him.
The dying centaur said to her,

> " Hearken,—for this at least wilt thou have as a gift from me,
> Thou that wast the last whom I ferried across the stream,—
> Gather the blood from my breast—'twill be to thee for a charm,
> Winning Hercules' soul, gripping the love of his heart,
> So that he never will love another woman but thee."

Remembering this she sends to him now a sacrificial robe
anointed by the centaur's blood.[2] But when the herald has
departed with the gift of Deianeira, she begins to fear; for,
having left the tuft of wool which she had used in the
anointing, in the full blaze of sunshine, contrary to the order
of him who had given it to her, she saw it shrivel away and
crumble to powder, while the very earth on which it fell
seethed with clots of foam. So she begins to doubt whether
the monster had not perhaps a double purpose, and a devilish
meaning in his charm, and that the poison of the arrow
which slew him, passing into his blood, was intended to be
diverted upon Hercules himself.

Even while she doubts, her son returns,—tells how his
father, her lord, about to dedicate altars on a sea-washed
headland, had put on the robe his wife had sent him, and,
as the fire kindled, the venom, like a viper in its cruelty,

---

[1] Nessus symbolises the fierce roar of a torrent. *Cf.* Curtius, " Etym." § 287 b.
The rescue from Nessus had been treated by Archilochus and Pindar.

[2] The tragic blindness again—so dear to the poet, of using a gift of evil to bring
forth good.
Cf. The gift of Medea. Both point to some form of sun-myth. Love-charms are
usually seen to be harmful. Antiphon's first oration is on behalf of a woman who
has poisoned her husband by a love-potion.

began to bite into his soul, till, in a frenzy, cursing her who
had slain him, he fell into a swoon, begging that he be
borne across the sea to die.   To the curse of Hercules is
added now the curse of her son.

> " May justice and the furies visit thee,
>   For dark design and deed against my sire.
>   Cruel art thou to slay that noble heart
>   Whose like the world shall look on never again."

Deianeira moves away in grief, and with her own hand,
takes her life, the only proof of her love that seems possible
to her.[1]

Hercules is brought into the courtyard ; and, awaking
from his swoon, suffers the renewal of untold agony ; but
ere he dies, he learns the sorrowful error of his wife, and
sees in it fulfilment of the oracle of heaven—as did Macbeth
himself ere the light went out.   He begs his son to wed the
captive Iolê, and then is borne away, that his body may be
burned on Mount Œta.

The Chorus see in this the terrible workings of the gods.

> " No man the future foreseeth,
>   But the present for us holdeth sorrow,
>   And shame for the gods up in heaven ;
>   But anguish, earth cannot compare,
>   For him who endureth such doom."

A striking summary and impeachment of life's incompati-
bilities, and the folly of the gods.   Further, one sees the
madness wrought by sin.   The passion of Hercules for Iolê
thus brought destruction on her household, the unjust impiety of which recoiled upon his own, awakening superstition in the heart of Deianeira, whereby she wrought upon
her lord the wishes of his foes ; teaching how perilous it
ever is for mortals to put forward their hands in interference
with the unseen purposes of heaven.

There is no hint in this drama of any glory to be given

---

[1] The curse has a messenger that does its bidding. *The woman* has to suffer for
her blindness.

to Hercules in recompense for his life of suffering and toil :
yet it strangely completes the circle of the passion of this
demi-god, bearing such sorrows as fall to one who is set, as
it were, between earth and heaven, with human desires at
war with divinest aspirations, and falling at the last into the
net of simple human love, which unwittingly destroys what
was dearest to it,—an embodiment of the eternal heart-
breaking irony of destiny here below.

The fate of the children of Hercules after his death, is
dealt with in the " Heracleidæ." [1]

Iolaus, who had accompanied Hercules in the slaying of
the hydra, speaks the prologue in front of the altar of Jove
at Marathon, telling how, driven by the rage of Eurystheus,
from city to city, they seek shelter now in the Athenian
territory. While he speaks, Copreus, the herald of
Eurystheus,—a blustering bully, akin somewhat to the
Egyptian herald who, in a similar scene of Æschylus's
" Suppliants," hustles and domineers.[2] He tries to drag the
children from the altar, to take them back to death by
stoning at Argos. Iolaus, however, invokes the aid of the
Athenians against this insult, which is alike a shame to
their city and an outrage on their gods.[3] But the citizens
will not have their hospitable reputation wronged.
Demophon, son of Theseus, who now rules the realm, enters,
and demands the reason of the uproar. The herald, windily
inflated with provincial pride, tells how he has pursued them,
Argives, daring to flee from an Argive doom of death,—
outcasts turned away from city after city, which justly feared
to risk a war with Argos. There is a touch of contemporary politics in the warning,[4]

[1] One of the earliest of Euripides' plays—probably standing, like the " Alcestis,"
fourth of a Tetralogy.
[2] To Euripides, a herald is always a bully, presuming upon his inviolableness.
See " Suppliants " and " Trojan Women."
[3] Schlegel points out how prone the Athenians were to represent themselves as
outshining all Greece in hospitality, generosity, and chivalry. *Cf.* Æschylus,
" Suppliants," and Sophocles, " Œdipus at Colonus."
[4] Its purpose, indeed, was to challenge and rebuke Argos for having entered into

" O forbear
To follow the usual custom of your state,
Making with worthless people leagues and bonds,
When mightier allies could be bound to you."

Argos was evidently recovering her status, and people
had to be reminded, in a day of possible alliances, how faithless Sparta had been to her allies in the past.   Iolaus, speaking by permission of King Demophon, praises first the
glorious gift of freedom of speech which is enjoyed by
Athens, while he denies the right of Argos to claim the
return of those whom she has uncitizened, and made state-
less by her own decree of exile.   Demophon remains firm.
He has history on his side, for, the Athenian state protects
the rights of strangers.

" The altars are a shelter sure to all
Who seek asylum there.   The Athenian state
Is not an Argive appanage.   We hold,
And I defend, our freedom as our right."

The Argive herald withdraws, and Demophon, urged by the
Chorus of citizens, resolves to prepare for the war that has
been threatened against him.   Soon he informs Iolaus of
the coming of the hosts of Argos against him, but, alas, the
prophets declare that a maid must be sacrificed to Ceres.[1]
He admits his zeal on behalf of the suppliants, but he says,

" My daughter I can never sacrifice,
Nor ask my citizens to give the gods
Such sacrifice abhorred.   For never man
So void of feeling, so bereft of wit,
Who'd yield his own loved children up to death
On altars.   Think some plan to help us out."

Iolaus offers to surrender himself, and save the children :
but this is absurd.

alliance with Sparta, and joining in the war against Athens.   At the same time it
reminds Sparta how Athens had protected the ancestors of the Spartan kings from
the demands of Argos, and consequently of the shamelessness of joining Argos in a
coalition against Athens.

[1] As in "Hecuba," " Iphigeneia in Tauris," etc., the propitiatory power of human
sacrifice forms the touching point.

> " Not the old worn-out corpse, Eurystheus needs,
>   But these, the hope of a great race of kings,—
>   Dreadful, with memory of their father's wrongs,
>   To those that wronged them."

But now Macaria, one of the suppliant daughters of
Hercules, comes forward, asking if any new ill has emerged.
She hears without fear the dread oracle of the prophets, and
then, calmly, and with a frank courage offers herself.

> " Here stand I of free will, a sacrifice.
>   Athens has ta'en our burden on herself,—
>   Shall we fear death if need be, for our freedom?
>   What, when the city fell to Argive arms,
>   Would men not scorn us?   Or, in other towns,
>   As we come suppliant, would they not exclaim,
>   ' Hence, cowards, loving life before dishonour.' "

Her calm entreaty overcomes the opposition of Iolaus, and
she goes forth to die. Macaria! Truly the blessed one!
Blessed in giving her life for others, facing the unknown,
the unravelled mystery, with its question never to be
answered here!

And here, evidently, a lacuna occurs in the text.
Macaria is no more heard of, nor does Demophon again
appear. The old fire of fight smoulders again within the
ashes of the soul of Iolaus, at the thought of the coming
battle. The servant of Hyllus, a son of Hercules, enters,
and when Iolaus hears his news he insists on girding himself
for the fight. In vain he is reminded of old age, of debility,
his changed appearance, no longer qualified to encourage
his friends, or to dismay his foes. Nevertheless he will out
to the fray, though the servant cannot put the armour on
his decrepitude, and has to lead him forth by the arm like a
child. Here, undoubtedly, Euripides is caricaturing some
prominent citizen of Athens, keen for generalship, while ripe
rather for the grave! The story of the fight is told by a
messenger to Alcmena,—how Hyllus had proposed to
Eurystheus a decision of the quarrel by single combat

between them twain, but Eurystheus was not bold enough
to risk the fight.   And then the terror of the battle
broke.

> " In thickest fight they closed,
> Crash went the brazen shield ; with groans and cries
> Resounding, intermingling.   Through our lines
> Broke the strong host of Argos, and anon,
> Were driven by us apart : then, knee to knee,
> And man to man, till crowds of slain lay stricken."

Iolaus begged of Hyllus to be admitted to his car, and,
mounting, prayed that for one day he might have strength
given him to punish his foes.   And now a marvel out of
heaven appeared.

> " The stars stood o'er his chariot.   Young again,
> He caught Eurystheus, bound him in his car
> With chains, and brings him hither, all luck lost ;
> A warning both to kings and men to wait
> Till their last sunset, ere they measure life
> And talk of happiness."

Alcmena   cannot   understand   why   Iolaus   has   spared
Eurystheus' life.

> " Unwise it seems
> To spare the lives of foemen when our wrongs
> Are unrevenged."

The captive is led in for the satisfaction of Alcmena's eyes,

> " For 'tis most sweet to see one's enemy
> From the high levels of good fortune fallen."

He gets some plain speaking from her, for Euripides dearly
loves to paint a shrewish woman.   The messenger who
brings Eurystheus in, prevents her slaying him.   He blames
his persecution and oppression of Hercules and his children
on Juno ; and, still a king, he cares not whether he die or
live.   The question of the slaying of a captive is debated
keenly, but Eurystheus relieves the situation by revealing an
oracle of Phœbus, whereby, in return for the kind defence

of his hapless condition from the fury of Alcmena's vengeance, his corpse will be a blessing to the realm, and a bane to its foes. Was this a laugh at Œdipus?

But Alcmena puts the case pro and con very clearly.

> " Living a foe, yet dead a blessed friend?
> Off with him,—to the dogs fling out his carrion ! "

CHAPTER XVII

"THE PERSIANS," "SUPPLIANTS," AND "PROMETHEUS BOUND"

LIBERTY, hospitality and generous suffering for others form the themes of three Tragedies of Æschylus which we shall bind together here. All these were topics dear to the poet's heart, and all three were, to him, like starlight over Athens.

The pride of native land, the bravery of his countrymen, and their triumph over the enemies of Greece, in which he had no small share, inspired Æschylus to noble song in "The Persians."[1]

This drama is Homeric in its rush, in the grandeur and ghostliness of its conception, and in the flood of national pride which sings of the glory of victorious Hellas. Only eight years before, the life-and-death grapple with the Persian multitudes by "sea-born Salamis" had issued in the vindication of Grecian liberty, and in the unspeakable disaster and utter overthrow of the invading hosts. With a power somewhat akin to the Hebrew prophet, he makes even the realms of the dead stir at the desolations which the ambition and arrogance of Xerxes had dragged upon the East; and the shade of Darius is evoked from the very grave to accentuate the solemn lessons of defeat. The awe of such a scene, the spectacle of the wailing Persian Councillors, the recital of the messenger, hot-foot from the scene of Persia's shattered hopes, and, finally, the advent

---

[1] Acted B.C. 472, seven years after Salamis. (Phrynichus's "Phœnissæ" had gained the prize the year before.) It is the earliest specimen of Greek history we possess, probably giving a more correct account of the battle than Herodotus.

of Xerxes dejected, dishevelled, and in despair, must have
thrilled and swayed the crowd of Athens with a national
pride that yet had pity behind it.   The poet whose arm
shared in the battle-shock, doubtless feeling for the loss of
so many valiant foes, tried to impress upon his countrymen
that the sure anger of the gods, and the victory of the
brave had brought sufficient retribution on the enemy, and
that the peace now sought by Persia, with humiliating
enough concessions, should be granted, even though
Themistocles opposed.   Here, surely, was sufficient revelation of the punishment of obstinate pride, to make the
nation fear lest they themselves might pass to the shadow-
side of the favour of heaven.

The Tragedy opens at Susa, near the Council Palace, and
adjacent to the tomb of Darius.   The Chorus consists of the
Councillors of Persia, who feel anxieties and forebodings
over the prolonged absence of the king, and his innumerable army.

> " For Asia's youth I sigh.   Her strength she sent
> Across the seas for conquest.   Chiefs and kings,
> Drawing their hosts behind them in the train
> Of the great sovereign king whose sway they owned."

All the glory and the valour of the Orient resound through
the lines.   The flower of Persia have gone oversea; and
the souls of the women and the weak, left behind, tremble
with unveiled anxiety alike over their silence and their
non-returning.

There are countless touches of the eyewitness in the
descriptions of the Chorus.   You feel the flash of the armed
men, the tramping of horses; and " the billows whitening
underneath the gale."

The Queen-mother Atossa enters and imparts her fears
lest the pride of wealth have dragged the curse of heaven
upon the happiness of the state which Darius had reared
with such toil and pain.   She tells how she has dreamed of
a Dorian woman and a Persian, whom Xerxes had tried to

yoke equally in his car, but the Greek with indignant fury
spurned the car, and overthrew Xerxes in the dust, even
before the sorrowing presence of his father's shade.   Nor
was the morning free from vision and portent.

> " I rose and bathed my hands in the gentle stream,
>   And on the altars of the kindly gods
>   Laid woe-averting offerings.   Lo, I saw
> An eagle full of fear, in hurried flight,
> For shelter seek the altar of the sun ;
> And, while I wondered, from the welkin blue
> A hawk swoopt swift upon the cowering bird,
> And with wild furious wings the victim beat,
> And tore the proud plumes from his shuddering head,
> A king dishonoured, cringing to the blows."

She asks for information about Greece ; and each line is a
throb of glory to the Greeks.   In the words of Darius
himself, which had stung the pride of Athens to anger,[1]
she enquires,

> " Where, in what clime, do the towers of Athens rise ? "

They answer,

> " Far westward, where imperial suns go down . . .
> The steady shield, the stalwart spear are theirs . . .
> Lords of themselves—no king's word makes them slaves."

While they debate, the messenger of woe enters, crying
sorrow to all the Persian towns.   Eyewitness, with no
carried story caught at second hand, he tells how

> " Strewn on the strand of Salamis they lie,
> The hapless dead ; and on the adjacent shores
> Heaped,—O unhappy comrades,—in the waves,
> Whelmed out of conflict, 'mong the shattered wrecks
> Of war-broke ships, they roll among the foam."

Then the dread catalogue of slaughtered princes bitterly
falls on the hearers' hearts, till the messenger involuntarily

---

[1] Herodotus, v. 105 ; vii. 10.

is compelled to cry the compliment that must have made a
sea of murmuring applause break along the benches,

> " Impregnable the walls of Athens stand,
>   Her fearless children are her bulwarks sure."

Through glowing lines the story of the battle flows, the
whole course of it a eulogy of Grecian intrepidity, all the
greater because, through the skill of the poet, it is represented as falling from the lips of a foe.   How the exhorta-
tion of the Grecian host, reported by this messenger, must
have rung through every heart.

> " Sons of the Greek, advance ; from serfdom save
>   Your country, and your children and your wives,
>   The temples of your gods, the holy tombs
>   Where sleep your fathers' honoured dust ; to-day
>   One common cause demands your bravest deeds."

Land and sea beheld the driven disaster of the Persian
forces ; and Xerxes from the seat he had chosen to watch
his victory, fled in dismay.   It means more than immediate
defeat.   The Chorus see that it means more than present
disgrace.   It lays a hand upon the future.

> " No more the tribes of Asia shall revere
>   Great Persia fallen and shamed ;
>   No more the king's behest shall nations fear,
>   Nor pay the cess he claimed."

Now out of the grave rises the shade of Darius, asking
why the people wail, and by what loss the state is crushed?
When told, he recognises the rash impetuous risk of the
anger of heaven which Xerxes had undertaken.   He had
bridged the Hellespont, uniting what the gods had sundered.
He had cut a passage for his ships through Mount Athos.
When Hellespont had wrecked his first bridge of boats he
had ordered it to be lashed like a disobedient slave, and
had flung fetters into its depths, in token of its bondage to
his imperious will.   Ah ! cries Darius,

" How swift to fulness heaven's dread doom doth speed,
Like lightning Jove's revenge hath smote my son.
. . . . . . Madman! that hoped to chain
The sacred Hellespont, and cast in bonds
Rude Bosphorus! How, with vain passion blind,
He deemed his power more god-like than the gods
And Neptune's seaborn night. Heaven struck his soul
With madness for the thought."

This is the old theory of the envy of the gods, but
lifted into quickened meaning. Herodotus records the
warning of Artabanus to Xerxes on the inception of the
plan of Invasion. " Do you not see how the deity casts his
bolts against the loftiest buildings. For he is wont to cut
off everything that is too highly exalted ; for the deity will
not suffer anyone but himself to have lofty thoughts."
This was a very ancient conception—the hostility of heaven,
watching man as he emerges from his primitive level, grudg-
ing his every step higher, and ready in any moment to hurl
him back again. Man was a dangerous rival, restless and
forward, frequently threatening trespass on the fields of the
very gods themselves.[1] The names of the martyrs and
helpers of men who had suffered for their labours on behalf
of mankind—heroes like Prometheus and Hercules were
written large in popular mythology. This idea of the
divine jealousy had its tendrils of origin in the heart of an
early age, when a balance of power seemed fixed as between
things divine and human—so that all that earth gained
seemed to be won through a raid over the frontier-line of
heaven. Especially was the judgment provoked by such work
as Xerxes had ventured upon—altering the divine decrees,
making, by bridges, a path where the gods had fixed the
sea, or bringing water where dry land had been established.
It was a presumptuous interference with the laws of heaven.
Xerxes, further, was a victim of the daimonic infatuation.
When a man gets enslaved, so far, by pride, and selfwill, the

---

[1] *Cf.* Genesis for the early Jewish parallel to this idea. See also Prof. Butcher's
" Aspects of the Greek Genius," p. 105 *et seqq.*

divinity seems to blind him, "hardening his heart" as Scripture puts it. In this Tragedy, we find it expressed—

> " When a man on his ruin is rushing,
> Heaven gives him a lift to the goal."

The popular mind was apt to confuse Jove and Fate: but as man, in the epic age, had created the gods in form and passions like himself, the shape and colour of them remained through much fluctuation. Behind both gods and men was stern Destiny. The gods themselves were subject to sorrow, joy and disaster, just like men, but the gods were nearer fate than men were, and dominated man's destinies, and got entangled in his purposes. To elevate this from the low level of superstition, and to reconcile human freedom with divine destiny, Æschylus took these old ideas and tried to teach that what seemed to be the mere freak of the deity was in reality the natural consequence of moral guilt. He felt this very deeply, for to him Jove was not blind Fate, but a personal god of justice and discernment, knowing the human heart and human purpose through and through. He tried to show, too, that time was on the side of Destiny, and drew the lines of men and gods finally together, into a resolving unity, making a universal justice. The arrogant will of Xerxes, uplifted by his wealth and power, drew him away with his eleven hundred ships, and over five million soldiers, despising the power of his enemies and counting himself as a divinity ; and his sin had its own reward with it, like its shadow—blind disaster, disgrace, and the long line of staggering retreat, marked by the birds of prey hovering above his wounded and dying.

The teaching of the Tragedy is intensified still more by the appearance of Xerxes himself, loathing the light and crying out for death. He is addressed by the Chorus—

> " The realm, robbed of its people, and bare of its youth,
> Laments all the pride of its manhood, by Xerxes misled
> To slaughter and death oversea,—till the halls of the dead
> Are glutted with Persia's heroes. The flower of the realm
> Are fallen in fight far away ! "

Again, in the impassioned sorrow of the Chorus the roll-call of the mighty dead is repeated; and then they lead the fallen monarch to his house, to wait the doom of Persia.

> " For War, rising aloft,
> With the ships of the Grecians around
> Gave the Greeks the blessing of conquest,
> Their arms with victory crowned ;
> While the blighted host of Persia, dashed on the shore,
> Or whelmed in deep gloomy ocean, can battle no more."

The shattered ruin of an imperious attempt at conquest was never better shown—the proud victorious assertion of a nation's freedom never more nobly sung; while, over all, flicker the warnings and the evidences of divine doom on mortal pride, worthy to be set in the great shadowy vision of prophecy and portent of the Hebrew seers.

Love of liberty is the expression of a generous heart. The truly brave have ever an open hand. The law of hospitality has always ranked in the heroic times of nations as among the most sacred laws of heaven. Athens, like ourselves, and sometimes with as little reason, vaunted her liberality, her justice, and her hospitality. These themes as well as the old haunting shadow that lies at the threshold of all enquiry, were represented on the national stage as sacred things. In "The Suppliants" Æschylus therefore makes hospitality, and especially the hospitality of Athens to the stranger and the persecuted, an object of the greatest piety, and of the deepest approval of the gods.

The story is the familiar one of the fifty daughters of Danaus, who have fled from the threatened marriage with their cousins, the fifty sons of Ægyptus, because the oracle had prophesied that Danaus their father should be slain by one of his sons-in-law. It is here apparently, as with "Prometheus," the middle play of the Trilogy that has survived. The scene is near the shore, in a grove adjacent to the Altar and shrine of the gods of the sacred games,—on

the one side, the sea and the ships of Ægyptus, and, on the
other, the towers of Argos.

The fifty daughters of Danaus are discovered suppliants,—
fugitives,

> " Not doomed for crimes, but, of our own free will,
> Flying from hateful union with our blood,
> Across the rolling deep."

They lay claim to Jove's protection, through kinship with Iö.
The gods above, and the awful powers beneath are invoked
to hinder the landing of the pursuing sons of Ægyptus.
They appeal to the justice and integrity of the gods against
what they plead to be almost an incestuous marriage. They
put the gods to the proof.

> " Show that ye guard the right : and in our cause
> Prove that the laws of life are holy laws."

Their hope is in the righteousness of Jove.

> " Jove's firm resolve, no mortal eye divining,
> Still, through the gloom, a deathless thing is shining.
>   From heaven's high height
> He keeps the sinner's impious deed in sight,
>   And when his wrath
> Is ripe, the gods are sent,
>   Hot-foot upon the path
> Of punishment."

They threaten that, unless the gods protect them, they
will go, voluntary victims, to the shades, thus, by impiety,
putting to shame the impotent powers of heaven.[1] But
Danaus warns them that even death does not liberate the
haughty deed from its due punishment ; for in the lower
realms of darkness sits another Jove, apportioning to the
guilty shades the wage which they had earned.

Pelasgus, king of the land, next appears and wonders to
see so many strangers, unannounced, thrown on his shores for
hospitality ; but, in a long dialogue they prove their Argive
lineage through Iö, and they beg the king's support. He

---

[1] And at the same time desecrating the altars.

hesitates to provoke new wars, but they urge that Justice always holds her shield over the deliverers of the needy. He is in a dilemma. Prudence prompts him to refuse: but the duty of hospitality forbids the rejection of their prayers. The Chorus emphasise the case.

> "Jove weighs each action fairly, and he gives
> To cold impiety, its own revenge:
> But duty done, he leaves not unrepaid."

The king is still in a strait. He must not, for the credit of humanity and religion, alike, in Argos, allow them to be arrested by force, nor to be dragged from the Altars; nor must he have them betrayed or handed over by his people, as they are, like all strangers, "hostages of heaven." So he decides to face it.

> "Like a ship at anchor riding,
> I must risk the storm."

Yet, while he says so, he begs the suppliants, when his people come, not to speak of him.[1]

> "For liberty gives license to this folk
> Freely to blame their rulers as they choose."

The people, however, agree that protection shall be given, and the Chorus, in a fine ode, pour their gratitude to Jove as the righteous, kindly king, adored above the highest.

Meanwhile the father Danaus sees the pursuers drawing near the shore—a fine sea-picture from the poet's heart.

> "The ships in pride
> Across the billows ride.
> The foremost furls her sails, as, near the shore
> She draws her keel, while the shouting crew bend to the flashing oar."

Still, they must trust in the protection of the holy place.

> "Fear not. Who dares insult the gods shall feel
> Heaven's hour, in vengeance, strike above his head."

---

[1] Lest, of course, their suspicions be awakened that they are having some of their constitutional rights interfered with.

The pictures are like memories of the imaginative soul that fought at Salamis, so true they are.

> " Their massy ships
> Frowning, upon the gloomy waters heave,
> Eager to fling their swarthy bands ashore."

The Chorus are comforted by the reflection that there may yet be time given to them: for

> " Slow are the movements of a naval host,
> The order and the mooring of the ships.
> The skilful leaders watch the anchoring ground.
> And then the night adrift is full of care ;
> Nor do they risk a landing ere they ride
> In all security "

But soon the messenger from the fleet appears, and finding threats in vain, begins to drag the victims from the sanctuary by violence; when king Pelasgus comes upon the stage. He cries

> " How has thy folly dared
> To put this cruel outrage on the land
> Where dwell Pelasgian men ? . . .
>   Our dignity—
> The dignity of Greece, thy rude hand soils,
> Barbarian ! "

He gives his word he will defend those who have been received by him into the state.

> " My resolution shall stand fast and firm,
> Though uninscribed on tablets, nor enrolled
> In seal-stamped parchments."

The Chorus gives its approval to the king's resolve : and there meanwhile the matter ends.

This play vindicates the duty of hospitality, especially incumbent on the piety of ancient races. It does not speak highly of the Egyptians, sneering at them as enervated by their climate, and their barley-wines,—probably remembering how they were alien to those of Argive blood, and hateful to the gods of Greece, and at the same time foreseeing losses of good men and ships through contact with "darkbrowed Egypt," for the poets' politics were often truest prophecy, and they had their hand upon the pulse of history oftener than they knew. This is one of the earliest plays, and it is noteworthy in this connection to observe that in point of bulk the Chorus occupies by far the largest place throughout it.

Liberty and hospitality alike involve self-denial and endurance of hardship for the sake of others,—but the greatest heroes were those who, to secure gifts for men and progress for the world, involved themselves in conflicts with the jealous powers of heaven.

In the surviving plays of Æschylus we have one that seems to be almost a blasphemous attack on the popular ideas of religion, as these affect the relations of men and the gods. The "Prometheus Bound," for its great strength, and its interest of desolation and oppression, its cruel tyranny of blind gods exerted against a divine open-eyed human-heartedness, is of eternal power. It is, as it stands, a daring impeachment of the common religious notions regarding Jove, full of scathing scorn flung from one god, who has been wronged, at the other god who has used his strength brutally to oppress him. And, besides, the oppression and punishment were occasioned by the desire to do good to man, poor, naked, helpless, fireless. But perhaps, as has been pointed out, had we the other dramas of this Trilogy, the blasphemy would lose its startling force.[1] We only have the second of the series, the first of which probably displayed Prometheus carrying the sacred gift to humanity, the second (which alone has survived) shows him chained to Caucasus : while the third revealed the generous god released.

The " Prometheus Bound " has a unique fire and strength,

---

[1] Further, the utterance of such sentiments on the lips of Æschylus has an entirely different significance from what it would be on the lips of Euripides. There is no scepticism in Æschylus. He believes, with terrible earnestness, in his gods.

with a rugged dignity and sublimity of conception which makes one mourn the loss of the other two tragedies, on the same subject. It opens in the desolate domain of Caucasus, with one wild rock frowning above the sea,—the sons of Pallas and Styx holding the fallen god, while Vulcan fixes his chains upon his limbs. The mournful piteousness of Iö, who also has tasted the violent tyranny of Jove,—the sympathy of Ocean's daughters, with the anguish of the god himself, all combine, in beauty, freshness and power, to make this a most moving drama. His offence is grounded deep on the old, archaic, epic idea of the relationship of gods and men.[1] Thus, Strength, addressing Vulcan, fitly uses the Titanic notion.

> " Flame, moulding all things to the will of art,
> The gods' own pride, he stole, and gave mankind.
> Here, then, the gods' just punishment he drees,
> That he may learn submission to heaven's will,
> And temper wisely his esteem for man."

There is something very touching in the reluctance of Vulcan to do the task appointed to him.

> " My spirit shrinks from binding to this cliff
> A kindred god,—left to the desolate storm;
> Yet need compels me. I am bound to Jove,
> Nor dare neglect our monarch's dire command."

There are not a few beautiful nature-glimpses, as when he warns Prometheus that he must be left riveted to this savage crag, all through the scorching day, longing for the approach

> " Of gentle night, drawing her spangled veil
> Across the burning heat of the weary day,
> Till melt the frosts before the morn once more. "

And all this is the reward of the kindness of a god !

> " This the reward of thy deep love of man—
> Heaven's anger for thy meed. This desolate cliff
> Thy dreary home—chained, sleepless, unreclining ;
> For Jove, new-crowned with kinship, no grace knows."

---

[1] The legend is one of the oldest in the repertoire of humanity. The parallel of the theft was found in that of Tantalus, who stole nectar and ambrosia and gave them to mortals.—Pindar, " Olym." i. 60.

There are hints, also of rival dynasties, of rebellion and dissension among the gods,—some, evidently, like Prometheus inclining to man's side, others, with the old distant suspicion, opposed to him; and now this generous one lies,

> " Hated by all the gods, himself a god,
> Who prostituted fire, the pride of heaven,
> To man's mean service."

Vulcan is reminded of the relentlessness of Fate.

> " Jove alone, is free ! "

Even he, though a god, must be more cautious in his sympathies for a kindred god, and when he wails the misery of Prometheus he is warned,

> " What ! Pitiest thou the foe of Jove most high ?
> 'Ware,—lest thou wail ere long, thine own sore case.
> Stern is the god, whose eye is all-beholding."

The sufferings of Prometheus are, of course, further intensified by the fact of his godlike prescience, and he has to nerve himself for the long vigil's pain, every stage of which he must clearly foresee in all its horror.

> " My doom I needs must bear
> Patiently : for 'tis vain my strength t'oppose
> 'Gainst Fate's Necessity.   Even speech and silence
> Alike are all in vain ! "

Left in his chains, he breaks into wailing and complaint.

> " O look, ye powers of Nature ! swift-wing'd winds,
> Rivers and fountains, rippling ocean-waves,—
> Thou generous earth !   Thou all-beholding sun,
> See my sore woe—a god by gods opprest !
> Through all the countless years, my eyes, in pain,
> Must vainly seek relief, and I must bear
> Those chains imposed by heaven's unpitying king."

The Chorus of Ocean-nymphs approach—daughters of old Oceanus,

> " That folds
> The wide earth round about with sleepless sound,"

and their deep sympathy finds beautiful expression as they
behold him, withering in the parching wind, a spectacle to
men and gods ; nor are even they without dark hints of a
doom that dogs the very footsteps of Jove himself.

> " Among the gods can gladness be,
>   To view the pangs that torture thee,
>   Pitiless, knowing what thou art,
>   And ne'er a tear within their heart ?
>   Nay, Jove, alone,
>   Tyrant of heaven, from his high throne,
>   Curbing with wrath the pride
>   Of all the gods beside,
>   Till folly blast, or, in some later days,
>   Some power defraud him of the strength he sways ! "

Marvellously daring is the statement put in the lips of the
agonising Titan regarding Jove.

> " That tyrant of the gods shall need my aid,
>   To read the riddle of the schemes unkind,
>   Against his reputation and his throne,
>   Flattery nor frowns shall win one word of mine.
>   The veil'd doom veil'd shall stand, until these chains
>   His hands unbind from mine, and his remorse
>   Plead for a pardon from my outraged heart."

What the fatal secret is, we know not, but on it hangs
the integrity of Jove's kingdom. And he draws aside the
veil of heaven, and shows how, when discord in the courts
of heaven was roused, Prometheus had espoused Jove's cause
among the divided gods, and so aided the overthrow of
Saturn and his confederate powers ; but now,

> " This is Jove's gratitude—these galling chains !
>   'Tis but the rule.   Serve any tyrant well
>   And dark mistrust's the richest wage you win."

And now, having won supremacy in heaven, he showered
benefits on the chief gods, to bind them to his throne by
favours well-remembered.

> "But hate for man darkened his earthward view—
>   He would extirpate manhood from the world.

> I, only, out of heaven, opposed his will.
> And, pleading fearlessly, preserved the race,
> And saved them from the doom of blackest night.
> So now, for mercy to mankind, I lie
> Here, bound, cut off from mercy and the gods."

That, after all, seemed little enough reason why an eternal god eternally should suffer.   What aggravation was there?

> " I veiled from man the vision of his fate.
> I made men's hearts a dwelling place for Hope.
> I bore to him the gift of generous flame,
> By whose warm help he masters many a craft."

And this offence was voluntary,—open-eyed he risked the anger of the tyrant deity. His was the struggle of a beneficent will against the malevolent, overbearing spirit of Jove.

Oceanus now appears, a friend, but a Job's comforter, the plain speaker, who sits by the sufferer, and admonishes him to be silent, as this is for his good! It is a weak prescription for a broken limb, or a breaking heart! Polonius is poor comfort in a sick room.   " Purge the soul from wrath and pride,—so lies the way of peace. Learn to know thyself and to be silent.   Mischief still attends the petulant tongue," is the gist of his talk.

Oceanus departs pledging himself to plead with Jove; and the Chorus again break into song.   They listen while Prometheus still further unfolds his constant thought of men, and all the good he did with constant labour for them.   He taught them knowledge, drew order out of mental chaos; revealed to them the wisdom of the stars; then gave them Memory, the mother of all wisdom, Medicine with healing comfort, peaceful industries and civilising arts, dream-wisdom, portents, and every useful gift.   He then hints his own future fate and Jove's.

> " Through the low door of pain for others borne
> I am free.   Necessity than art is stronger,
> And Jove, too, is Fate's bondsman."

Yet, what fate, ask the Chorus, is Jove's fate, except to reign forever? But Prometheus keeps the secret to himself as the key to unlock his chains.

Anon, Iö enters, the distraught maid, driven by the spite of Juno, suffering through the passion of Jove, another of heaven's victims: and she questions her fellow-sufferer, What wretch art thou? His answer is—

> "Thou lookst upon Prometheus. He who gave
> Heaven's flame to men, is bound in anguish here,"

and now, as she puts it,

> "Thou who hast blest mankind, art suffering thus,
> Pierced by the pitiless wrath of ruthless heaven."

He tells much that still awaits, and reveals that her fate and his are bound together, since of her blood must come the divine deliverer.[1] The impeachment of the god supreme is deepened and intensified by the story of Iö, disfigured, degraded and torture-driven through the lust of heaven's ruler ; but Jove's tenure is tottering, and the dissolution of his kingdom shall arise from within itself.

> "Have I not seen two tyrants overwhelmed,[2]
> And I shall see third, whose cruel sway
> Now graceless rules, dishonoured and o'erthrown."

Refusing disdainfully to disclose even to Mercury, the messenger of heaven, the secret that he holds, he is dashed, in earthquake turmoil, into Tartarus. The closing words have cataclysm throbbing in them.

> "Lo ! now the solid world
> Shakes to its socket. Thunder's redoubling roar
> Deeps its rage, with frequent flashing flames,
> The sands caught up by whirlwinds, eddy and wheel

---

[1] Iö's son, thirteen times removed, was Hercules, the son of Alcmena.

[2] In the poem of Hesiod, and in the prose of Apollodorus Heaven and Earth are the rulers of the first world-dynasty. Their offspring, under Kronos or Saturn, form a second dynasty, after a violent episode of dethronement, while he, thrown out of heaven by Jove, gave way to his conqueror, who forms the third dynasty of Olympus. See page 48.

> Torn with conflicting storms the welkin groans,
> And waves confuse the bounds of sea and sky,
> While on my head heaven's wild impetuous blast
> Terrific rolls its dark doom-driving rage."

And so it stands, a terrible impeachment of the envy of the gods, a tragic and epic topic ever near the soul of the Greek.

The conflict of the suffering Titan is titanic. The myth, always of intensest interest to humanity, pointed to some sort of solution of the origin of evil and suffering. Hesiod's tale is that Prometheus instigated mankind to cheat Jove of his offerings. In requital Jove deprived men of the blessing of fire ; but Prometheus stole it back from heaven, restoring it to men. Here, however, the poet follows no known version. He treats the story freely.

Mrs Browning finds in the gigantic figure of Prometheus the real influence which sank deep into the imagination of Milton and quickened there that poet's majestic Satan. But yet the impulse of each is far apart as the poles. Satan, for ambition and his own hand, was flung from heaven; Prometheus, for the sake of others, endured divine anguish.

Victor Hugo finds in him a sort of divine Hamlet with the agony of the Vulture at his vitals ; but the Vulture with Prometheus is neither the pain of conscience, nor remorse.[1] He has dared and he is not repentant : while the other gropes in shadow trembling, letting "I dare not" snatch away "I would."

The struggle against Fate and Necessity,—the unwearying, unmastered indomitable vindication of Freewill even against Jove, and especially in the interests of a kindlier rule of the universe, is most strikingly the note of this great drama.[2] It has often been pointed out that the idea of a self-devoting divinity has been mysteriously inculcated in many religions ;

---

[1] It is the injustice of heaven that stings him.

[2] The notion of a progressive order from Moral Chaos towards a moral and religious Cosmos is clearly perceptible even in the " Suppliants," but it finds its highest embodiment in the Orestean and Promethean Trilogies.

but here it is actually displayed in antagonism to religion as popularly accepted. Prometheus suffers for opposition to the divine powers that meanwhile hold sway over things, and his offence is simply the endeavour to give the human race perfection.[1] He thus becomes a type of the human race itself, tied to a narrow environment, beating in vain against the hindrances that hedge it round, friendless yet fearless, with a will unshaken and upheld by its own lofty aspirations ; while the very catastrophe is the acme of the triumph of the human spirit against adversity and oppression, —even through disaster unmastered and unmasterable. His agony shakes the gods upon their throne in the human heart.

In this play Æschylus made the important innovation of introducing a third actor on the stage.[2] Here, too, for the first and last time, he rebels against Jove, and leaves the soul, as it beholds the awful loneliness, and unspeakably desolate agony of the friend of man, entirely in sympathy with Prometheus, rather than with the imperious, capricious and jealous ruler of the Councils of the gods.

[1] *Cf.* Apollo in the " Alcestis." This is the sole example of a kind of play different from the rest of Æschylus,—a religious Mystery, as it were, allegorising a profound speculation on the attributes of deity.

[2] Prometheus may, however, have been only a dumb figure. *Cf.* Müller's Dissertation on " Eumenides."

CHAPTER XVIII

"PHILOCTETES," "AJAX," "HELEN," "TROJAN WOMEN," AND "ANDROMACHE"

THE suffering, which like a garment of mystery enfolds human life around, for which frequently no tangible explanation can be discovered, is often traced by the Tragedians to its source. They take humanity softly by the hand and lead it back to some rash unremembered word or action, some burst of passion uncontrolled, which had in the past let loose the judgments of the Invisible upon men's lives.

Thus, in the "Philoctetes" of Sophocles, we see the agonies arising though rash intrusion on divinely separated territory, and the trials, individual and national, which spring from non-recognition of the will of heaven.

Hercules, when he died, had left his invincible bow and poisoned arrows to Philoctetes, who was his armour-bearer, and was said to have kindled the demi-god's funeral pile.[1] This hero on his way to Troy with seven ships to join the fleet of Agamemnon, landed, along with others, in obedience to an oracle, to sacrifice to Chryse, whose altar was on a small island in the Ægean Sea. As he rashly approached the holy place he was bitten on the foot by a guardian serpent. His cries of pain prevented the execution of the sacred rites, and the odour of his putrid wound made him such an annoyance to his shipmates, that, while he slept, Odysseus put him ashore on Lemnos, an uninhabited island,

---

[1] He is spoken of in the Second Book of the "Iliad" as a skilful archer. He is mentioned in the "Odyssey" as being the best bowman in Troy, and as having come safely home. His adventures are to be, however, fully gathered from the poems of the Epic Cycle.

leaving him his bow and arrows, and sailing on to Troy.
Nine long years passed, and still Troy was untaken.
Achilles was dead and Ajax had destroyed himself; and
now the prophet Helenus,[1] the captive son of Priam, declared
that only by the son of Achilles and the bow of Hercules
should the city fall. Neoptolemus, the son of Achilles, is
therefore sent with Odysseus to Lemnos to secure the magic
talisman of victory. On the way, Odysseus (to the Greek
the type of diplomacy—the Jacob of the Homeric epos), well
noted for his cunning, having learned, in a long experience,
that words win where weapons fail,—instructs the young
man in guile. The honest soul of Neoptolemus revolts,
however, against deceit. My wish, he says,

> " Is to do right, and lose the mark
> Rather than win my end by shameful fraud."

But his crafty tutor pleads with him,

> " Nay, lend thyself to me, one roguish day ;
> Then all the days that heaven may give to thee
> Let them be called most honourable by men."

The young man is astonished. He looks this leader of the
Greeks straight in the face, and asks :—

> " Thou think'st it then no shame to speak a lie ? "

No, replies Odysseus,

> " No, if the lie bring victory to my craft." [2]

The cave of Philoctetes is discovered in the face of the
cliff, but it is empty. Soon the pitiable exile himself,
painfully dragging his weary limbs, appears, and enters into
converse with Neoptolemus and his sailors. Neoptolemus
is touched with deepest compassion for this hapless victim,
who, for almost ten long years has been left in continuous
suffering on this lonely place, within hearing of the ceaseless

---

[1] Calchas has referred the Greeks to Helenus, through whom speaks the irony of
fate.; for the deserted Philoctetes is, after all, to be the guarantee of victory.
[2] He can be honest when there is a price for honesty, but his first object is to gain
his end.—JEBB.

surge. Yet, following at least part of his teaching, he
pretends that he is now on his homeward way, having been
harshly treated by the Atreidæ and Odysseus.   This
fiction at once wins the sympathetic attention of Philoctetes.
The thought of home reawakens life within his weary heart,
and in the most human way the relationship between the two
is deepened, till sudden sleep overcomes Philoctetes, following
a spasm of pain which breaks down exhausted nature ; but
ere he sinks into slumber he gives the coveted bow and quiver
into the hands of Neoptolemus to be guarded till he wake.
Unconsciousness falls from his spirit as swiftly as it sank
upon him, and while he is assisting him to the shore
Neoptolemus rebels against his own deceit and confesses the
intrigue to which he has made himself a party.   So he tells
him he is being taken to Troy, and not home to Greece.[1]
And then the passion of Philoctetes breaks out kinglily.

> "Thou flame, thou monster, master of deceit.
> How canst thou look on me, who turned to thee
> Suppliant for pity.   Give me my bow again.
> It is my life.   Ah, rob me not of it !
>
> O lonely listening world all round about—
> Crags, creeks, and capes, and all wild creatures, hear,
> See the vile knavery of Achilles' son
> Against his plighted troth with hand in mine !
>
> Nay, give it me.   Be thy true self again.
> What sayst thou,—nothing ?   Then, indeed, I'm lost."

But Neoptolemus melts before his entreaties and despairs, and,
while he wavers, Odysseus emerging from covert, draws him
away with the bow.   The young man, however, deeply
repenting the deceit which he has practised, returns, followed
hastily by Odysseus, and, notwithstanding protestation, restores
the precious weapon to its rightful owner in the hope that
he will go with them to Troy.   But Philoctetes is still

---

[1] He naturally hates those who had abandoned him to his fate.   His loneliness is
accentuated further, by the constitution of the Chorus, all attached to the Greek
interests.

obdurate. His solitary sufferings and complainings have deepened in his mind a horror of that city, till, at length, Neoptolemus flings aside his own ambition and declares that he himself will accompany him on the homeward journey, no matter what the Greeks shall say or do. But the purpose of the gods intervenes in Hercules himself, who shows to Philoctetes that his sufferings have not been in vain. He reveals how he himself

> " Having endured sore labours to the end,
>   Won deathless glory. And for thee the fate
>   Is writ that, through thy sufferings thou shalt win
>   The glory of thy life. Seek Troy's fair plains.
>   There shall thy wound find health, thine anguish pass.
>   There, bravest of the brave among the hosts,
>   Troy shall before thee fall, and Paris die. . . .
>   Thou, too, Achilles' son, art with him joined,
>   Nor canst be sundered. Lions twain are ye,
>   Together each the other's life to guard. . . .
>   Show reverence to the gods even in thy strife.
>   Piety is eternal, all things else
>   Are nothing in the judging eye of Jove."

Philoctetes submits to the command of the voice of him whom he reveres, and beautifully bids a yearning farewell to the place of his sufferings.

> " Farewell, cave of my lonely watchings,
>   Nymphs of the meadows and streams, a long good-bye ;
>   Farewell, deep-sounding voice of the thundering waters,
>   Filling my cave with cries from the storm-beaten cape ;
>   Where, with the wind-borne spindrift, often my head was drenched,
>   And the crags re-echoed my wailings when sorrow was wild,
>   Like a tempest around and above me. Lemnos, adieu—
>   Girt by the waters ! I leave you at last, and obey ;
>   Bowing my will to the gods' will, who finish all things,
>   Bringing fulfilment out of men's obdurate pride."

This is the tragedy of bodily pain, a personal interest somewhat alien to our idea of Tragedy. Prometheus endures his bodily agony in silence, and his cries are against injustice, and the ungenerous gods ; but Philoctetes is Suffering eating its own heart out, until he learns that the will of Heaven is not to be forced by man's violence, and the soul which has suffered, first from the abuse of human power, and again by astuteness and craft, is strengthened at last to carry the purpose of the gods to its end. Heaven passes by the strong and rude, and leaves the secret of victory with the unambitious, the abandoned, and forgotten.[1]

The development of contrasts and combinations of character is very notable : the new-found, freshly formed friendship between Philoctetes and Neoptolemus, grappling and struggling with the spiritual surrender of honour to the diplomatic duplicity of Odysseus, till shame at the betrayal of his better soul drives the son of Achilles to victory over self, displays as subtle a psychological advancement as is to be found in any play of the moderns. The sure tidal progress from the " Persians " of Æschylus to the characterisation of this drama should not be overlooked.

Leaving the lesson of suffering through inadvertent trespass, we see now an example of soul-destroying passion, dragging madness in its train, as a man's fate can never be separated from his conduct, nor his conduct from the dominion of his conscience. The uncontrolled, unguided following of the worse or weaker side of a man's nature, till it topple over into judgment, whelming him altogether in woe, gives the tragedian often his strongest provocation for a warning manifesto on the stage.

In his " Ajax," Sophocles displays, with that wondrous human power which gives him his own place among the dramatists, a soul whose honour has been betrayed, and whose pride, hurt by a slight, has rushed into unworthy violence, and so won shame and pain.

Ajax, the hero in the Trojan enterprise, next in glory to Achilles, was passed over when the award of the armour of

---

[1] The "Philoctetes" was produced in 409 B.C. and won first prize. Some have considered that the return of Alcibiades was the question which influenced the poet.

that dead hero was to be given to the Grecian warrior
worthiest the gift. The trophy was bestowed upon
Odysseus, whose wisdom had saved the army. In bitter
anger, therefore, the disappointed chief goes forth by night
to slay Agamemnon and Menelaus, but at the door of their
tent he is confronted by the goddess Athene, who, striking
him with madness, suffers him in his vengeful rage to fall
upon the herds and flocks of the Greeks, cutting down their
keepers and themselves, and leading some of the animals
captives to his tent, in the frenzied belief that they
were some of the chiefs by whose verdict he had been
wronged.

The Chorus consists of sailors of Salamis, from the train
of Ajax himself. Odysseus has tracked the footprints
through the camp to the tent of Ajax, when Athene meets
him and shows him the hero in his pitiable plight. The
Chorus mourn over the rumour of the night's work.

> " O thou, whose wave-girt Salamis
>   Is set above the sea,
> When thy fortune's fair
> And free from care,
>   Great joy it gives to me ;
> But when from heaven
> Grief's to thee given,
>   And rumour brings thee shame,
> I shake with fear,
> And sorrow's tear
>   I drop upon thy name.
>
> 'Tis on the great that envy creeps,
> Though in thy presence close it keeps ;
> Like chattering birds, that, when the eagle come,
> Cower in silence, fearful, stricken dumb.
> Fare forth and face thy foes,
> For unrestrained, among the glens, their mocking slander goes."

Ajax, in his tent, when he opens his eyes out of his
madness and sees what he has done, is crushed with
shame.

"Now what remains to me,
 Hated by men and loathed by gods on high?
Shall I set off across the Ægean Sea,
 And homeward fly?
Yet how my father's questioning shall I face,
In my disgrace?

Nay, who would choose
The chance of peace to lose,
When woe and pain abide?
Oh, who would, day by day,
Follow deceiving hopes that fade away,
 Across the tide?
Nay, he who is noble turns from griefs and cries,
And fearless dies."

Tecmessa, his bride by conquest, tries to awake within him a brave scorn for his enemies, but in vain; and the Chorus in exquisite phrase pour forth their lamentations.

"Ah, Salamis renowned, the blue sea laves
Thy happy shores, and laughter from the waves
Each heart delights that turns its gaze to thee,—
O severed from thee thus, death would bring joy to me!

For what to me consolings can afford,
Heart-broken, by the sorrows of my lord—
Hearing his mother mourning, far away,
The pain that now obliterates her day?"

Ajax emerges from his tent with a sword in his hand, ostensibly to seek solitude and to bury his blade, giving it over to Night and Hades.

"This was the sword of Hector, erst my foe;
Sure foemen's gifts can only bring us woe.
. . . .
Now, as the winter softens to the sun,
And Night makes way that light round heaven may run,
So to the gods and chiefs of men I bow—
They may befriend me who oppose me now."

The Chorus are misled into the belief that the cloud has been lifted by the destroying god; and Teucer, his half-brother, having arrived at the camp, sends a messenger with instructions to keep Ajax in his tent till he shall come, as Calchas, the seer, has declared that if he leaves that tent he shall not again be seen alive. For the seer knows of the impious speech of Ajax, who, when his father had warned him to seek victory in arms, but ever with the help of heaven, had vaunted his own ability, without that aid, to bring glory within his grasp. And, further, he had provoked the goddess Athene by refusing her proffered help, saying—

> " Stand thou beside all other's needs, and never think of mine ;
> Where Ajax bides in battle-front no foe shall break the line."

Now, Sophocles makes a daringly unique breach of stage convention,[1] for the Chorus separate and rush off in search of the fugitive.

The scene changes to a lonely place by the shore, and Ajax is found preparing for death. For the second time, here, the poet departs from convention, for Ajax falls upon his sword, and dies in presence of the people.

> " By an enemy's sword I fall, the sword of Hector my foe ;
> Now Jove and Hermes hear me, and grant my prayer as I go ;
>   Let my poor body be found,
>   As I lie here dead on the ground,
> By a kindly hand, that shall pity my pain as I sleep by the deep sea's
>   sound.
>
> O sun that westward wheels in glory along the sky,
> When thou seest the shores and fields of my home beneath thee lie,
>   Whisper, through listening day,
>   To my parents, old and grey,
> How their son lies dead, by sorrow sped, in this sad land far away.
>
> Salamis, Salamis, sacred isle, far over the waters blue,—
> Athens my glory, race of my pride, my long good-bye to you.
>   Sunlight around me shed,
>   Fields where my life has bled,
> Farewell, no longer I speak with you. I go to the house of the dead."

---

[1] *Cf.* pages 15 and 25.

The Chorus return, having searched in vain. Their hearts are wrung with sorrow over the distraction of their hero. They can but cry aloud their anxieties.

> " O for some fisher, sleepless at his quest,—
> Or nymph that lingers by the flowing stream,
> To tell me if he wander in wild dream,
> Or lies at last in rest."

Suddenly Tecmessa announces her discovery of the self-slain hero, exclaiming—

> " Let no eye behold him ;
> Close in his robes I fold him ;
> Ah, thou my lord, from glory fallen low,
> Worthy of wailing even by thy foe."

Teucer, when he comes, fittingly mourns his lost brother—

> " Alas, my brother, by thy fate accurst . . .
> Come, lift the covering,—let me see the worst.
> O form of dread ! true valour was thy breath—
> What grief is mine forever by thy death ?"

And now emerges the same tragic motif as inspires "Antigone," for Menelaus refuses his burial on the ground that he had proved himself an enemy of the host.

> " Let no man dare to entomb him ; on the yellow sand let him lie,
> A feast for the fierce sea-birds,—unpitied by earth or sky."

The elegy which the Chorus sing is one of the most pathetic things I have ever read ; and while they sing it, Agamemnon, in great rage, comes upon the scene. A colloquy between Teucer and him is ended by Odysseus whose pleading wins the cause of the dead, and the poor sad clay finds burial. Odysseus warns Agamemnon that it is not the dead, but a law of heaven, he would outrage by refusing the last sacred rites, even to a foe.

> " When a brave man dies thou must not do him wrong,
> Though even with hate thy heart is charged against him.
> Yon man was once my foe, and yet his worth
> Outweighs with me the enmity we felt."

In Ajax we see the proud spirit broken into despair, yet re-
taining its majesty, and his act of frenzy becomes a deed of
sacrifice to the gods and to honour. His own arrogance,
however, it is which first sets in motion the slow avalanche
of destruction; his heart, by hyper-introspective morbidity,
is made feverishly susceptible to injury and hate against his
foes, and yet he owes the last pious rites of burial to the
very man whom in life he hated as his bitterest enemy. It
is a warning against rash feud, and a commendation that
wisdom is stronger than swords.

Of course much of the suffering and hardship which were
ever present to the Grecian mind circled about the struggle
of Troy which inspired the Homeric lays.

The "Helena" of Euripides deals with that form of the
myth in which she who provoked such strife was, by magic,
translated to Egypt, while only a phantasmic resemblance
of her misled both Trojans and Greeks at Ilium,[1] so that it
was all for nothing—the bloodshed, the destruction, and
the slander on a woman's name! In this play there are really
two prologues. Helen herself tells the story; and then
Menelaus appears after Teucer has told her of the returning
Greeks, and she and the Chorus have poured forth their
lyrical lament. Next follow the dramatic recognition of
the twain, the departure of the phantom, and the development of schemes whereby they successfully manipulate a
flight from Egypt and from the awkward amorous attentions
of the Egyptian king. It is remarkable as an illustration of
the free hand-grasp which Euripides laid upon the mythical
material. The story which he adopts owed its invention to
Stesichorus, and had been told to Herodotus by the priests
in Egypt.[2] It was a daring thing on the part of the poet to

---

[1] A similar docetic episode is in "Iliad," v. 450, where Apollo makes a spectral image
of Æneas. Homer, in "Odyssey," Book iv., had already spoken of a visit of Helen to
Egypt. Herodotus, Book ii. 113, tells of her having been carried to Egypt by
adverse winds, when on her course from Sparta to Ilium, with Paris.

[2] The source of these plays was the " Epic Cycles," especially the poems of Arctinus
and Lesches.

put boldly on the stage a version which contradicted the popular legend, incorporated, as that had become through time, in the very life and history of the Grecian people.

There is in this play a remarkably friendly tone adopted towards Sparta, and it is also worthy of note that the finest personality in the drama is a prophetess, whose knowledge is unswervingly true, and yet, alongside of this, the sceptical agnosticism of the poet finds plentiful expression.

The character, also, of Menelaus receives an elevation above the usual Euripidean portraiture. Helen, too, is not the Helen of either the "Trojan Women" or of the "Orestes."

These facts show the difficulty, already alluded to, of holding the poet as identified with the utterances, opinions, and point of view of dramatic persons in the play of his creation. It is clear, too, from this, that Euripides held the myths to be convenient enough frames on which to drape the passions and the characters of men and women, but they possessed for him little, if any, other worth.

The "Hecuba," of the same poet is a picture of the trials and griefs of Priam's widow, in which the sacrifice of her daughter Polyxena to the shade of Achilles is demanded by the Greeks,[1] which, when conceded to them, finishes the first episode. Another immediately begins in the finding of the corpse of Polydorus, murdered by Polymestor, the King of Thrace, to whose hospitality he had been entrusted. The closing episode is the artful revenge exacted by Hecuba and her women from her son's murderer by enticing him into the tent and then blinding him. The choruses are beautiful; the speeches of Hebuca awaken pathetic sympathy; while the picture of her rising out of despair to the wildest fury of revenge is a marvellous bit of psychology. But the play is, after all, more of a march-past of the sorrows of a queen than the tragic utterance of one great grief.

---

[1] Failing this, the fleet is kept by contrary winds at the Chersonese—an exact parallel with Iphigeneia's case at Aulis.

In the "Trojan Women"[1] Euripides displays the sorrows
and wretched experiences of the captives of Ilium, in the
last day in which they look upon the city of their pride.
Cassandra and Andromache appear, drawn with outstanding
power.   It is the "Lochaber no more" of Troy.

Poseidon himself speaks the prologue and tells how
Hecuba, the queen of grief, lies before the gates, wailing
for Polyxena, for the death of Priam, and for Cassandra,
who is to be led to a dishonoured captivity by Agamemnon.
Athene gets him to agree to vex the returning ships of the
Greeks with storm and disaster.   Hecuba learns, in her
sorrow, from Talthybius, the fate that is allotted to her,
and Cassandra enters, frenzied—pours forth now cries for
bridal wreaths, and anon dark prophecies of woe.

> " Lead me forth, for the wedding of my lord,
>   To go home to the dark halls of Hades.
>   Ah, captain of the hosts, thou art base,
>   And base is the burial that awaits thee,
>   In the night, dark and deep,
>   When thy day of pride shall die."

Adromache appears, carrying the doleful tidings of the
sacrifice which has taken place at the tomb of Achilles; and
Hecuba, in one of those fine sea-similes of Euripides, commits
herself to the tempestuous surge of her griefs.   Their
remaining hopes, centred on Astyanax, the child of Hector,
are rudely dashed aside by the decision of the Greeks to
cast him from the walls of Troy, and he is brought in dead,
on Hector's shield.   How true is every phrase of Hecuba
then!

> " O little hands, so like your father's hands,
>   Limp now ye lie before me!
>   Dear mouth, so often filled with tremulant music
>   In words of pride and promise,
>   Death has sealed thee.
>   And I, who am old, and seeking for my grave,

---

[1] 415 B.C.   Schlegel says the soul gets wearied out by the overdone anguish of
these people.   The sentiment of compassion gets palled.

> Bury thee, young, in whose brave heart the flame
> Should be so freshly burning.
> What shall they write above thee on thy grave?—
> 'Greece feared this child, and slew him in her fear.'"

The play is an episodic drama of the piteousness of the deprivation of home, love, and friendships, and the facing of the great, cold, lonely world by the victims of the wrath of men at variance with heaven.

His "Andromache" is really a political attack on Sparta through Hermione and Menelaus. Andromache, formerly Hector's wife, but now concubine of Neoptolemus, tells the sorrows of her persecution, alike at the hands of Hermione, the lawful wife of Neoptolemus, and of Menelaus, Hermione's father, who desires to take the life of her child. She laments her bitter, undeserved slavery, so different from her former lot. The old, old reflection of the Greek finds utterance once more.

> "Call not a son of the human race happy until
> Thou seest his departing and how he goes out of the world
> To the land of the shades."

The Chorus cannot enter into her woes. They admonish her rather to submit.

> "See what thou art, in bondage far from home
> No friends are near thee, in thine evil day."

Hermione is proud, cruel, and cold, jealous of the motherhood that has blest the slave, though it be withheld from her the lawful wife—an old jealousy, that has made more dramas than one in the world's history.

Andromache is voice for some thoughts of Euripides on womanhood. Alas, she cries!

> "Alas, the gods can find
> Cure for all venom but a woman's spite."

Menelaus, by threatening to destroy her child forthwith unless she leave the altar, draws her away from the shelter of the gods, but then immediately has her seized, and sends them both forth to die. She cries—

> " Think'st thou heaven's hand is shortened, and thy deed
>   Can go unpunished ? "

But Menelaus cares not.

> " Come when that may, my heart shall bear it all.
>   But thy life shall be mine."

And so an opening offers itself for a cry against Sparta.

> " O bane of all mankind, ye lords of lies,
>   With crooked modes and minds and no true thoughts,—
>   Why should ye thrive in Hellas ?   What of crime
>   Is lacking from your lists, ye murderous thieves?
>   Your lips and hearts at variance, on the one
>   A word that gives the other still the lie."

The Chorus comment on the evils of rivalry in family life and in the State.

Meanwhile the two victims are outside, ready to die, when Peleus enters in haste, and protests vigorously against the crime. He flings scornful imputations on the virtue of Spartan women in general, and on Helen in particular, and he sets Andromache and her child at liberty. And then Hermione, agitated with fear of her husband's return, agrees to fly with Orestes ; but a messenger enters with the news of her husband's murder at Delphi, apparently through the machinations of Orestes himself.

The corpse of Neoptolemus is brought in upon a bier, and Peleus bewails his empty halls and his old and helpless state, "a lonely dweller in a lonely home."

And then Thetis is seen hovering over all, giving the solutions of the gods.

There is little, in a play like this, of consolation or of enlightenment for the pain and mystery of life. Few are the sorrows that find a god to tell them all the reasons why!

It is perhaps a pity that so many of the plays of Euripides have survived, for, undoubtedly, those that come down to us cannot be taken to represent his very highest utterance, beautiful in many respects though they be. It is remarkable, on the other hand, that so few of those of Æschylus and Sophocles have been preserved ; but there can be no question that these are amongst their very best. In the matter of criticism, of course, just as in warfare, it is not of advantage to present too long a line to the enemy. As has been well shown, it would have been better for Euripides had only the fragments which are extant of the whole three dramatists survived, for the scraps of Euripides which remain have a far higher power than those of the others, so striking are they for the thought they carry, and for the phrase in which they are clothed.

CHAPTER XIX

" MEDEA," " HIPPOLYTUS," AND " THE BACCHANALS "

A WOMAN's revenge for wrong and scorn, a woman's spiteful
lie because her illicit passion has been slighted, a woman's
murder of her son, the king, under the frenzy of the genial
god of the glens and the grapelands—these, with the disasters
that followed them, form the topics of three Tragedies of
Euripides.

The first is shown us in the fire and fury of " Medea." [1]
This Tragedy was eclipsed in popular favour when it came
out, by a play by the son of Æschylus,[2] which obtained
the first prize, while the second went to Sophocles. That
this was deemed its due may be gathered from the censure
in the " Poetics " of Aristotle. Of course it needs no vast
erudition for any one to perceive that this is rather a picture
of the passionate rage of one woman, a truculent dame,
evolving schemes of retribution on those who have hurt her,
than a regular Tragedy, while the other characters in the play
are but moving shadows beside her.

Jason,[3] the husband of Medea, where he does not strike
one as a fool, is evidently an unprincipled worldling, lured to
his confusion-making step by his flickering inclinations.

When she rebukes him for his faithlessness to her as a
wife, and his ingratitude, besides, for all wherein she has
given him her help, crying out—

---

[1] B.C. 431, the year after the outbreak of the Peloponnesian War.
[2] Euphorion.
[3] Leader of the Argonauts in the voyage for the Golden Fleece. Through the
magic of his wife Medea he overcomes every obstacle and wins the prize he seeks.
Then he looks for a more royal consort.

" O Jove, thou hast given men tests to know the alloy in gold ;
  Why hast thou never yet branded the mark of a rogue on his brow ? "

Jason replies—

" Well, now it seems I must turn speech-maker, and try,
  Like a shipman with sails close-reefed, to weather the storm of thy tongue.
  Not that I loathed thee, or hated thy children, or longed for new bride,
  But to help on the good of the house, to have brothers for those thou hast
      borne."

Medea will have no such lame defences.   She will not palter
with truth.

" 'Tis a well-arranged speech—had it only been true, but thou know'st it
  is false.
  Thou hast sinned—that's the short of it, sinned hast thou, Jason, in basely
  betraying thy wife."

The play contains a fine patriotic ode on the glory of
Athens, but the provocation of that ode seems quite in-
adequate, seeing that the Chorus is only moved to its
utterance by the fact that the Athenian Ægus has agreed
to give shelter in his city to Medea when she shall have
become outcast on account of her necromancies and murders.

Creon and his daughter, whose deaths are compassed by
the poisoned robe which Medea's magic skill prepares, are
not outstanding, and, by comparison with the " Trachiniæ "
motif, the episode is poor enough.   Yet a great actor could
make of Medea a great part.   It might become a Sarah
Bernhardt monologue of passion, hate, and fury, with an
accompaniment of minorities.   Like a creature out of another
world, this wild woman whom Jason's outrage has kindled to
unquenchable fury moves across the stage, till Corinth rings
with her lamentings and her rage ; and one sees not so
much a woman as an elemental passion unconfined, fateful,
winged with destruction, dreadful to provoke.   Hence, when
the time came, not of great plays but of great actors, when
the medium stood out beyond the material, and the character
eclipsed the setting of circumstance, this might easily become
a piece that would crowd the largest house in Greece.

Especially thrilling in interest is that battle scene of a
mother's love at conflict with the stern resolve to slay her
children in order to harrow her husband's heart, a scene
which forever remains secure in the world's esteem.

> " Ah, why do you smile, my children, in my face?
> My heart surrenders to your laughing eyes.
> Farewell all schemes of gloom.   I'll take your hands,
> And seek with you a shelter far away.
> Why should I pour a double load of pain
> Into my heart already full of grief?
>
> .   .   .   .
>
> And yet—Out, coward, letting the soft words slip
> Over speech threshold !   No, the babes must die. . . .
> Alas, the deed I dare not.   Go, farewell.
> My sorrow wins the day." [1]

It was a popular subject ; but, away above all who touched
it, with all his faults, Euripides stands supreme.

The " Hippolytus Crowned " [2] deals with the dreadful god-
sent curse of the passion of Phædra for Hippolytus, which
strangles all the beauty of her nature, obliterating every trace
of good, and culminating in her dying accusation against
the object of her lust, for the fostering of revenge.
Hippolytus, by his very purity, involves himself in destruction ; for he rouses the hate of Aphrodite herself through
his neglect of her.   He is not a strong character, but
becomes, in his innocence, practically a plaything in the
hands of Aphrodite.   It is in this play that the line occurs,
already referred to—

> " My tongue has sworn it, but my mind is free,"

which has been often used to the detriment of the morality
of Euripides,[3] though no falser use of words was ever made.
It applies, certainly, to Hippolytus, in the circumstances in

---

[1] Some carpers at Euripides even object to this relenting of the mother-heart.
Surely this, at least, is a true nature-touch in the play !

[2] Gained the first prize in 429 B.C.   Schlegel sets it in the forefront.

[3] It is, indeed, alleged that the poet was summoned to the Court for encouraging
perjury.   It contains, however, the true definition of a valid oath.

which he was placed, but in no wise whatever to Euripides, any more than expressions of Odysseus in "Philoctetes," isolated from the context, could legitimately be employed in condemnation of Sophocles. It is difficult to know what impulse a critic was following, sometimes, when he stumbled into utterance; though it would be easier to understand the origin of ideas if lesser critics, in their carping, only let us know whose opinion they were quoting as their own. So many men are content to appropriate what lies to their hands, like an old coat, and are satisfied if it comfortably hide their own deficiencies, and give them somewhat of a figure when they walk abroad.

Theseus, his father, finding her declaration on the corpse of his wife Phædra, banishes Hippolytus, putting him under one of the maledictions of which his own sire Poseidon has promised to bring fulfilment for him. It has not long to wait; for, as he goes along the coast to his banishment, a monster, rising from the deep, scares the horses, and the hapless youth, entangled in the reins, is dragged to his death.

Through this play we find references and allusions to Pericles, who, just the year before, had perished of the plague.

"The Bacchanals" which may perhaps be taken as the closing utterance of the poet in exile, in regard to human life and passion, has above it the soft wonder and glamour of wild places, and seems to embody the poet's reflection on the lessons himself has learned in regard to the accepted religion of his time; [1] for King Pentheus reaps, from his determined opposition to the popular worship of Dionysus, shame, madness, suffering, and death, the usual reward for such a course. Euripides himself had undoubtedly suffered, and been misunderstood, through his agnostic attitude

---

[1] The idea that this exquisite drama is the palinode of Euripides, a reaction to the orthodox worship of the divinities he had doubted, and the superstitions he had in his earlier years assailed, is opposed by Hartung and Pfander.—See PATER, *Macmillan's Magazine*, 1889.

towards the popular beliefs of his time. Very naturally and
pathetically therefore this voice of his speaks from the grave;
for it was reproduced after its creator had died in exile. It
is the only extant Greek Tragedy dealing with the wander-
ings of the god in whose worship was the wellspring of
Greek Tragedy itself.

Dionysus, the Asian god, has come across to Greece, and
kindled in the hills and glades the frenzy of his worship.
He tells how he has passed through many lands, leaving
behind him, everywhere, his revel-shout, and his dancing
crowds of worshippers skin-clothed, ivy-crowned.

Now, in Thebes, Cadmus and Teiresias themselves have
joined the throng, and, when the young king Pentheus returns,
he finds even his mother Agave [1] amongst the Bacchus-
possessed. So he resolved to crush this new madness.

" They tell me a stranger has come, a trickster with magic from Lydia.
With hair of gold, and a wine-flushed face, and eyes all soft with dreaming,
Speaking of Dionysus, the mystical child of Jove."

So he orders the arrest of this visitant, decreeing likewise
his death. Vainly Teiresias warns him.

" Beware ; for he whom thou hatest will rise throughout Hellas to power,
Greater than soul of mine can ever through time foresee.
She the foodgiver is great, Demeter the mother of corn,
But blessing is also on him who gives us the gladness of wine,—
Wine that hushes men's griefs, sealing up softly the doors
Through which remembrance of ill comes creeping into the heart.
Balm-giver, calm-giver, giver of slumber and ease,
Such is the god whom thou scornest. Beware of the judgment he pays.
Fear-flinger, sight-bringer—think not thy might can oppose him.
The grape and the god are against thee ; the pride of thy wisdom is vain."

The Chorus of Bacchanals express their impression of the
doom involved by such an action as the king contemplates.[2]

---

[1] Dionysus himself sent this madness upon her, because she had cast aspersions on
his mother Semele, denying the Jove-paternity of her child.

[2] Paley takes the play as rationalistic in tendency, yet strangely blent with praises
of the ancient faith ; Müller, as a protest against reasoning about the gods ; Ovid
("Metamorphoses," iii. 514) calls Pentheus "contemptor superum." The king is the

> " Wretched and sad is the end
> Of speech unrestrained
> By law or the fear of the gods."

And now Dionysus is led in, a captive, his divinity un-suspected. He has not resisted. He feared nothing. He held forth his hands to be bound, but, in his arrest, all the Bacchanals who had been in chains and prison, miraculously released, had rushed forth hymning his praises in the wild frenzy of their orgies. Cast into the stables, he warns the king that for this impiety to Dionysus he will have to pay. And soon again he emerges, and declared himself, to the Chorus. When the king enters, enraged at the escape of his prisoner, a messenger appears from the mountains, narrating the mysterious rites which he and some shepherds had observed, and in which the mother of the king had shared. The king resolves to seek them out and behold their revels for himself. Under the spell of Dionysus, and disguised in woman's garb, he goes forth, but when they reach the place where the Bacchanals are gathered, he is torn to pieces by them at the instigation of the god ; and his mother Agave, their leader, comes bearing his head, which in her madness she deems to be the head of a lion from the desert. Her frenzy passes,[1] under the speech of Cadmus, whose eyes have been opened, and who has seen, in lone Cithæron's glen, the mangled limbs of the king,

> " Scattered amid the dark and tangled thicket."

Agave, awake now in her grief, utters a most pathetic lamentation, full of the pitifulness of a mother's love.

It is remarkable, how, in the " Christus Patiens "[2] of

embodiment of the ancient ὕβρις. At the same time he represents the traditional character of the Thebans.

θρασεῖς καὶ ὑβρισταὶ καὶ ὑπερήφανοι . . .

Dicæarchus.—Müller, " Frag. Gr. His." ii. 258, 14.

[1] Tyrell draws attention to the subtle patho-psychology of Euripides, herein : for Agave forgets the past, when the obscuring mist is lifted, but Ajax does not.

[2] A cento of verses, taken chiefly from the " Bacchæ," "Rhesus," and " Trojan Women," the reputed authorship of which is very questionable.

Gregory Nazianzen, some lines of Agave in this play were transferred to the Virgin Mary's sorrow over Christ, and so these lines were omitted from all later texts of Euripides. Milman very successfully makes restitution.

Dionysus, this time in all his godhood, enters and settles the future of Cadmus and Agave.

There is, all over this drama of the mystic god, an atmosphere unique.[1] The Choruses are now exquisite reflections of the joy of worship,—now wild cries of the chase; while sometimes into your very room comes the spell of the quiet solitudes in hill countries everywhere, god-haunted.

> "Hushed grew the sky, and in the grassy glen
>   Each leaf hung still; nor through the listening world
>   Awoke one creature's cry."

The king's punishment is the retribution of heaven on his obstinacy, and his resolve to arrest the worship of the god by violence and murder, while at the same time there is a certain personal remonstrance by the pensive poet, against rude persecution for religious differences, and over matters not wholly understood nor fully revealed to all.

---

[1] This supplied countless subjects for art representation on vases, etc.

CHAPTER XX

THE topics which had drawn the greatest minds of Greece on through the labyrinths of Thought to the very edge and margin of the Unseen were dragged into the life of Elizabethan England, and were beckoning the thinkers and the poets into pursuit of them almost before men knew. The ethical issues of action: the certainty with which the hand of judgment clutches the heel of the deed: man and God, death, doom, and all the conflicts of the soul, rose out of the deeps and walked about the platform of Thought, challenging question.

The Elizabethan thinkers, contemplating the phantasmic evolutions and disasters of historic and legendary characters, alongside of the defeats and trials of contemporary personages,[1] put upon the stage what developed into English Tragedy—a study of mental pathology, a representation of abnormal conditions and circumstances of the soul. Like the Greeks, they put crowns on their puppets, or set them on thrones, or made them great warriors clothed with high renown, only to overwhelm them with shame and failure, through sin, pride or folly. There is virtue for the Tragedian, in remoteness thus, of place, time or circumstance. For when the tragic elements of human passion are at war there is no safe vantage-point of observation. The Charybdis of spiritual strife is apt to draw all near it into its vortex, and a

---

[1] *Cf.* The Rise and Fall of Essex and Southampton.

tranquil observation of the conflict can only be obtained
through securing a long perspective.   This principle threw
upon the early Elizabethan stage the thunder and the flaming
rant whose echoes sound sometimes even among the words
of Shakespeare.

The stream of pre-Shakespearian Drama was fed by
the work and imagination of the wits of the Universities.
Lyly [1] was the earliest of these, standing, however, apart
from the whirl of passion and Bohemian dissipation which
marked and marred the lives of so many of them.   Dilettante,
select, somewhat of a courtier, his plays were represented
" before her Majesty," and not in the rush-strewn, tobacco-
fume-laden theatre, in the presence of the vulgar mob.
Marlowe, Greene, Peele, Lodge and Nash compose one
great group, all intimately connected in life and writing;
except that Lodge was free from the Bohemianism of the
rest, and untainted by the loose morals of a free and easy
age which had ruined them.   Like all planets, they were
wandering stars.   Kyd was of this School, though it is
uncertain that he belonged to either of the Universities.
Little is known about him.   He is silent in his work, and
yet his "Spanish Tragedy" was not without influence on
Shakespeare.

Undoubtedly the work of this School had many blemishes,
but, at the same time, many beauties of its own shine
through its imperfections, and it stands most often, in reality,
misjudged, owing to the difficulty, if not impossibility, of
the light-hearted critic of this century putting himself into
the position of the period in which those poets wrote, free
from the blinding glory and super-excelling mastery of
Shakespeare.   There is, amongst their splendour, more than
sufficient of bombast and rant, violence and blood.   But it
was considered at the time that a tragedy, to be worthy of
the name, must have abundance of such material.   Thus in
1581 Wilson, of Leicester's Players, received orders for

[1] 1580-1601.

a play not only original and entertaining, but also including all sorts of murders, immoralities and robberies! They make the error of quite naturally putting in the mouths of their created characters, irrespective altogether of position or time, anachronisms and classical absurdities; nevertheless, there is in their utterance a loud, big, growing heart-beat, which makes one regret the loss which the student of literature and the lover of poetry must have sustained, through the destruction of countless specimens of their work, in the havoc of the great London fire.   Above all, there was within them, and can still be felt, the music of Shakespearian promise.   Occasionally your soul comes into the presence of some utterance, some voice with a power like the spell of a hidden cataract's cry among the glens, making you pause, and silencing your heart,—a spell, indeed, which is found in this School, as a new thing, and for which you vainly search in all before them.   Nor is it wonderful. These are the angels singing of the day that was to be!

Thomas Kyd[1] in his " Spanish Tragedy" shows us the very ghastliest vein of popular tragic writing.   This play was retouched by Ben Jonson and others.   Its identification with the name of Kyd is confirmed by Heywood's allusion in his " Apology for Actors," where he says—

" Therefore Mr Kyd, in his ' Spanish Tragedy ' upon occasion presenting itself, has thus written—

'Why, Nero thought it no disparagement,
And Kings and Emperors have true delight,
To make experience of their wits in plays.'"

The play has been associated with the " First Part of Jeronimo," but this latter, published first in 1605, fifteen years after Kyd's death, seems to be a later production, amplifying the story already abundantly told in the opening scene of the " Spanish Tragedy,"[2] and, indeed, called into

[1] Born in London, 1557.   Died in poverty, 1595.   Coupled with Marlowe by Ben Jonson—" Sporting Kyd and Marlowe's mighty line."
[2] Licensed 1592.

being by the success of Kyd's production. The influence of classical studies is shown in this play, when the ghost of Andrea is brought in by Revenge to see retribution wrought upon his enemies, through whose influence he had been slain, reflecting the "Thyestes" of Seneca, in which that hero's spectre appears to Ægisthus his son, and instigates him to the murder of Agamemnon.

Revenge and the Ghost are Chorus, waiting to see " Love turned to hate, and hope into despair.". Andrea's ghost grows impatient, as he feels the promised satisfaction too long deferred; and he has to wake Revenge from sleep at the close of the fourth act. Jeronimo's lament gives Jonson food for laughter in " Every Man in His Humour," [1] though I am not sure but Jonson might have found plenty of less poetical matter to laugh at in his own writings. The revenge of Jeronimo is accomplished through the medium of a mock play,—where may be found the germ of Hamlet itself,— in which all the deaths are real tragedy, and the daggers are stained with the heart's blood of the actors. Jeronimo is prevented from hanging himself by the spectators, who only learn, when he brings in his dead son, how real has been the conflict at which they have been sitting. He bites out his tongue, then signs for a pen, next for a knife to mend it, and then with the knife he slays himself and the father of Lorenzo. Andrea's Ghost and Revenge rejoice in bloody satisfaction, as well they may, and arrange most telling tortures for the shades of their foes,—certainly a sumptuous feast of horrors!

The popularity of " Jeronimo " is strikingly testified in Prynne's " Histriomastix," [2] in which he quotes from

[1] 1598.

[2] " Histriomastix," 1633 —" The Scourge of Players "—by Wm. Prynne, b. 1600. Graduate of Oriel, Oxford, author of Puritan and Anti-Arminian diatribes. In " Histriomastix " he reflected on the virtue of Henrietta Maria the Queen, and in consequence was sentenced to have his Book burned by the hangman, to pay a fine of £5000, be expelled from Oxford and Lincoln's Inn, lose both ears in the pillory, and suffer perpetual banishment. Three years later for a libel on Laud, he was fined another £5000, again pilloried, branded on both cheeks, etc. See "Documents relating to Prynne," edited by Gardiner, Camden Society, 1877.

Braithwaite, the story of a late English gentlewoman who had frequented the theatre over-much and when exhorted at her deathbed to repentance and invocation of the mercy of God, she could only reply " Jeronimo, Jeronimo,—O let me see Jeronimo acted," and so she died. Kyd's translation of Garnier's " Cornelia,"[1] is the only one to which he attached his name in publication.

His work is not inspiring to the present day, but he could write such hauntingness as this:

> "There is a path upon your left-hand side,
> That leadeth from a guilty conscience,
> Unto a forest of distrust and fear.
> A darksome place and dangerous to pass.
> There shall you meet with melancholy thoughts,
> Whose baleful humours, if you but uphold,
> It will conduct you to despair and death."

Thomas Lodge,[2] whose " Rosalynde," a work oftener referred to than read, helped Shakespeare not a little in " As You Like It," had sailed with Cavendish on his last voyage, and seen some life and adventure upon the deep waters, and in the mystic lands below the horizon. He became a doctor of physic, through a degree of Avignon, and translated Josephus, and Seneca's " Works both Moral and Natural."[3] Though a friend of Greene he escaped the Circe wiles of Bohemia, and died aged sixty-five years, a physician in good practice. He wrote "The Wounds of Civil War "[4] setting forth the tragic history of Marius and Sylla. It is based upon Plutarch, and notwithstanding its crudities, its tricks of rhetoric, and its imperfect vision, it doubtless touched the miscellaneous crowd that was before its author's mind when he wrote it. It is not a little remarkable and startling, however, to find ancient Gaul represented by a ridiculous figure of a Frenchman, speaking broken English, thus—

[1] Garnier (1530-1590) was the most distinguished predecessor of Corneille.
[2] Born 1558 : died 1625.　　　　　[3] 1600.　　　　　[4] 1594.

" O me no can kill Marius : me no dare kill Marius.
Adieu, messieurs, me be dead, si je touehe Marius. Marius
est un diable. Jesu Maria sauve moi."

The conservatism of Lodge finds. expression in his
sentiment declared through the mouth of Sylla, that the
secret of misery in the state lies in the people's seditious
innovations, and their fickle minds inclined to foolish
change.

George Peele, born about 1558, arranged pageants at the
University of Oxford, where he took his master's degree in
1579. For seventeen years he lived a Bohemian life in
London, and died in poverty between 1596 and 1598.
Greene has designated him [1] as "no less discerning than the
other two, in some things rarer, in nothing inferior, driven
as myself to extreme shifts." He wrote the "Arraignment
of Paris,"[2] which was a court pastoral, with flattering
allusions to Elizabeth. Juno and Pallas summon Paris
before the assembled gods on the ground that he has
delivered an unjust sentence. As they will not depart from
their appeal, the decision is left with Diana, who awards the
fatal apple to the wise, chaste and potent Eliza, passing the
three goddesses by! These, however, agree in the decision,
and lay their gifts at the feet of the Queen ; and even the
Fates appear and give up their emblems of power to her
whom the gods have favoured. It is, thus, altogether a
court play, and yields no measure of a man's spiritual
teaching. It would be too polite to speak plainly on what
might be unpleasing to a royal ear like Elizabeth's.

His " Edward I."[3] was, in spirit, a slanderous attack against
Eleanor of Castile. This is a chronological sketch,—pictures
in a mirror, dimly passing. Queen Eleanor murders the
Mayoress for the sake of her rich dresses ; and, then, on
her deathbed confesses a double adultery, and with all her

---

[1] In his "Groatsworth of Witte." "The other two" were Marlowe and Nash.
See page 221.
[2] 1584.   [3] 1593.

nobility of spirit, is proud, wicked and hard. The Queen, swallowed, in answer to her imprecation, by the gaping earth, to be flung forth again in another part of London, is an expression, however clumsy, of the popular faith in the interfering guidance of providential wisdom, almost worthy of Euripides at his worst.

The "Battle of Alcazar,"[1] anti-Spanish and anti-Popish, is tragic enough, if blood and murder, and goriest utterance make up Tragedy. It retains the old Dumb-shows, of which a good example is seen in the play which is represented before the King in "Hamlet," filling up with information the space before the acts and between them.

> " Of death, of blood, of wreak, of deep revenge
> In blood, in death, in murder, and misdeed,
> This heaven's malice did begin and end."

Muley Hamet, revelling in utter abandonment of a truculent and villainous mind, cries out—

> " Sith they begin to bathe in blood
> Such slaughter with my weapon will I make,
> As through the stream and bloody channels deep,
> Our Moors shall sail in ships and pinnaces,
> From Tangier shore unto the gates of Fez."

Surely this was heart-curdling enough for any band of quarrelsome 'prentice boys in England !

Stukeley, a character in this play, was a real adventurer, who, with ambition for power, had aimed at colonising Florida ; but, being impecunious, he had gone to Rome, and offered his service for the conquest of Ireland to the Pope. Receiving Irish titles, and furnished with eight hundred soldiers by the King of Spain, he sailed to conquer that western island, but finding, at Lisbon, that Sebastian, King of Portugal, was fitting up an adventure of war against Africa, he and his men went as volunteers ; and, in Africa, with Sebastian, and with the Kings of Barbary and Morocco, at Alcazar, in August 1578, in their defeat, he was slain.

[1] 1594.

In Peele's play this English captain utters his ambition to
have a crown, and to be companion of kings,—

> " King of a mole-hill had I rather be,
> Than richest subject of a monarchy."

There is also in this play, amidst all its rant, a direct
appeal, as powerful as in Æschylus, to the pride of country,
and especially reminding the English listeners of England's
glorious victory over the Armada, fresh in every heart.
The Portuguese King, endeavouring to dissuade Stukeley
from his project, says,

> " Were every ship ten thousand on the seas,
> Manned with the strength of all the eastern kings,
> Conveying all the monarchs of the world,
> To invade the island where her highness reigns,
> 'Twere all in vain. . . .
> The wallowing ocean hems her round about,
> Whose raging floods do swallow up her foes,
> And on the rocks their ships in pieces split ;
> The South, the narrow Britain-sea begirts,
> Where Neptune sits in triumph to direct
> Their course to hell that aim at her disgrace ! "

Good, gentle Shakespeare puts in the mouth of Pistol
some raillery at the bombast of this play, and Ben Jonson in
"The Poetaster"[1] joins him in a chuckle. The piece is as
full of the clatter of battle and camps as "Tamburlaine,"
while it lacks the passion, the romantic vigour, the pathos,
the thunder-and-lightning glamours of Marlowe's play,—the
richness of word and phrase and haunting music of his work.
It was evidently a hurried throwing together of a verbal
garment to clothe a spectacular representation built for
popular appreciation.

His " David and Bathsabe "[2] has some soft sweet writing,
and gave, to such a mind as his, a most fit subject, full of
opportunity for sorrow, and clang of conflict, and human
stress and passion. This is his best work, bearing traces of

[1] 1601.   [2] Published 1599.

Shakespeare's overmastering power of influence on the literary workers around him. The basis of the piece is the Jewish idea of the transmission of punishment from parents upon the children. David's lust for Bathsabe, draws upon him the shadow of the murder of Uriah, and the door of the king's house is opened to the sin and feud involved. The rape, by Amnon, of his own sister, the fratricide and unfilial rebellion of Absolom, are the inevitable results.

Poor Peele, in time, got his feet entangled, like Greene, in the net of tavern dissipation, and its concomitant sins. It is pathetic to see him, in penury and ill-health, sending to Lord Burghley his eldest daughter, " Necessity's servant," for help, with playful allusion to the prologue of Persius, where Hunger was the Master of Arts. The letter is his last trace. Death, the examiner of all human Finals at the " Great Go," called him to a higher degree.

Standing high in poetic power above Peele, Robert Greene, born in 1560, a Master of Arts of Cambridge,—perhaps in holy orders, though an unholy man, lived a lamentable life, and died undoubtedly a melancholy death. He had not a high idea of love, and I question but the words of his play spoke somewhat of his own true feeling, and at the same time the deeper religiousness of his training, and regret of his better self, when he says,

> " Now the touch of such aspiring sins
> Tell me all love is lust, but love of heaven ;
> That beauty used for love is vanity."

His muse had a skilful touch in painting female characters ; and he was a friend of Lodge.

In his tragedy of " Selimus " you sup " full with horrors." The scene is crowded with curses and blood. Aga's eyes are plucked out upon the stage ; and when he exclaims that his hands are left him still to work revenge, Acomat gives orders to have his hands cut off, and thrust into his robe, asking with truculent scorn,

> " Which hand is this ? right or left ? Canst thou tell ! "

Bajazet, having " cursed himself dry," is poisoned in a draught given him by an aged Jew, who proffers the cup to Aga also, after he himself has drank of it, because age has made him weary, and he prefers to go to the shades in such brave comradeship.

Greene's letter to his wife throws a pathetic light upon him. He had been told by a friend, the night before his death, that she, from whom he had been separated, had sent him " commendations, and that she was in good health, whereat he greatly rejoiced, confessed that he had mightily wronged her, and wished that he might see her before he departed." Then, feeling that time pressed, he wrote to her.—

" Sweet Wife,—As ever there was any good-will or friendship between thee and me, see this bearer, my host, satisfied of his debt. I owe him ten pounds, and but for him I had perished in the streets. Forget and forgive my wrongs done unto thee, and Almighty God have mercy on my soul. Farewell, till we meet in heaven, for on earth thou shalt never see me more. This second of September 1592.   Written by thy dying husband,
" Robert Greene."

The age was a dramatic one, and, unthinkingly, had pathos round it in its simplest acts. When Greene's corpse was laid out for burial, his poor landlady tenderly placed around the dead poet's brow a wreath of bays!

Greene, out of his closing hours, gave utterance poignantly to the feeling of disappointment which was in his heart at the treatment of the University poets by the professional actors for whom they wrote.[1] He speaks especially to three dramatic writers. The first he styles—

" Thou famous Gracer of Tragedians,"

and he warns him—

" Defer not like me till this last point of extremity, for little knowest thou how in the end thou shalt be visited."

This has been identified as undoubtedly Kit Marlowe, the

---

[1] " Groatsworth of Witte bought with a Million of Repentance," published after the death of Greene by Henry Chettle.

greatest of this school. To the next, who has been identified as Nash, and whom he called—

> "young Juvenal, that biting satirist,"

he advises—

> "Get not many enemies by bitter words."

And, to the third, undoubtedly Peele, he says that he is to cherish the true life, to seek better masters than the players, and to—

> "Remember Robert Greene, whom they have so often flattered, perishes now, for want of comfort."

It is in this tractate that the first certain allusion to Shakespeare's outstanding position among the players is found.

His work has not that greatness of plan so necessary in dramatic writing. There is not distinction among the persons; but, when his lyrical vein breaks through, he finds speech in exquisite tones. His "Pandosto" helped Shakespeare with the "Winter's Tale." At least seventeen editions of this are known—it was so popular.

It has been conjectured that in "A Midsummer Night's Dream"[1] the lines—

> "The thrice three Muses mourning for the death
> Of Learning, late deceased in beggary,"

refer to Greene.

He was filled with classical learning, and his imagination was quick, but he lacked himself the character to make character live upon the stage. Yet, though his blank verse had not the stride of Marlowe's, he had the gift of true expression. See this alone from "Pandosto."

> "Sovereign of beauty, like the spray she grows,
> Compassed she is with thorns and cankered flower :
> Yet, were she willing to be plucked and worn,
> She would be gathered though she grew on thorn."

Outshining and outstanding all others of this school,

[1] Act V., sc. i.

Christopher—or, as he was called in the familiar appellation of the period, " Kit " Marlowe,[1] worthily, through the radiant poetry of his lines, the turbulent, imaginative march of his music, and especially for the marvellous perfecting by him of blank verse as a medium of tragic utterance, takes his position as the immediate pioneer of Shakespeare.

A short life and a merry one, indeed, was his. When one remembers that he fell in a tavern brawl, having lived for only twenty-nine swift, fiery years, one wonders at the position which he achieved in our literature. Around his death and character much mystery and scandal have gathered. Truly applicable to him, however, is, it seems to me, that exquisite couplet which Shakespeare puts in the mouth of his dying Hamlet—

> " O good Horatio, what a wounded name,
> Things standing thus unknown, shall live behind me."

The little that has come to us regarding him is obscured by jealousy and prejudice ; but even Nash, that virulent scourge of all his contemporaries, has a word for—

> " Poor deceased Kit Marlowe."

Greene, on his deathbed, as we saw above, addresses him earnestly as—

> " Thou famous Gracer of Tragedians."

Gabriel Harvey,[2] in his own quaint way, cries—

> " Weep Powles. Thy Tamburlaine voutsafes to die."

Thorpe the bookseller, in his dedication to the translation of Lucan, writes—

> " To the memory of that pure elemental wit, Chr. Marlowe " ;

while Shakespeare, surely in tenderness, addresses him, in " As You Like It "—

> " Dead Shepherd "—

---

[1] 1564-93.   [2] 1545-1630.

a sweet, sad phrase. To my mind, Mr Stopford Brooke hits the mark when he says—

"Marlowe lived and died an irreligious, imaginative, tender-hearted, licentious poet."

The variety and inconsistency of the records of Marlowe's death, garbled, as most of them undoubtedly were, by Puritan feeling against the drama and players, as seen in Beard's "Theatre of God's Judgments"[1] six years after Marlowe's death, make the circumstances altogether uncertain and judgment insecure. Moreover, Bame, the informant upon whose authority the one specific accusation against Marlowe rests, was hanged very shortly afterwards at Tyburn for a misdemeanour.

Marlowe's fame, however, is not dependent either on his morals or his lack of them, but it rests securely on the work of his heart and brain, on the full-sail beauty and glory of his utterances, some of the masterpieces, indeed, of English literature. All his heroes are of the gigantic mould and voice, though in his productions Pegasus often has the bit in his teeth, and courses through the thunder clouds. He towers above his fellows, but he falls short of Shakespeare. There is in the web of life represented by him, undoubtedly, much fustian, but yet there are whole threads and checks of living gold through it all. His contribution was an undefinable majesty, ring, clang, and verve, poured into the blank-verse line of Tragedy, making it a kingly medium full of blood and breath, of life and fire. His work is a heap of jewels. It is the great poetry of a soul that did not live long enough in a raging world to find the pathos that would have led it to the still high reaches of calm.

Peele, in his prologue to "The Honour of the Garter,"[2] wrote—

"Unhappy is thy end,
Marley, the Muses' darling, for thy verse;
Fit to write passions for the souls below."

---

[1] 1599. [2] 1593.

It is, indeed, remarkable, that this man, before the age of twenty-one, had produced the first Tragedy really worthy of the name, and perfected the verse medium of dramatic writing, in English literature; and thereby won his right to undying record on the historic page. He has left us " Tamburlaine," in two parts; " Faustus "; the " Jew of Malta "; " Edward II. "; and " The Massacre of Paris." " Dido, Queen of Carthage," was finished by Nash—a fit precursor of Swift, but not at all an adequate successor of Marlowe.

" Tamburlaine "[1] is a whirlwind of flame, and yet, often, the still small voice is heard. It is not fair to test it with all the pomp, majesty, and music, the psychological insight, human pathos, laughter and awfulness, of Shakespeare, in our hearts. It stands alone, by the wonder of it, created by this artist in a turbulent Bohemia, with no worthy model to aid him in its shaping, and Hunger often at the door, clamouring for copy.

No more striking picture of the madness of ambition victorious, ever came upon the stage than that of Tamburlaine,

" Drawn in his chariot by the Kings of Trebizond and Syria, with bits in their mouths; reins in his left hand, and in his right hand a whip with which he scourgeth them."

" Holla, ye pampered jades of Asia !
What,—can ye draw but twenty miles a day,
And have so proud a chariot at your heels,
And such a Coachman as great Tamburlaine? "

It has been suggested that this wild collegian may have trailed a pike in the wars, so full of the camp and the shouting of armies is his verse. But wherever he went he saw Nature on the sea and under the starry night, with full eyes wide-open, noting,

" The golden ball of heaven's eternal fire,
That danced with glory on the silver waves."

---

[1] 1587 : published 1590.

How an inferior poet would have watered such a sight into weak moralisings!

When Tamburlaine finds the army of the Christians breaking their truce, he cries, invoking the aid of the Christ he does not acknowledge against the Christians who are false to their faith,

> " Open the shining veil of Cynthia,
> And make a passage from the empyreal heaven,
> That He who sits on high, and never sleeps,
> Nor in one place is circumscriptible,
> But everywhere fills every continent
> With strange infusion of His sacred vigour,
> May, in His endless power and purity,
> Behold and 'venge this traitor's perjury.
> Thou Christ that art esteemed omnipotent
> If thou wilt prove thyself a perfect god,
> Worthy the worship of all faithful hearts,
> Be now revenged upon this traitor's soul."

The Tragedy bristles with classical allusions, some of them clear as a picture; as when he speaks of the blasted banks of Erebus,

> " Where shaking ghosts
> Hover about the ugly ferryman,
> To get a passage to Elysian."

Nor has the poetry of his reference to his own art ever been surpassed.

> " If all the pens that ever poets held
> Had fed the feeling of their masters' thoughts,
> And every sweetness that inspired their hearts,
> Their minds, and muses on admired themes;
> If all the heavenly quintessence they 'stil
> From their immortal flowers of poesy,
> Wherein, as in a mirror, we perceive
> The highest reaches of a human wit;
> If these had made one poem's period
> And all combined in beauty's worthiness,
> Yet should there hover in their restless heads
> One thought, one grace, one wonder, at the least,
> Which into words no virtue can digest."

Passages like these are true poetic touchstones, for all time.

His " Faustus " [1] was admired by Goethe, who thought of translating it into German. "Tamburlaine " is thunder and blood, with wayward snatches of windcaught music; but this is a tragic poem of a soul in eternal dilemma between good and evil, salvation and perdition. Yes; a soul lost; sold away to hell,—pitiable dilemma, a Tragedy of the tragic conundrum of the heart's deepest life. On the one hand, his good angel pleads,

> " Faustus, repent ; yet God will pity thee."

But the bad angel interposes,

> "Thou art a spirit. God cannot pity thee."

Faustus, stirred by their pleading and counter-pleading, exclaims,

> " Who buzzeth in mine ear I am a spirit ?
> Be I a devil yet God may pity me ;
> Yea, God will pity me if I repent."

The evil angel, however, with knowledge and insight and a sneer, says,

> " Ay, but Faustus never will repent."

Then, when he is left alone to the silence of his own thought, and the stillness of reflection on himself, he says,

> " My heart is hardened : I cannot repent."

The anguish of a soul sinning against the beauty of God's universe, could scarcely be more strikingly represented than in the line,

> " When I behold the heavens, then I repent,"

while the answer of the tempter, who has successfully lured

[1] Earliest edition 1604.

the spirit to destruction, is most true in its harsh shifting of blame,—

    " 'Twas thine own seeking. Faustus, thank thyself."

Even when Faustus pleads Christ, and calls upon Him for help, Lucifer bars the door upon his wavering spirit, deepening his despair.

> " Christ cannot save thy soul, for He is just;
> There's none but I have interest in the same."

Inexpressibly beautiful is the Vision of Helen, brought from the shades to satisfy the curiosity of some scholars. An old man enters, admonishing and pleading with Faustus,—

> " O stay, good Faustus, stay thy desperate steps,—
> I see an angel hover o'er thy head,
> And with a vial full of precious grace
> Offers to pour the same into thy soul;
> Then call for mercy and avoid despair."

Again repentance knocks at Faustus' heart, only to be driven forth by the craving of lust for Helen.

> " Was this the face that launched a thousand ships
> And burnt the topless towers of Ilium?
> Sweet Helen, make me immortal with a kiss.
> Her lips suck forth my soul: see where it flies!
> Come Helen, come; give me my soul again."

At last the time draws near when the bargain with Hell comes to its completion; and Faustus must surrender his soul. Lucifer enters with minor angels of evil, and he speaks to Faustus as chief among

> " The subjects of our monarchy,—
> Those souls which sin seals the black sons of Hell,
> Faustus, we come to thee,
> Bringing with us lasting damnation
> To wait upon thy soul; the time is come
> Which makes it forfeit."

Surely there is insight here, when Mephistopheles
exclaims,

> " Fond worldling ; now his heart-blood dries with grief ;
> His conscience kills it, and his labouring brain
> Begets a world of idle phantasies,
> To over-reach the Devil, but all in vain.
> His store of pleasures must be sauced with pain."

And now, in agony of remorse and a late repentance, his
scholars find him and he confesses all.

> " O gentlemen.   I gave my soul for my cunning."

They can but pray for him.   And now, when there is no
way of escape, and the door to good is barred by his own
hardness of heart, Evil unmasks itself, denying not that it
was by its temptation that Faustus had been robbed of
eternal peace.

> " I do confess it, Faustus, and rejoice.
> 'Twas I that, when thou wert i' the way to heaven
> Dammed up thy passage ; when thou took'st the book
> To view the scriptures, then I turned the leaves,
> And led thine eye.
> What, weep'st thou ?   'Tis too late.   Despair.   Farewell !
> Fools that will laugh on earth must weep in Hell."

His good angel leaves him, and then the unspeakable
torture of a soul self-slain racks him as he waits the midnight hour.   Here Marlowe rises to marvellous passion.

> " O Faustus,
> Now hast thou but one bare hour to live,
> And then thou must be damned perpetually.
> Stand still you ever more-moving spheres of Heaven
> That time may cease and midnight never come.
> Fair nature's eye, rise, rise again, and make
> Perpetual day ; or let this hour be but
> A year, a mouth, a week, a natural day,
> That Faustus may repent and save his soul.
> See where Christ's blood streams in the firmament :
> One drop of blood will save me : O my Christ.
>
> O soul be changed into small water drops,
> And fall into the Ocean, ne'er be found."

This is the Tragedy of intellectual pride leading the way to madness, crime, and death. Marlowe, in quiet moments, when the tavern was empty, and the night outside lay still, and he was left alone, had lived and known this drama ere he wrote it,—known, too, the bitterness that he set in the lips of a fiend, when Faustus asks,

> " How comes it then that thou art out of Hell ? "

The fiend replies

> " Why, this is Hell, nor am I out of it ;
> Thinkst thou that I, that saw the face of God,
> And tasted the eternal joys of Heaven,
> Am not tormented with ten thousand Hells,
> In being deprived of everlasting bliss ? "

John Milton felt the strength of that, and was not ashamed to touch again that string.[1]

The Chorus express the lesson of the Tragedy,—the waste of heaven-given opportunity, the horror of the hell-bought soul, the hope that is slain by sin.

> " Cut is the branch that might have grown full straight,
> And burned is Apollo's laurel bough,
> That sometime grew within this learned man ;
> Faustus is gone ; regard his hellish fall ;
> Whose fiendful fortune may exhort the wise
> Only to wonder at unlawful things ;
> Whose deepness doth entice such forward wits,
> To practice more than heavenly power permits."

His " Jew of Malta "[2] is a drama of ambitious greed and scathing spite, succeeding in its devilish devices, but in the end caught in its own mesh. It was a popular play, being acted thirty-six times in four years. Such a figure was somewhat of a favourite on the Elizabethan stage, for the populace dearly loved a villain.

The play opens with Barabas counting his fabulous wealth.

---

[1] " Paradise Lost," i. 253.   [2] *Circa* 1588: published 1633.

" What a trouble 'tis to count this trash.
The needy groom, that never fingered groat,
Would make a miracle of thus much coin,
But he whose steel-barred coffers are crammed full,
And all his life-time hath been tired
Wearying his fingers' end with telling it,
Would in his age be loth to labour so
And for a pound to sweat himself to death."

He has one sole daughter, who, even in his greedy isolation, has made him speak of her as one

"Whom I hold as dear
As Agamemnon did his Iphigen :
And all I have is hers."

Meanwhile Malta is in terror of a Turkish fleet, that
demands from the Knights of Malta ten years' tribute,
which is to be levied and raised from the Jews.   It can be
met easily by the Jews giving up half of their possessions,
but Barabas demurs, and so his all is forfeited, his home is
made into a Nunnery.   But, with the prudent acuteness of
his race, he has secreted considerable treasure under a plank
in his house, so he persuades his daughter to become a Nun
in order that, by her aid, he may recover what he has hid.
With clever duplicity he curses her before the Friar, while,
in his " asides " he directs her to the treasure, which she
succeeds in throwing out to him, under cover of darkness.
The hatred which he feels towards the Christians, and his
natural malevolence against all mankind, find exercise in his
playing with the passion of Lodowick and Mathias for
Abigail.   Ithamore, employed by Barabas, sets the two
gallants at each other's throats in jealousy, and they kill
one another.   Abigail, who has left the Nunnery, now
re-enters it of her own choice, and her father, in blind rage,
sends an offering of poisoned rice, to be set down in the
dark passage where gifts for the Nuns are received.   The
whole Nunnery is in this way poisoned, and, amongst them
Abigail herself; who, in her dying confession, reveals the

secret of Barabas.   Now rival priests, who know the secret
and hunger after his money, are drawn to his house by
trickery, the one to be strangled by the Jew, and the other
to be hanged by the State as a murderer of his fellow, while
Barabas pretends that such a revelation of cruelty in
Christians has turned him back from a meditated apostasy.
But retribution haunts his doorstep.   Ithamore deserts him,
and would betray him, blackmailing him with threats.   Well
does the Jew understand his danger; knowing his own
soul he knows greed through and through, and how

> " Every villain ambles after wealth."

But, by the Jew's craft in drugs, the traitor and his comrades
are murdered, and Barabas only escapes by simulating death
through the influence of mandragora; and, in the trance
thereby induced, his body is thrown over the wall.   When
he awakes among the Turks he betrays the city, and after
it is taken he receives the Governorship in recompense.

But his thirst for mischief does not leave him satisfied.
He offers to feast the chief of the Turks and his officers in
his own house, while the soldiers will be entertained in a
Monastery outside.   At a given signal the monastery and all
in it will be destroyed by gunpowder, while he intends,
through an arrangement of a false floor, to precipitate the
Turkish chiefs into a cauldron beneath, in exchange for a
reward of a hundred thousand pounds from the former
Spanish Governor.   While having it shown to him, however,
the Governor cuts the cord, and Barabas is himself precipitated to the terrible destruction he has designed for others.
The man then truly speaks, in the snarling curse of a soul
stripped naked of all goodness,

> " Die life, fly soul ; tongue, curse thy full and die."

He was the unhuman anatomy on which Shakespeare clothed
his Shylock ; and his hopeless spit-fire malevolence was
carried into the creation of Aaron, in " Titus Andronicus."

The Jews were not understood by the Englishmen of
this period, and the popular idea was a grotesque caricature.
All kinds of ridiculous charges had been made against
them, a favourite one being that they abducted Christian
children in order to crucify them. This was alleged against
them in the ninth year of King Stephen's reign at Norwich.
At Bury St Edmunds, the monks displayed the mangled
remains of an infant alleged to have been so maltreated.
Matthew of Westminster even gives the boy's name to
have been " William." They were continually used as a
convenient means of raising money when the kings required that useful and often scarce commodity.

Richard I. forbade them to draw near Westminster at
his coronation, and many who dared to approach were slain
and their homes burned. The dreadful holocaust in York
Castle is one of the most terribly bloody things on record
in the Middle Ages. There could be little love between the
common people and this persecuted race, and the picture
each had of the other must have been contorted by all
manner of spites and fears.

Marlowe approaches Shakespeare most nearly in his
" Edward II.," [1]—a strong Tragedy of the doom of pride and
fatuous favouritism, standing very close to Shakespeare's
Richard II. and forming, indeed, a model for that drama.
This lifted the historic play out of Chronicle into Art. The
material is hewn from Holinshed, Fabian, and Stow.

Gaveston, a friend of Edward, who had been banished, is
recalled by the King on his accession. He is a light, weak
spirit of vanity, who aims at intimacy with the monarch,
while absolutely scorning all inferior. The two insult the
Bishop of Coventry, who had previously exiled Gaveston,
and they send him to the Tower. The nobles thereupon
rebel. Queen Isabella, insulted and forsaken, will yet not
have a levy of arms ; but Gaveston is banished, and made

[1] About 1590. Swinburne, indeed, prefers Marlowe's character-painting, though
few will agree with him here.

Governor of Ireland, the King refusing to see the Queen again till she shall win the recall of his favourite. The nobles prevail upon her to agree to this, with the resolution that, if he be still insolent, they will slay him.

Never was there a stronger picture of a weak monarch, the slave of changing whim, neglecting to protect Normandy against France, nor caring for the threatening dangers of Ireland and Scotland, so keen is he for his friend. In vain the nobles confront the King, casting in his teeth the sarcastic song sung by the Scots over the English defeat—

> "Maidens of England, sore may ye mourn,
> For the lovers ye have lost at Bannockburn,"—

a telling affront, although in the play an anachronism.

For Gaveston he throws away the loyalty of his brother Kent, and thrust aside the Queen, with an impure imputation on her honour. Then civil war runs wild across the land, and Normandy is lost. Gaveston is slain by the nobles, and Edward plunges after revenge; but, defeated by the army of his Queen, the young Prince, and his nobles, he is, at Killingworth, discrowned, then carried through the country in disguise, insulted, degraded, thrown into a dungeon in Berkeley Castle, where, by Mortimer's command he is ruthlessly murdered.

It is a tale of twenty years, but it passes as with the action of a single day: and, though the King is contemptible, cruel, fickle, wavering, and the State declining at his hands through a worthless affection for an unworthy favourite, yet the suffering which his life entails upon him, the unutterable horror of his captivity and death, wring pity from us; and the man whose follies made us scorn him, claims, by the true tragic pathos of the retribution which he drags upon himself, the sympathy and tears of all who look into that dingy cell, unclean, in which he lies.

The persons are admirably characterised with masterly portrayal.

Gaveston stands out, gibing, strong, scornful. Feeling
the nobles against him he is contented to rest in the strength
of the King's favour.

> " Which, whiles I have, I think myself as great
> As Cæsar riding in the Roman street,
> With captive kings at his triumphant car."

The sin of Edward which involves him in destruction is
impiety first, bringing with it the blighting malediction of
the Bishop of Coventry,

> " For this offence, be thou accurst of God ! "

Next follows his headlong course of folly, " trampling
the good and lifting the depraved." The result, of course,
is that his

> " Court is naked, being bereft of those
> That make a king seem glorious to the world."

There is an ineffable open-air charm in such lines as Kent's,
worthy of the writer of the finest pastoral love-song in the
language—

> " Fair blows the wind for France ! "—

a line which is a ballad in itself, through which one feels the
breeze upon one's cheek. The Queen is a clear and vivid
portraiture, strong in outraged pride ; yet when her husband
is defeated, and she thinks of him a captive, her woman's
heart is pained.

> " I rue my Lord's ill-fortune ; but, alas !
> Care of my country calls me to this war,"—

a true tragic dilemma of a soul in doubt between pride and
rage on the one hand, and love and duty on the other.
Edward, in his misery at Killingworth, feels her strong, just
indignation, branded on his conscience. He dare not have
her brought.

> " Isabel, whose eyes, being turned to steel,
> Will sooner sparkle fire than shed a tear."

This drama has more than one concentrated picture whereby we see, as by the sudden lurid flame of lightning, features and character start right out of the dark. Thus, when Edward, with the Abbot, Monks, Spencer, and Baldock, are in flight, Spencer, whose keen eye has been watching as they fled, acknowledges that they may sit secure if they have not been observed,

> " But shrewdly I suspect
> A gloomy fellow in a mead below.
> He gave a long look after us."

The poor King's weariness and despair are most pathetically depicted, along with his hate of Mortimer. When someone mentions this name he cries,

> " Mortimer! Who talks of Mortimer?
> Who wounds me with the name of Mortimer?
> That bloody man! Good father, on thy lap
> Lay I this head laden with mickle care.
> O might I never ope these eyes again,
> Never again lift up this drooping head,
> O never more lift up this dying heart! "

The misery of his captivity in Berkeley Castle is brought before our hearts with compassion—commanding simplicity. Mortimer sends Lightborn to murder him. Even Gurney and Matrevis have a kind of pity for him, being a king. The assassin enters the cell. Let the scene speak for itself.

" EDWARD.

Who's there? What light is that? Wherefore com'st thou?

LIGHTBORN.

To comfort you and bring you joyful news.

EDWARD.

Small comfort finds poor Edward in thy looks.
Villain, I know thou com'st to murder me.

LIGHTBORN.

To murder you, my most gracious lord?—
Far be it from my heart to do you harm.
The Queen sent me to see how you were used,
For she relents at this your misery.
And what eyes can refrain from shedding tears,
To see a king in this most piteous state?

EDWARD.

Weep'st thou already? List awhile to me,
And then thy heart, were it as Gurney's is,
Or as Matrevis', hewn from the Caucasus,
Yet will it melt ere I have done my tale.
This dungeon where they keep me is the sink
Wherein the filth of all the Castle falls.

LIGHTBORN.

O villains!

EDWARD.

And there in mire and puddle, have I stood,
This ten days' space ; and lest that I should sleep
One plays continually upon a drum.
They give me bread and water, being a king,
So that for want of sleep and sustenance
My mind's disordered, and my body's numbed ;
And whether I have limbs or no I know not.
O would my blood dropped out from every vein,
As doth this water from my tattered robes.
Tell Isabel the Queen I looked not thus,
When, for her sake, I ran at tilt in France,
And there unhorsed the Duke of Cleremont.

LIGHTBORN.

O speak no more, my lord, this breaks my heart.
Lie on this bed and rest yourself awhile.

EDWARD.

These looks of thine can harbour nought but death.
I see my tragedy written in thy brows.

LIGHTBORN.

He sleeps.

EDWARD.

O let me not die : yet stay, oh stay a while.

LIGHTBORN.

How now, my lord ?

EDWARD.

Something still buzzeth in mine ears,
And tells me if I sleep I never wake.
This fear is that which makes me tremble thus,
And therefore tell me, wherefore art thou come ?

LIGHTBORN.

To rid thee of thy life.   Matrevis, come !

EDWARD.

I am too weak and feeble to resist.
Assist me, sweet God, and receive my soul.''

I question if in any literature there is a deeper bit of tragic
writing than that.[1] It is so simple, so direct, and so
heartbreakingly pathetic, it drags back to the wretched King
the sympathy which his folly had almost repelled. Tragedy
here is knocking at the door of a greater time, and that door
was bound to open wide to knocking such as this.

As in the old Greek tragic world this sin of blood has its
own wage-giver with it.   The murderer Lightborn is stabbed
by Gurney above his royal victim, lest he blab.   Then
Gurney betrays the whole dark deed to the young King,
whose pride makes him believe he stands secure.   Queen
Isabel knows the fibre of her son's resolve, and warns
Mortimer, as she sees the King enter with his lords—

"Now, Mortimer, begins our tragedy ! "

Mortimer is at once impeached and taken away to execution ;
but, before he goes, he gives expression to his feeling, in

[1] Brandes condemns, but without ground, this murder scene.   In this, as in some
other things, his judgment is too material.

regard to fortune, as old and as true as when men first began
to think upon the problems of the soul of man all shadow-
haunted and destiny-driven.

> " Base Fortune, now I see that in thy wheel
> There is a point to which when men aspire
> They tumble headlong down : that point I touched.
> And seeing there was no place to mount up higher
> Why should I grieve at my declining fall?
> Farewell, fair queen : weep not for Mortimer,
> That scorns the world, and as a traveller
> Goes to discover countries yet unknown."

And so he walks out bravely to his doom—a sort of Macbeth
stirred first to action by his country's need, and then, seeing
himself strong enough to lead, he stretched forth his hand
to the governing rein of the State. The parallel of the
Queen's duty divided between the State and her husband's
imperious will, the murder of the King and the relations she
has with his murderer, and, finally, the judgment at the
prince's hands, might well echo with the sad step of doom
through the palace of Agamemnon.

Marlowe's "Massacre of Paris" is a mutilated survival,
chiefly reflecting the feelings of English Protestantism over
such an event, with heaven's retributions on the House of
Guise; while the Tragedy of Dido scarce bears the evidence
of the touch of his dead hand.

CHAPTER XXI

SHAKESPEARE

THESE—a somewhat motley band, yet men who had looked life in the face, and drunk deep of the well at the world's end, prepared the way and perfected the weapons for the king of dramatic poets. The day of the "University wits" was past, and the actor-playwrights were making their own material. There was in every theatre by this time an accumulation of plays of all kinds, mostly filled with the blood-revenge and rant so dear to the play-going people of a period in whose ears rang still the echoes of old fightings.

It was not quite enough to face an audience with mere strings of thundering recitation; for the Stage was developing and advancing with the improvement in theatres, and the man who walked the boards knew best what was required for the staging of a piece. Hence the neglect of the scholarly writers, and that independence of the playwrights of which Greene complained. The actor or manager took the material that was lying as so much lumber, and, if he had genius, recast the old story, retuned its music, humanising the lay figures which had become grotesque, and burning new wonderful colour into the half-forgotten clay with the flame of fervid poesy. Shakespeare's first efforts were of such a sort. He touched what was lying dead and cast aside; and still, to-day, amid the bombast and ranting crudities which were left, the mark of his masterly hand, and the spell of his unspeakable glamour, can be seen and felt by those whose hearts are responsive to the mysteries and music of the poetic and sublime. It was in reference to the position Shakespeare was attaining in such work that Greene made his bitter allusion, so valuable to the student of literature, warning his friends in "A Groatsworth of Wit" against the ungratefulness of the players.

"Yes, trust them not; for there is an upstart crow, beautified with our feathers, that, with his tiger's heart wrapt in a player's hide, supposes he is as well able to bombast out a blank verse as the best of you; and, being an absolute Johannes Factotum, is, in his own conceit the only 'Shake-scene' in a country."

The allusion is evidently to some play of Marlowe and Greene used by Shakespeare, and apparently, under his improving touch, a greater success than it had previously been.

Shakespeare's biographical material is the whole world of Nature. We do not look for note-books of a soul like his. He put his impressions into his work, especially his dramatic work. "All thoughts, all passions, all delights," of humanity came under his observing eye, passed through his sympathetic heart. The world of all things was his Commonplace-book. The wind and the rain, the laughter and the tears, the storms of passion, the hurricane movements of the human heart, the cloud chasing the sunshine over the water and the land, found meaning and interpretation at his glance and word. And especially in his noble Tragedies[1] do we find the greatest concentration of life's teaching, as understood by him, in regard to love and sorrow, death and pain, sin and its reward, not as these are found grouped and tabulated in a "Dictionary of Illustrations," but as they are thrown together in the lives of men and States,—stalking across the stage of history, and leaving their footprints in warning, in deserts and in battlefields, in hovels, halls, and streets, and in the courts of kings. We shall see what we speak of in "Romeo and Juliet," under

---

[1] Goethe says, "They are no mere poems. We could imagine we were standing before the gigantic Books of Fate, through which the hurricane of life was raging, and violently blowing its leaves to and fro."—*Wilhelm Meister.*

the blood-warm suns, the dreamy moons and pulsing stars of
Italy, where feud and friendship, love and romance grew
together, as passion-flowers of an impetuous people: in
"Hamlet," where Doubt shrinks from Duty along the verge
of Madness, among the shadows of the Court of Denmark:
in "Othello," where the devil whispers desolating jealousy
into trustful hearts, and kills all joy eternally; in "King
Lear," where Simplicity, grey-haired and old, involves a
whole state in disorder, through Greed begetting Ingratitude
in selfish natures: till, in "Macbeth," all hell is brought
into the homes and lives of men, because Ambition calls in
Murder to its aid, and opens the sluice-gate for the unsleep-
ing horrors of the damned;—a vast Cathedral full of ancient
shadows and weird heart-moving glimmerings: and, in the
crypts, men groping, mourning, dying in the dark, with
laughter just the other side of the wall, because they
clutched the phantom and missed the real of life.

The Roman streets, and Pompey's statue with a gashed
body lying in its cloak; the fickle breath of the world's
mob, now banishing, now blessing; the great "Might-have-
been," lying charmed in the bondage of Egyptian wiles and
luxury; disappointed Prodigality turning, ere it creep into
its sea-washed grave, to snarl at men's ingratitude; and the
swirl and strife of English camps and blood-shed,—these, too,
speak forever Shakespeare's criticism of life, looked at from
without, but as a man, whose raft has felt the anger and the
awe of all-night tossings on the deep, might stand upon the
shore, and read the incessant moanings of the winds and
waters, the sorrows of the darkness, the hopes and fears of
dawns and gloamings, the change and mystery of the lonely
surf-beaten sands.

CHAPTER XXII

" ROMEO AND JULIET "

THE EULOGY OF YOUTH

In "Romeo and Juliet " [1] we find the passion of the young heart of Shakespeare overflowing towards the pathos, and tragedy, of a love far-off but unforgotten. The groundwork of the tale is found in the mediæval romance of Xenophon of Ephesus ; then later, in 1476, in a novel by Masuccio of Salerno, and so it passes along until Bandello wrote his version which made an English writer compose a long-lost play upon the subject. Arthur Brooke [2] the English poet unearthed it from Bandello, and wrote on the topic an iambic poem of some length, upon which at last Shakespeare based his own immortal drama. It is the " eulogy of youth." It is the Tragedy of Love, triumphing over family feud, entering through locked doors and high-walled gardens, mastering even life itself, in Love's scorn for its inferiors. It is the conquest of young affection over ancient hate, working, by Love's magic, reconciliation between two sundered families, although over an open grave.

The play runs on like a tide ; and what in Brooke's poem extended over months, is, in the Tragedy, only a matter of days. It bears all the marks of being a youthful work. It

[1] Published in quarto 1597. In 1580 there was an earthquake in London. *Cf.* Act i. sc. 3, l. 23.
[2] 1562. " The Tragical Historie of Romeus and Juliet "—a free paraphrase of Bandello's novel. Brooke was lost by shipwreck in 1563 while passing to Newhaven. Shakespeare found Mercutio and the nurse in Brooke's poem. A prose version of it was also printed in 1567 by William Paynter, in " The Palace of Pleasure." Paynter was clerk to the Armoury of Queen Elizabeth.

is full of rhyme-endings, internal rhymings, aud sonnet forms : it has blank verse that is truly blank, and echoes of the rant of the dead tragedians, while it is studded like the sky of a mid-summer night with stars of poetic fancy. One can hardly keep from believing that we have here an old rhymed form either by himself or another, adapted and dignified into blank verse by Shakespeare. Further, that ancient shadow of the past, the Chorus, is retained and makes periodical appearance.

Romeo, like Hamlet, enters the stage of interest wrapped in gloom, the cause of which arouses anxious enquiries. He is a mournful night-walker with his grief, weeping till the dawn. Sadness lengthens his hours, not so much that he is in love, but rather that he is out of love's favour, while yet in love with love.[1] It is the thought of Rosaline, the haughty cousin of Juliet, that disturbs him so. He is tempted to venture with Mercutio and Benvolio, his friends, to the festival at the house of Capulet. And Fate gets her fingers on him. He feels it, even on the threshold of the house in which he is to see that radiant presence which shall be so full of gladness for his soul. He surely saw a shadow walking before him as he entered, when he says

> " My mind misgives
> Some consequence, yet hanging in the stars,
> Shall bitterly begin his fearful date
> With this night's revels, and expire the term
> Of a despised life closed in my breast,
> By some vile forfeit of untimely death."

There, however, he sees Juliet ; and in a flash he falls pierced by her beauty.

> " Oh, she doth teach the torches to burn bright ;
> It seems she hangs upon the cheek of night
> Like a rich jewel in an Ethiope's ear,—
> Beauty too rich for use, for earth too dear.
> Did my heart love till now ? Forswear it, sight,
> For I ne'er saw true beauty till this night."

---

[1] *Cf.* A. Symons.

Tybalt, the nephew of Lady Capulet, a quarrelsome gallant, recognises the speaker as a Montague, but is restrained by Capulet himself, who, when he hears that it is Romeo, says,

> " Let him alone,
> He bears him like a portly gentleman ;
> And, to say truth, Verona brags of him
> To be a virtuous and well-governed youth."

Juliet is the only child of old Capulet, all whose hopes, beside, " the earth has swallowed." He has designed her to become the bride of Count Paris, but here she, like Romeo, falls headlong in love at sight. She moans to her nurse—

> " If he be married,
> My grave is like to be my wedding-bed."

Romeo's nature, of course, has all the while only been waiting for the spark of Juliet's eyes to set his heart aflame. Alas, it is to be but love's dream, to wither in the grey heart-breaking dawn!

The garden-scene, where Romeo, lingering within sight of his lady's lighted window, hears her sighing over his name, is like a bit of living moonlight; and the love, confessed with maidenly mingled modesty and passion, is like a voice out of the youth of the world in warm Italy.

The character of Father Laurence is drawn with a steady hand. He is the embodiment of Reason in this play of passion. It has been pointed out how delicately this picture has been drawn by the master-hand, entirely free from any bias against the Church of Rome. Herein Shakespeare infinitely transcended his original, for Brooke in his moralising preface to his poem, says—

> " A couple of unfortunate lovers, thralling themselves with unhonest desire, neglecting the authoritie and advice of parents and frendes, conferring their principall counsels with dronken gossypes and superstitious friers (the naturally fitte instruments of unchastitie) attempting all adventures of peryll for thattaynyng of their wished lust, usyng auricular confession (the key of whoredom and treason), etc."

Not alone in charity towards the Catholic faith, but in purity of innocent true elemental love, does the picture of the later poet soar above the other. With some scheme within his heart of obliterating the ancient feud through the union of these young loves, Father Laurence agrees to wed them in his cell, while he says, warningly,

> "These violent delights have violent ends,
> And in their triumph die, like fire and powder,
> Which, as they kiss, consume."

Meanwhile, Mercutio and Benvolio enter in a public place— kindly Mercutio, whose heart is like a spring of laughter and of mirth, while yet he is a true man, faithful and brave. Sudden upon them come Tybalt and others, and, while Tybalt tries to force Mercutio into a quarrel, Romeo, entering, refuses contemptuously to be drawn, meanwhile, into a conflict, which would thwart the purpose of his life. Mercutio, hurt at what seems like pusillanimity, challenges Tybalt, who, when Romeo interferes, stabs Mercutio treacherously under Romeo's arm, and flies. Sore hurt, thus, through his friendship with Romeo, he forces himself to jest about his wound.

> "No, 'tis not so deep as a well nor so wide as a church door, but it is enough,—'twill serve ! "

and so, with the joke on his lips, he is carried off to die ; and when Tybalt re-enters, insolent from his victory, Romeo, swung passionately into revenge, fights with him, till he kills the murderer of his friend.

> "For Mercutio's soul
> Is but a little way above our heads,
> Staying for thine to keep it company :
> Either thou, or I, or both, must go with him."

Such a nature as Mercutio's could scarcely escape such a death. Laughing, and with a light estimate alike of love and life, he is as ready with his sword as with his tongue, and both, with such as he, are dangerous. But one cannot help a hankering kindness for the soul that could have such a light creative fancy as made him speak thus of Mab, the fairy mid-wife, who presides at the birth of world's dreams.

> " She comes
> In shape no bigger than an agate-stone
> On the fore-finger of an alderman,
> Drawn with a team of little atomies,
> Athwart men's noses as they lie asleep ;
> .   .   .   She gallops night by night,
> Through lovers' brains, and then they dream of love ;
> O'er courtiers' knees, that dream on court'sies straight ;
> O'er lawyers' fingers, who straight dream on fees ;
> O'er ladies lips who straight on kisses dream ;
> And sometimes comes she with a tithe-pig's tail,
> Tickling a parson's nose as a' lies asleep,
> Then dreams he of another benefice ;
> Sometimes she driveth o'er a soldier's neck,
> And then dreams he of cutting foreign throats,
> Of breaches, ambuscadoes, Spanish blades,
> Of healths, five-fathom deep ; and then, anon,
> Drums in his ear, at which he starts and wakes,
> And, being thus frightened, swears a prayer or two,
> And sleeps again."

Now when, in revenge for this gay spirit's death, Romeo slays Tybalt the bully, and leaves him lying in his blood upon the street, while he flees, feeling he is fortune's fool, the prince, nobles, and citizens of all kinds enter on the scene, and Romeo is declared outlaw, and banished from the State. Naturally, to the lovers, such a sentence is fraught with harsher consequence than death itself. At first, however, Juliet, when she sees not only a kinsman slain, but all her hopes of sanction for their union, through reconciliation between the sundered families, shattered and dispelled by Romeo's violent deed, has a revulsion of hate against him.

> " O serpent heart, hid with a flowering face !
> O nature, what hadst thou to do in hell,
> When thou didst bower the spirit of a fiend
> In mortal paradise of such sweet flesh ? "

But, with the sudden alternations of a passionate soul, she plays upon another stop.

> " Ah, poor my lord, what tongue shall smoothe thy name,
> When I, thy three-hours' wife have mangled it ?
> Romeo is banished !—to speak that word
> Is father, mother, Tybalt, Romeo, Juliet,
> All slain, all dead,   Romeo is banished !—
> There is no end, no limit, measure, bound.
> In that word's death ; no words can that woe sound."

Romeo meanwhile is in hiding in the cell of Friar Laurence, and to him, also, banishment is unspeakable anguish.

> " 'Tis torture and not mercy : heaven is here,
> Where Juliet lives ! "

Into his frantic grief the nurse enters, bearing Juliet's message ; and the priest advises him to go to Mantua,

> " Where thou shalt live till we can find a time
> To blaze your marriage, reconcile your friends,
> Beg pardon of the prince, and call thee back
> With twenty hundred thousand times more joy
> Than thou wentst forth in lamentation."

Even now there is a meeting between Capulet and Paris, when the very day of the marriage of Paris and Juliet is arranged, though, under the same roof, she and Romeo are together, for it is their wedding night.

The dialogue of the lovers in the dawn is, as has been pointed out, based on the lyrical form of the ancient Morning Songs.   Juliet pleads,

> " Wilt thou be gone?   It is not yet near day :
> It was the nightingale and not the lark,
> That pierced the fearful hollow of thine ear :
> Nightly she sings on yon pomegranate-tree : "

While Romeo replies,

> " It was the lark, the herald of the morn,
> No nightingale : Look, love, what envious streaks

Do lace the severing clouds in yonder east :
Night's candles are burnt out, and jocund day
Stands tiptoe on the misty mountain tops ;
I must begone and live, or stay and die."

Then, with a tragic fore-note in their words, she says,

"O now begone ; more light and light it grows."

And he mourns,

"More light and light ; more dark and dark our woes ! "

And now the tragedy of their love deepens ; for Juliet is
to be thrust into this union which her parents have devised,
with a man whom she detests. She turns, in her distress,
to Father Laurence, who, with his knowledge of drugs
devises a way of escape. He gives her a vial which shall
clothe her with the appearance of death.

"The roses in thy lips and cheeks shall fade."

Then, being carried in an open bier to the vault of the
Capulets, she shall wait the coming of Romeo, to bear her
away from her distress. The plot works. The wedding
day of Paris is a day of lamentation, and distress, and she is
carried to the tomb.

Romeo, now in Mantua, elated with a dream of being
waked from death by Juliet's kisses, meets Balthasar his
servant, who tells him of her death which he had heard of,
and her burial which he had witnessed, ere he had left
Verona. In sudden distraction of grief he summons an
Apothecary from holiday rest, and forces him, against the
law, to sell a deadly poison. Nowhere does his impetuosity
so much cut the thread of the purposes of the stars, as when
he bids them defiance, and sets off to Verona, to his doom,
and the ruin of his love. Friar Laurence's letter with the
disclosure of his scheme having been detained, owing to the
plague, has never reached his hand, and so the tragic end
draws nigh.

Paris, whose joy had been snatched from his hand, comes, in the darkness bearing flowers to lay upon the corpse of his lost bride; but, while addressing her in melancholy verse, Romeo enters, determined to descend into the tomb; and, giving as excuse to his servant, that he goes to take a ring from the dead finger of his sleeping love. He forces the tomb open, but, while thus engaged, Paris intervenes, and in the struggle, is slain by Romeo. Then with the heart-broken cry,

> "O my love, my wife,
> Death that hath sucked the honey of thy breath
> Hath had no power yet upon thy beauty.
>   Ah, dear Juliet,
> Why art thou yet so fair?
>   O here
> Will I set up my everlasting rest,
> And shake the yoke of inauspicious stars
> From this world-wearied flesh."

He drains the draught of death, and dies besides his Juliet. And now, too late, Friar Laurence comes, finds the tomb open and the two men lying dead; while Juliet awakes from her trance, and, in an agony of grief, kills herself with Romeo's dagger. Then, soon, there is alarm running wild-eyed through the streets; and Montague and Capulet, with the Prince, arrive to read what their feud has written in the blood and sorrow of these two sweet lives; and by the open grave their hates are reconciled.

The drama is a Tragedy of the wreck of love and hope through the tyranny of human passions, and the pride of human will.

> "A greater power than we can contradict
> Hath thwarted our intents,"

confesses Friar Laurence. Beautiful as love may be, and sweet as the affections of Romeo and Juliet are, they yet allow passion to overbalance them. Excess is their sin, which displaces the centre of gravity of their universe, and topples them to disaster. The constant association with the aged nurse and her gross nature, through the proud neglect of Lady Capulet, her mother, has given an undeniably sensual bias to the love of Juliet, which, finding its counterpart in the hot nature of Romeo, draws them both blindly to gratification of appetite. He is stubborn, impetuous—all the faults of his feud-driven race meet him with his own virtues, in secret conflict which rends his soul. How near the truth was Hazlitt when he said that "Romeo is Hamlet in love." Their speedy marriage without consultation, which, indeed, considering the relations of their families, would have been fruitless of aught but recrimination and outrage, plunges them straight into the vortex of destiny. The same passionate haste has made the world of Verona too narrow for the hate of the heads of their houses, and stains the streets with the blood of Mercutio; while the unbalanced, unrestrainable spirit of Romeo which carries him headlong into his matrimonial complication, leads him to the further disastrous deaths of Tybalt and Count Paris. The tragic pathos is, that the hapless victims are entangled in the disastrous issues of the feuds of others, and the cup of love dashes to atoms, just as its full gladness, after all their pangs, was at their lips; while those others emerge out of the shattered lives and loves of their most dearly beloved, to have their eyes and hearts opened and chastened by the humbling sight of the price which destiny has asked and taken. As the Prince, who, in this cauldron of bitter brew of fate and feud, stands for ethical security and stability, remarks,

> "Where be these enemies?
> See what a scourge is laid upon your hate,
> That heaven finds means to kill your joys with love."

Love is, thus, to them all, the gladness-slayer, turning their instruments to melancholy bells, their solemn hymns to sullen dirges, and making their bridal flowers serve for a buried corse ; while, at the same time, from the grave of love, slain through their blind and stubborn selfish hate, which has driven a passion like Romeo's and Juliet's to a corner, wherein confined, it had burned out their young lives —from that very grave, and only thence, springs the humbling pain, which was the effluence of love that had not feared even to die, seeking that peace in union, somewhere, in the great vast unexplored, which no Verona ever could bestow.

"Othello" is the sorrow of love undermined, sapped, sundered, shattered by insidious devilment of spite and envy, whose pride has been hurt : but this is the pathos of love, deep, passionate and complete, leaping off the world's narrow round, because it cannot dwell in the same small House of Life with Hate !

CHAPTER XXIII

"HAMLET"

PRINCE OF DENMARK

THAT the interest in the story of Hamlet [1] was widespread is evident from the fact that the legendary material was to be found in Shakespeare's time in Saxo's chronicle, in Belleforest's French version of Bandello's Italian romance, afterwards rendered into English, in which Hamlet becomes King of Denmark, marries twice, and subsequently dies in battle; as well as in a contemporary drama, conjecturally by Kyd : while an Icelandic version, in a Saga, has also been later discovered. An old play, full of bloody revengefulness, existed also in English, as we gather from a reference by Nash ; [2] and again by Lodge,[3] who speaks of

> "the ghost which cried so miserably at the Theatre, like an oister wife, 'Hamlet—revenge!'"

For a parallel in historical circumstance Shakespeare did not need to go to Clytemnestra; for, in 1567, Mary Stuart of Scotland had been cognisant of the murder of her husband Darnley, and yet had married Bothwell, his murderer.

The magic spell of Shakespeare transfigured the old material. The cunning prince of the tale becomes a man of genius and culture, with an ever-present sense of the ideal about him, while hedged and beset by an environment of

[1] Registered 1602 : printed 1603. See Goethe's Exposition of the purpose of "Hamlet" in "Wilhelm Meister," bk. iv. chap. 13. See also Coleridge's : and Prof. Lewis Campbell's "Tragic Drama in Æschylus, Sophocles, and Shakespeare."
[2] Epistle prefixed to Greene's "Menaphon," 1589.
[3] "Wit's Miserie and the World's Madness," 1596.

fraud, suspicion, and down-right villainy. Only in the Rosencranz and Guildenstern episode, when he, by a clever substitution, transfers to them the death designed for himself, does the old craft come in.

"Hamlet" is human nature, or at least a wide range of it. Hence, probably, no two minds can ever contemplate Hamlet from exactly the same point of view, as no two men can ever regard human life under exactly the same aspect. No man who has looked into his own heart with knowledge, and with questioning of the sleepless monitor within, but must, when he looks, thereafter, into the heart of the Prince of Denmark, see his own face reflected from the shadows. So, all who have brooded with him over his perplexities, betray themselves in their discussion of him. He is each of them, and they, and all besides, see but a part of his soul.

Hamlet is a psycho-pathology. It is the sick thought-life of the hero that is the play. The whole drama, the life and destiny of all around, depend upon the inner rage and conflict of the thoughts, sentiments and passions of one character, a nature divided against itself, a soul with an internal cleavage between action and contemplation. He cannot solve the problem of evil, and it haunts his life like a questioning ghost, plucking his sleeve and demanding answers. The tragedy arises from the ruin which this enigma wreaks upon his sensitive moral nature. He tries to adjust life to his fixed ideas, to steer the world by an ideal within himself, rather than steer himself by a star that is without ; and so he moves only around his own soul's pivot, never getting beyond the shadow of himself.

Hamlet finds no real philosophy of life. He is victimised by events over which he might have conquered, had he moved at first. The contradictions of his soul within intensify the contradictions which baffle him without, and so doubt and disgust alternating demoralise his will. His own irony only deepens the irony of fate which the empty universe in which he moves holds for him.

The Queen is not imaginative like her son. She does not
see visions, nor hear the voice of repentance speaking to
her, nor can she understand her son.

> " Alas, how is't with you,
> That you do bend your eye on vacancy,
> And with the incorporal air do hold discourse ?
> .   .   .   Whereon do you look ?
> .   .   This is the very coinage of your brain,
> This bodiless creation ecstasy
> Is very cunning in."

Like Lady Macbeth, and the daughters of King Lear, she
has no shadow-sight to keep her from her sins. To her,
therefore, Hamlet is mad ; for we always judge others by
our inability either to see or not to see what they apparently
behold or dream they are beholding.

He cannot read or interpret the outward circumstances
that press upon him, nor unriddle the mingled tones stirred
in his heart by the breath of augury and dream.

> " How weary, stale, flat and unprofitable
> Seem to me all the uses of this world."

So life becomes a cloud, with rumbling voices unintelligible,
—and lightnings, without revealings or guidance of any kind.
He grows out of love with life, yet has no confidence in the
great conjecture over which meanwhile he broods. He is a
man in a darkened place, entangled in the threads of countless circumstances which have neither meaning nor intent
clearly seen by him. He has lost the hand of purpose, if he
ever held it fast ; and then he begins to question if it ever
had been there. Hope, with him, is always having her
candle blown out by Mistrust. When he resolves to do his
great intent, he asks himself so often if it be enough, that
it never becomes aught. He is a soul doubled-back upon
itself in interrogation of a question to which no answer can
be found.

The King, Polonius, and the Queen all try to probe the
mystery of Hamlet's gloomy and distracted conduct. Polonius

thinks it is love for Ophelia, but the Queen's conscience suddenly hits the mark with true womanly quickness,—

" His father's death, and our o'erhasty marriage."

Lear's passion, the humour of the melancholy Jacques, the entanglement of Othello's soul, are all found in Hamlet. The old Greek cry seems thrilling over him, the wail as in the " Agamemnon," over Cassandra, the wail that embittered Euripides,—" Knowledge is grief." Not madness, but pain, through vision of the soul itself, is Hamlet's sorrow. Melancholy, which has exiled all lightness of heart, has also crushed all impulses of action, and bound his spirit in listless misery. The still waters have lost their music : the green pastures of the soul are buried underneath volcanic dust and now are sterile wastes.

" I have of late, but wherefore I know not,—lost all my mirth, forgone all customs of exercises. . . .
. . . What a piece of work is a man,—how noble in reason, how infinite in faculty.
And yet to me, what is this quintessence of dust ? man delights not me."

He is not mad. He is never irresponsible for word or deed, and his reflections and ironies alike have wisdom of the deepest in them, although steeped in bitter gall of his own heart. Indeed, at the offset, he resolves to ape madness, and he swears his friends to secrecy regarding his intent.

" How strange or odd so'er I bear myself,
As I perchance hereafter shall think meet,
To put an antic disposition on."

And this he does, at first, not to protect himself, as in the older story, from the hate of the King, but to conceal his suspicious and revengeful gloom. Yet, by this very artifice, he risked failure of his purpose, for he might have been confined, as indeed the King seemed to devise after the death of Polonius, when he says,

" His liberty is full of threats to all.
How dangerous is it that this man goes loose."

Yet when more and more he sees the aim of his life flicker from the reach of his vacillating purpose, there are times when madness gives his heart a wrench, as though to remind him she is waiting there, having heard his summons.

His motives, like flickering spectres, hamper his purpose of revenge continually. He has no clear proof of the blood-guiltiness of the King, nor is he of a truculent nature, and so he holds continual inquest in his heart.

The theme of " Hamlet " at once suggests a comparison with the tragic cycle of the Atreidæ. Revenge for a king and father murdered through a queen's unfaithfulness, haunts a prince in both, like a shadow. But the later play has the greater gentleness of a Christian time over it. He is to be no parricide,' though, perhaps, had his blood been ripened under southern suns, he had become Orestes.

> " Soft, now, to my mother ;
> O heart, lose not thy nature ; let not ever
> The soul of Nero enter this firm bosom ;
> Let me be cruel, not unnatural :
> I will speak daggers to her, but use none ; "

and yet the Queen is not charged with the murder, not even with foreknowledge of it. She is even saved, by the special pleading of her husband's ghost, from the vengeance of her son.

Again, in the old myth-cycle, Orestes from his childhood is set apart, practically consecrated to revenge. Electra, his sister, schools him in his terrible task, which involves nothing less than the murder of their mother, as well as the death of the usurper, her paramour. And though he shrinks from the awful lifting of the sword against Clytemnestra, pleading as she does her motherhood to this vengeful son, not till the blood of his mother is on his hands are the sorrows of conscience awoke. In " Hamlet," however, conscience sits on the threshold of action, and stretches out restraining hands against the brooding heart of the unfortunate prince of Denmark.

The tragic soul, in ancient Drama, was he who broke out into rashness of action, for which he earned the judgment of the gods, but here, in " Hamlet," that for which he suffers is the nerve-shaking soul-confusing delay in taking up the punishment which is at once his task and his cross.   Thus he promises the ghost that he will obey his behest.

> " Haste me to know't, that I, with wings as swift
> As Meditation or the thoughts of love,
> May sweep to my revenge,"

and then, what is laid upon him makes him cry aloud in self-pitying agony,

> " The time is out of joint : O cursed spite !
> That ever I was born to set it right."

The delay in Hamlet's task makes him, like Orestes, begin to wonder whether it might not be a fiend that has spoken in the sacred image of his father, a thought which finds suggestion in Horatio's words—

> " What if it tempt you toward the flood, my lord,
> Or to the dreadful summit of the cliff,
> That beetles o'er his base into the sea,
> And there assume some other horrible form,
> Which might deprive your sovereignty of reason
> And draw you into madness ?   Think of it :
> The very place puts toys of desperation,
> Without more motive, into every brain
> That looks so many fathoms to the sea
> And hears it roar beneath."

Indeed, if Hamlet had had as much faith in the ghost as Macbeth had in the Weird Sisters, he would have had his blade red with his uncle's life's blood without further question.[1]

And yet Hamlet's delay only drags more doom upon the persons of the play, causing the death of Polonius, the feud of Laertes, the death of poor Ophelia, and finally of himself.

[1] See Bucknill, " The Mad Folks of Shakespeare."

He is at last moved to action by the clatter of Fortinbras on
his way to war.

> " How stand I then,
> That have a father killed, a mother stained,
> Excitements of my reason and my blood,
> And let all sleep ? while, to my shame, I see
> The imminent death of twenty thousand men,
> That for a fantasy and trick of fame
> Go to their graves like beds."

It is the Tragedy of filial love in a corrupt, unlovely world
of hollow treachery. Deepest compassion is roused within
us by the sight of his "might-have-been." And yet he is
passionate withal. Though not easily kindled he has then,
when the flame is up, "something dangerous within him."
He is angry, too, with the false culture of his age, while yet
he has himself cultured skill as an actor, veiling his feelings
with masterly control after his interview with the ghost.
At last, from fear of an unwarranted crime, he turns to
suicide as an alternative, but even that door he finds barred
against him by a great grim shadow of uncertainty. That
thought wakes within him conflict between religious belief
and desire of self destruction. The fear of future punishment stands like a dark angel by the door, till the sense of
brave duty masters the fear of mortal discomforts.

> " To die, to sleep ;
> To sleep : perchance to dream—ay, there's the rub ;
> For in that sleep of death what dreams may come
> When we have shuffled off this mortal coil,
> Must give us pause. . . .
> . . . the dread of something after death,
> The undiscovered country from whose bourn
> No traveller returns, puzzles the will,
> And makes us rather bear those ills we have
> Than fly to others that we know not of."

In Hamlet's introspection he grows fastidious. He sees,
apparently at prayers, the guilty king within whose soul the
deep sting of remorse is moving too late.

"A brother's murder!　Pray can I not,
Though inclination be as sharp as will :
My stronger guilt defeats my strong intent ;
And like a man to double business bound,
I stand in pause where I shall first begin,
And both neglect.　What if this cursed hand,
Were thicker than itself with brother's blood,—
Is there not rain enough in the sweet heavens
To wash it white as snow ?　Whereto serves mercy ?
. . . . What then ? what rests ?
Try what repentance can : what can it not ?
Yet, what can it, when one can not repent ?
O wretched state,—O bosom black as death."

The play which is designed to convict the King stirs
Hamlet's own purpose the deeper.　The King's guilt is clear,
and yet we see him also, like Hamlet, wavering between his
sin and its repentance, as Hamlet sways between his grief
and his revenge.　The red hand from which no dews of
heaven shall ever wash the stain,—what a thought for a sin-
ruined soul!　How it marks the page of "Macbeth."　How
it incarnadines the passion of Orestes.　How it shakes the
throne of Denmark!

Hamlet cannot slay him on his knees, for what if he slay
him in an holy act?

"Now might I do it pat, now he is praying,
And now I'll do't.　And so he goes to heaven ;
A villain kills my father : and for that
I, his sole son, do this same villain send
To heaven. . . .
O, this is hire and salary, not revenge."

And so he turns away and will not, when he could, so easily,
complete his purpose.　And yet the King rises from his knees
with the confession that he has been, all the while, unable
to pray !

But, he has not always been a failure, " sicklied o'er with
the pale cast of thought," for we find how heartily he greets
his friend Horatio from his old University of Wittenberg.
He speaks cheerily to the players, and he talks happily of

the old, glad, jocund days with Yorick.   Nor does speculation always hold him.   In the momentary flash, thinking it is the King behind the arras, he whips out his sword and slays Polonius, the miserable chattering courtier, eavesdropper, " Worldly-Wiseman." He thus, through his passionate nature, clasps the chain of destiny upon himself.   For Laertes, the son of the murdered man, no fine philosophising soul like Hamlet, speeds home from Paris to Denmark to wreak vengeance on his father's murderer.   There will be no hesitation in the execution of the young courtier's resolve. His is a bitter heart.   To make assurance doubly sure, he poisons his rapier, and enters into whispering plots with the King against Hamlet.   For he has now a somewhat parallel case upon his shoulders,—to revenge also a murdered father is his duty.   Only he will do it, and speedily, too.

Horatio is the one true friend that Hamlet has, — the Pylades who yet does not urge him on to the completion of the blood-feud of revenge.   But even this true friend does not understand him.   He has not Hamlet's windows; he can neither see into Hamlet's soul, nor can he look upon the world with Hamlet's eyes.   He is free from superstition, and is only a believer at sight.

> " Horatio says 'tis but our fantasy,
> And will not let belief take hold of him,
> Touching this dreadful sight twice seen of us."

When the ghost is passing away, he tries to stay it with his partisan, and challenges it like Banquo.   He is, indeed, a representative sceptic of the Renaissance epoch, one of those

> " Whose blood and judgment are so well commingled,
> That they are not a pipe for fortune's finger,
> To sound what stop she please.
> Not passion's slave."

Laertes is a fiery courtier of the times, with a strong dash of the sententious manner of his father.   This especially comes out in his advice to his sister Ophelia, where he warns her of the risk of giving her heart to Hamlet, pointing out the disparity of rank between them.

> " He himself is subject to his birth :
> He may not, as unvalued persons do,
> Carve for himself.
> Then weigh what loss your honour may sustain
> If with too credent ear you list his songs,
> Or lose your heart, or your chaste treasure open
> To his unmaster'd importunity.
> Fear it, Ophelia, fear it, my dear sister."

The father himself repeats the advice.

> " Lord Hamlet is a prince, out of thy star ;
> This must not be."

Polonius, his father, has evidently bequeathed, also, some elements of his cunning, for the son of this whisperer and keyhole-listener does not hesitate to stoop to arrant treachery in sword-poisoning lest Hamlet escape his rage. But heaven is just, and the poisoned blade and poisoned chalice, alike, recoil on the villainy that employs them. No small blame for the sneering attitude of Hamlet towards Ophelia, which helped to break her heart and craze her brain, could be laid at the door of that same craftiness which employed her as an unwitting instrument in the plots against the prince, of complicity in which he assuredly suspected her. Whatever may have been Hamlet's real feelings towards her, there is not any doubt but that the sweet sad maiden loved him deeply. Her cry on beholding him so distraught proved that much anyhow.

> " O what a noble mind is here o'erthrown,
> Like sweet bells jangled, out of tune and harsh."

His conduct towards her sometimes seems inexplicable, and arose undoubtedly from mixed reasons, probably first of all because he saw the whispering partisanship of her family with the murderess of his father, and last of all because the

Revenger of blood must always tear out of his heart all trivial fond record of foolish love. Take his own word for it —

> " I loved Ophelia : forty thousand brothers
> Could not with all their quantity of love
> Make up my sum."

But Love and Revenge cannot ever dwell together in the narrow house of one human heart.

The scene in the graveyard is as tragic as any, recalling the memory of happy days, when Yorick kept the table on a roar, even amid all the awful symbols of the worthlessness of human ambitions. His jesting is not frivolity. Many a man has stepped from Time's narrow platform with a jest upon his lips. Acutest grief has often its own laughter when the heart has lost its power of tears. In the midst of it, the bier of hapless dead Ophelia is carried in. The priests forbid the full obsequies, as "her death was doubtful ": and there is a direct thrust at the harsh dogmas of the church, when they declare the funeral must be

> " With maimed rites.
> We should profane the service of the dead
> To sing a requiem and such rest to her
> As to peace-parted souls."

Laertes' indignant protest spoke the spirit of the time,—

> " Lay her i' the earth :
> And from her fair and unpolluted flesh
> May violets spring : I tell thee, churlish priest,
> A ministering angel shall my sister be,
> When thou liest howling."

No, this man is not mad. He has seen the shadow behind life's shoulder, and laughter loses its mirth in the sight. There is only one door of escape ; but who knows what is within the darkened room it guards? He has lowered the bucket into self-consciousness, and realised what a deep well he has discovered in his heart. He is torn between the highest moral duty, and the crime of murder, of that kind anciently nicknamed "justice." It is no slight dilemma. Shall he himself slay the paramour mother, or prove Claudius to be the assassin of the king, and have him, by the laws which steady and protect society, dragged from the high place he has usurped? This latter drifts away from the grasp of possibility, and he has to draw the whole universe down about his ears in an act which sends his soul out into the infinite, about whose verges he has for so long been knocking, while, at the same time, he does catch Claudius in what has "no relish of salvation" in it, and drives him before himself to judgment.

And so he leaves his mystery unrevealed, and lives forever with the shadow brooding over him.

> " O good Horatio ! what a wounded name,
> Things standing thus unknown, shall live behind me ! "

CHAPTER XXIV

"OTHELLO"

"OTHELLO"[1] is a study of the desolating power of sheer, callous, calculating wickedness of nature. It is the Tragedy of Iago—a human devil far worse than any playwright's Mephistopheles, ruining a strong emotional soul filled with love's fire. One must beware of interpreting the plays of such a universal master of the human spirit as Shakespeare, as being simply cinematographs of single passions in operation. Shakespeare did not sit down to write ethical exercises. He set before him the task of reproduction of life and character, and what these signify.

The low passion of jealousy, so much more nearly allied to Comedy, is here made a means and instrument of the most terrific tragic power, entirely obliterating and slaying the sweetest emotions of life, and making what might be an idyl of tenderest beauty a dreadful dream of horror.

The novel of Cinthio[2] sets, in bare sententious phrase its purpose in Desdemona's words—"to serve as a warning to young maidens not to marry against the will of their parents, nor an Italian girl to marry a man alien to her race." How far the tragedy of Shakespeare transcends those crude beginnings and materials is evident to all who know the play. The leading character, or rather he who gives his name to the Tragedy, is a Moor, with royal blood within him,

---

[1] Date unknown,—probably about 1604. From entry in Record Office it would appear to have been produced in the autumn of 1605. In April 1610 it was acted before Prince Ludwig Friedrich of Wurttemburg. (Diary of his Secretary.) First printed in the quarto of 1622; again in folio of 1623.
[2] Cinthio's Collection, Decade 3, Novel 7, Ferrara 1565.

yet with a stain upon his birth. He is a Christian, and an adopted son of the Venetian Republic, and has shown his devotion to the land of his adoption in battles and campaignings. He knows little of the civil usages of men, as his life has been a conflict with opposing conditions; but now he has won a position in the State as a leader trusted and esteemed.[1] Yet, naturally, he has made enemies; for envy stalks at the footsteps of a man like him. He is, besides, credulous. Even Iago says of him,

> "The Moor is of a free and open nature,
> That thinks men honest that but seem to be so,"—

simple and imaginative; and yet his marvels which he narrates to the council, and Desdemona, are no more incredible on the face of them than those told in books of travel contemporaneous with Shakespeare himself. Undoubtedly he does love Desdemona, passionately,—excessively, somewhat. No greater slander can be perpetrated than to make him seem to pluck all at once the mask of gentleness and civilised conduct from his soul, and unveil the real savage that all the while was being kept by a master hand in subjection or obscurity. Such access of fury is not peculiarly the possession of a Moor. Men everywhere in paroxysms of jealousy, in disappointed love, have been driven full blast into direst murder,—but only when, like Othello, they are no longer, even the least, themselves,—changed to the foundation of their being, and with no fibre of their former selves remaining uncontaminated, unwarped, unwounded. No wonder Desdemona complains.

> "My lord is not my lord, nor shall I know him,
> Were he in favour as in humour altered."

And the Ambassador wondered when rage made Othello strike his lady to the earth in his presence. Is this the man

---

[1] Lest any of their leading citizens should use the soldiery for their own factions, it was customary for the Italian Free Cities to appoint to command over these, a vigorous stranger, alien to their parties and inured to war.

whom passion could not shake? He has mastered so far
the hot impetuous fire of his dark blood, which, in such as
he, is so apt to blind him to everything but his rage when
that is kindled. Still, he is sufficiently the child of his race,
circumstances, and environment, to be all the more a fit
instrument for the most hellish experiments at the hands of
an incarnate fiend like Iago.

Desdemona, quiet, pliable, affectionate, inexperienced,
clinging, and blind to risk, has seen and heard him. And
this great dark man, burned by the skies of dangerous
campaigns, catches her interest and her heart; and there
begins the first entanglement with fate. They wed without
her aged father's knowledge or consent, and so involve themselves in the father's displeasure, and an involuntary curse.
Nay more,—by her marriage with this alien she awoke the
whisper of all in Venice, and many a prophecy of evil would
follow them over the sea—many a headshaking, "I told you
so!" welcome the tidings of the wreck of a young fair life,
and a brave soldier's possibilities, while the true story would
be listened to with a condescending smile, "no doubt! no
doubt! but yet"—

> "O the pity of it, Iago!"

The simplicity of his upstanding defence before the Council,
when Desdemona's father lays his complaint against him,
wins all hearts; but Brabantio leaves the first sting in
Othello's soul, though unintended, when he says,

> "Look to her, Moor, if thou hast eyes to see,
> She hath deceived her father, and may thee."

This is the first cinder that sets fire to his nature, though
the fire smoulder till it is fanned by the human devil of the
play.

Iago!—Judas never touched so deep a bottom of deceit
as he! His soul is damned and blighted by cruelest envy;
but this is a malicious activity which rejoices in beholding

the hurt it inflicts on others. He is slighted ambition, sowing tares and trampling down all blossom and all beauty, all that makes gladness, as he sows. Sowing, moreover, only because hearts have been happy in the garden which he so wantonly destroys! He has desired to be Othello's lieutenant; and the tragedy opens with his complaint finding voice to his friend Roderigo—"I know my price. I am worth no worse a place." He argues falsehood with his own soul in order to make himself seem justified against Othello. He asserts, though he knows that it is untrue, that he suspects himself to be cuckolded by Othello. He displays throughout a mean gross mind. He is a low wily Italian, whose soul is as treacherous as the stiletto of his race. He is, besides, doubly dangerous, for he wears a clever mask,— the mask of rugged, plain speech, independent, according to himself, of the carping word or detracting thought of others. He is that most dangerous of all hypocrites,—the false out-spoken friend; and on that line he utterly deludes Othello, with whom it is always—" Iago is most honest."

> " This fellow's of exceeding honesty,
> And knows all qualities, with a learned spirit,
> Of human dealings."

His evil is a coldly directed thing, with the purpose of deliberate pain in it.[1] He must see his victim squirm, as he thrusts, with a smile, the bitter shaft home to the heart.

The action in the play presses on, like a prairie fire, to destruction. The plot steadily pushes to its crescendo, each step being a stride towards the next. Having been, as he feels, slighted by Othello in the appointment of Cassio as lieutenant, he designs to overthrow Cassio, and to work out upon Othello utter ruin of happiness in his love and in his life. His methods display him as a composite of personal jealousy, envy of rank, crude ambition, and bloodcurdling spite. He is always breathing honest, candid counsel to his

---

[1] Coleridge calls it " the motive-hunting of a motiveless malignity."

victims, and then, he blames the issue of it on the very
simplicity of their deeds. What strikes one very strongly
is the blindness of those to the true nature of the man.
And when, at last, all his villainy is laid bare, he knows no
repentance. He shuts his mouth,—he will reveal nothing,
and no confession or regret will ever knock for him at
heaven's door. He knows both good and evil well, but the
good only to do harm with it. He should have been
hanged early on the poison-tree of knowledge, whose fruit
he had so deeply tasted.

His wife Emilia is a simple common woman, an instrument
pliable in his hands, yet even she never truly knowing the
abysmal villainy of her husband. When she does discover
what a desolating horror he has wrought, she rises to the
dignity of true brave womanhood, and will not be silenced
by his threats, until, by a mean secret stroke, he slays her.

He first bleeds Roderigo,[1] a poor immoral, uncontrolled
creature, of money, for gifts, which he pretends he sends to
Desdemona; and he holds Roderigo bound to his foot by
the sensual love that poor creature feels towards her. Then,
when he has sucked him dry, he gets rid of him by
involving him in the plot against the life of Cassio, in which
Roderigo, being wounded, is despatched by Iago's hand in
pretended ignorance. Then, having got Cassio cozened into
a display of drunkenness and riot, and so led into disgrace
and dismissal from office, he sets the lieutenant to sue
Desdemona's good graces with her lord for his restoration.
All his cards take a trick, as he himself well knows,—revealing
in one of his soliloquies an intimate acquaintance also with
himself,

> "Whiles this honest fool
> Plies Desdemona to repair his fortunes,
> And she for him pleads strongly to the Moor,
> I'll pour this pestilence into his ear,

---

[1] Roderigo is not only Iago's, but, in Dryden's masterly phrase, God Almighty's
fool. And Shakespeare shows the poor devil no more mercy than Iago or than God.
—SWINBURNE.

> That she repeals him for her body's lust ;
> And by how much she strives to do him good
> She shall undo her credit with the Moor,
> So will I turn her virtue into pitch
> And out of her own goodness make the net
> That shall enmesh them all."

Next he sets to work with Othello, rousing suspicion over Cassio's interviews with the hapless woman, who in her innocence is always pleading with her husband for Cassio.

It is wonderful, the hypocrisy of the man, who, like Polonius, gives utterance to maxims of moral beauty so opposed to his own practice. It is this sink of duplicity that pleads, even while he is laying his nets with smiles,

> " Good name in man and woman, dear, my lord,
> Is the immediate jewel of their souls."

How cleverly too he sets the slow fire surely burning in Othello's heart, which by and by will blaze till it leave his life a blackened ruin. Mark the subtle sowing of the seed of hell. He names the thing that every lover fears, and then, having poisoned the soul's sight, prepares it to see evil everywhere.

> " Beware, my lord of jealousy,
> It is the green-eyed monster which doth mock
> The meat it feeds on. . . .
> . . . I speak not yet of proof.
> Look to your wife ; observe her well with Cassio."

Then, how he weaves circumstances together, filching the handkerchief, her first remembrance of the Moor, so highly valued by him as a token of his love, to be lost in Cassio's room ; and how he loves to see his vile work giving signs of growing.

Look, where he comes, sneers he,

> " Not poppy, nor mandragora,
> Not all the drowsy syrups of the world
> Shall ever medicine thee to that sweet sleep
> Which thou owedst yesterday ! "

For Othello now is torn by the pangs of the subtle poison working in his soul. He is divided between doubt and fear, and yet is not satisfied to trust the love of Desdemona.

> " By the world,
> I think my wife be honest and think she is not ;
> I think that thou art just and think thou art not.
> I'll have some proof. Her name, that was as fresh
> As Dian's visage is now begrimed and black
> As mine own face."

The very jokes of the clown only intensify the tragedy of poor Desdemona, sealing her doom all unwittingly with the oft-reiterated name of Cassio.

"My heart," cries Othello, "is turned to stone. I strike it and it hurts my hand." Othello believing that honour is gone, feels that all is gone.

> " Farewell the plumed troops, and the big wars
> That make ambition virtue.
> Pride, pomp and circumstance of glorious war,
> Farewell,—Othello's occupation's gone."

The mainspring of his life is broken. His heart can move no more, if he be put to shame. Then the Satan of the play plants in his hot brain the whisper, "Strangle her in her bed!" and leaves it to hell to make the seed grow there! Othello is convinced,—

> " And yet she'll kneel and pray ;
> I've seen her do it."

Then, maddened, he strikes her before the Venetian Ambassador.

The close comes swiftly, but, like a tropical night, plunged altogether into black, sudden darkness. There can be no greater pathos than the presentiment of Desdemona, as Emilia unconsciously prepares her for her goodbye to the world. It is almost too harrowing, dragging the soul through depths of tragic pain.

> " My mother had a maid called Barbara.
> She was in love, and he she loved proved mad,

> And did forsake her: she had a song of ' willow.'
> An old thing 'twas, but it expressed her fortune,
> And she died singing it: that song to-night
> Will not go from my mind; I have much to do
> But to go hang my head all at one side
> And sing it like poor Barbara! "

And then the horrid deed is done; and the blinded soul by its own act cancels bliss forever. His cry to his murdered wife surely wrung pity from the spheres.

> " Oh, ill-starred wench,
> Pale as thy smock,—when we shall meet at compt
> This look of thine will hurl my soul from heaven
> And fiends will snatch at it."

Othello's nature is not overdrawn. He is no match for the devil that destroys him; and he is slowly but surely hardened and degraded, till he can see no goodness even in the soul of good. Iago, by his skilful but fatal insinuations of evil, sensual, lowering thought, and lustful images, drives all generosity and purity from Othello's heart, and leaves love lying naked, unpitied, stark-dead, degraded, there. He cannot see beyond one thing—the honour that was so dear to him, now made him a thing for finger-pointing scorn. A sacrifice is needed, and she who, he believes, has betrayed what was dearer to him than himself, must die.

Though Shakespeare does not purposely make it so, yet in the Tragedy one feels something like atonement and retribution. The unhappiness which is a recoil from happiness that has been won at the cost of others, the grey hairs and broken heart of Brabantio, have the tragic pain laid whimpering at the doorway of doom. But the malicious envy that has wrought all the woe for its selfish ends, dies, justly slain by the edge of its own poignard, which, it forgot, could cut even the hand that used it for the hurt of others. Iago's duplicity and villainy exposed, means to him loss of all he had wished for. Even the sad ship-wrecked honour of Desdemona is rehabilitated, and Othello's madness made most deeply pitiable, and pathetic. Iago drops the mask. The plaster, and the fresco on it, come down with a clatter, and the lath stands bare, dismantled. Iago is found out, and is henceforward naked and not ashamed.

It is the tragedy of prurient curiosity, the unhallowed inquisitiveness of the nature of Œdipus, which will not suffer the happiness it enjoys to be disturbed, and will not master and repel the promptings and questionings of the doubts within, implanted and kept sleepless by malignity. So little would have set the music right again,—so little made the crooked straight once more, but Passion rends the chords, and Jealousy blinds all ways but the way to headlong ruin and eternal grief. Amongst the works of men born of women, nothing that touches so deep a depth as this has ever seen the world.

CHAPTER XXV

" KING LEAR "

In the great drama of "King Lear,"[1] Shakespeare lifts us into the region of such tragic presences as Œdipus of old. Œdipus was of a nature keen for power and dominion; and, by his impetuous actions and passionate soul, made himself a mere implement in the hands of the gods, whose judgments were roused against his father's house. Lear, on the other hand, a proud, imperious monarch, has allowed his three daughters to become spoiled children, with a love and ambition for worldly possessions, which finally overmaster any affection they may have had for their father. It is a drama in which we find, as the moving tragic potency, a threefold impiety, namely, rebellion and treason of brother against brother, of children against parent, and parents against their children.

As old age creeps over Lear, what had, in his earlier manhood, been a dignified majesty of kingship, becomes a wanton, impassioned, half-blind dotage, guided and impelled by whim and fancy.

Shakespeare, knowing that he is to set upon the stage such a Tragedy of blind ingratitude, and impious negation of the most sacred human duties, sets the action in an epoch

---

[1] Lear first appears in English literature in Geoffrey of Monmouth's "History of British Kings," about 1147. According to Geoffrey, Bladud the father of Lear, was a man of great genius and magical inventiveness, who succeeded wonderfully till he tried to fly, when he fell and was dashed to pieces on the Temple of Apollo, where St Paul's Cathedral now stands. Lear succeeded, and the substance of the tale as come to us, is given in Geoffrey's Chronicle and in the French and English rhyming versions thereof by Wace and Layamon

far remote from Christian times,[1] in a prehistoric age of Britain, but he dipped his pen in the gall of his own heart. He knew what he wrote of. Every man who rises like a star out of obscurity, through jealousies of mean contemporaries, knows what Lear most deeply signifies.

Again, as in " Macbeth," he is indebted to Holinshed for the weird old tale. The story had been told, first in Latin, by Geoffrey of Monmouth, and first in English by Layamon in the " Brut," about 1205. It carries the Celtic glamour of its Welsh origin with it. It is dealt with, too, in Sackville's " Mirrour for Magistrates,"[2] in Spenser's " Faerie Queen,"[3] and in a Ballad to be found in Percy's " Reliques," probably of later date than the play. It had also been treated in an old chronicle play of " King Leir,"[4] but in this drama of a simpler art than Shakespeare's, Cordelia and her father triumph over the vindictive cruelty of the wicked sisters. Such an ending was, at the time of the Restoration, considered more humane, and Shakespeare's Tragedy was actually rewritten, and concluded with joy-bells ringing. But the Master gave, towards the mighty culminating revelation of the gods and their judgment upon human sins and passions, the bigger interpretation of the tragic message of his whole soul's experience, as he had read it in the deep well of destiny, somewhere at the back of human life. The questioning spirit of Hamlet runs here like a maenad through the quiet places, calling mad echoes out of startled hearts.

The opening scene has been condemned and carped at by many critics, who, unfortunately for their criticism, have never themselves written as great a scene in any of their works. The King, desiring relief from the burdens of kingship, and of his wide dominions, proclaims that he

---

[1] According to Holinshed, Lear reigned in Britain contemporary with Joash in Juda. Cordelia reinstates her father on his throne, where he rules for two years longer, when she succeeds him in the year 54 before the building of Rome, Uzziah then reigning in Judah, and Jeroboam in Israel.

[2] 1563 [3] 1589

[4] 1593-4. See Analysis of this old and interesting play in Morley's " English Writers," vol. xi. p. 64.

intends to surrender to each of his three daughters a portion
thereof, according as their love to him is known.

> " 'Tis our fast intent
> To shake all cares and business from our age :
> Conferring them on younger strengths, while we
> Unburthened crawl toward death."

His daughters Goneril, wife of the Duke of Albany, and
Regan, wife of the Duke of Cornwall, have a fluency of
flattering sycophancy not possessed by the deeper-souled
Cordelia, who is his favourite. Her love is richer than her
vocabulary, while they can well express their affection for
their father, remembering the wage it brings. She can but
love, and be silent. She pleads as her excuse the depth and
strength of her truth, and Lear, in rage, exclaims,

> "Thy truth then be thy dower!"

He next, in hasty passion, pours denunciation on her for her
fancied coldness and untenderness.

> " I disclaim all my paternal care
> Propinquity and property of blood,
> And as a stranger to my heart and me
> Hold thee, from this, for ever."

So he invests the other two with Cordelia's portion, only with
this condition,—that he shall, monthly, with one hundred
knights, be maintained alternately in state by them. In vain
Kent pleads for Cordelia, that those are not empty-hearted

> " whose low sound
> Reverbs no hollowness."

The old King, in whom the whim of madness is already
beginning to quicken, will bear no argument.

Burgundy and France enter, the former being suitor for
the hand of Cordelia, now dowered with the father's curse,
and strangered with his oath. Burgundy shrinks, and turns
away from a bride "untochered," but the King of France,
stirred to the depths of his nature by the revelation of her

greatness, leaps to her side and takes her as his Queen. And now the tragic cross-currents and contending tides begin their play, and the Tragedy becomes a drama of treason within treason in palaces, and kingship mad and homeless on the empty moor.

The characters which are depicted in this play are drawn with power unequalled anywhere, but all subordinated, with a master skill, to that of the protagonist Lear himself.

In Lear, as in Œdipus, we seem to find a human weak creature, spoiled by greatness of position and power, led into tempting the gods.[1] His folly proceeds to its culmination in rapid strides. As in Œdipus, he becomes blind, in his own craze, to all around him. He banishes Kent, his most faithful noble; and drives away Cordelia, the one who loves him most; nor, when Goneril even rouses her servants to rebellion against him, can he see that she and Regan stand upon the same platform. He thus is driven out to a roused and angered Nature, in the storm, on the unsheltered moor, to herd in the straw-strewn, filthy hovel, with the outcast, and the crazed, himself as mad "as the vexed sea singing aloud." And sadder still, he has the tragic revelation given him of his cruel folly, when he finds that she, whom he had hurled from his love, and from her rights, was, after all, his true blessing, and his redeeming angel of sweet peace. What heart does not beat towards breaking to read his waking words beholding her?

> "You do me wrong to take me out o' the grave.
> Thou art a soul in bliss: but I am bound
> Upon a wheel of fire that mine own tears
> Do scald like molten lead.
>
> .   .   .   .   .
>
> You are a spirit, I know: when did you die?

---

[1] Shakespeare's kings are not, nor are meant to be, great men—rather, little or quite ordinary humanity, thrust upon greatness, with those pathetic results, the natural self-pity of the weak heightened in them, into irresistible appeal to others as the nett result of their royal prerogative. One after another they seem to lie, composed in Shakespeare's embalming pages, with just that touch of nature about them making the whole world akin.—WALTER PATER.

> Pray do not mock me.
> I am a very foolish fond old man,
> Fourscore and upward, not an hour more nor less,
> And, to deal plainly,
> I fear I am not in my perfect mind.
> I know you do not love me, for your sisters
> Have, as I do remember, done me wrong.
> You have some cause: they have not."

And, when, through the bloody treachery of Edmund and Goneril, the exquisite Cordelia has been murdered, the Tragedy rises to the point of absolute voiceless horror, when Lear, frenzied with madness and grief, staggers upon the stage with her dead body in his arms, and the old heart breaks at last in twain, with the piteous cry,

> "Thou'lt come no more
> Never,—never,—never,—never,—never!"—

Death then, like a great Physician, enters on his grief, and gives him peace. We feel intensely that the broken words of Kent are true.

> "Vex not his ghost. O let him pass. He hates him
> That would, upon the rack of this tough world,
> Stretch him out longer."

The dead march leads his worn-out body forth to its long needed rest, holding the audience, much as it might have done on the hillside of some city in ancient Greece.

The character probably of most intense tragic interest, next to Lear, is Edmund, the bastard son of Gloucester,[1] whose baser nature struggles with his better spirit, having seen, as in a dream, the cup of ambition near his hand for the draining. A nature like this stands in close relation to Macbeth and his lady, especially the latter; for Edmund has none of the compunction which made the Thane of Cawdor shrink from deeds of horror for ambition's sake. He has also in him the cold and clammy, selfish, calculating, blood-

---

[1] The story of Gloucester is taken as supplement to the tale of Lear, from Sidney's "Arcadia," which had been published twenty years before.

curdling logic of treason, the power of insidious poisoning of soul, so characteristic of Iago. His evil spirit drags down gloom on many. It means the blinding of his father Gloucester, the exile and misery of Edgar, the death of Cornwall, the defeat of the forces of France, the dastardly murder of Cordelia, and finally his own death. His father Gloucester is full of superstitious explanations of things. He feels "the times are out of joint," because Nature is off her balance. He blames the eclipses and disturbance of the planets for all that otherwise he cannot see and comprehend. These reference would be quite plain to the understanding of the time, which recollected the great eclipses of October 1605, followed by the Gunpowder Plot of the ensuing month. But Edmund has no superstition, allows no shadow to come between him and the glory of the heights towards which ambition beckons him. He is too conscious of his own strength for that. Nor is he quite a hypocrite, except to Edgar and his father; but he succeeds in ousting both of these from their legal title and possessions; and, having done so, he looks further, and tries to secure the heritage and kingdom of Lear's family through the lust of Lear's daughters, to both of whom at once he secretly betroths himself.

Gloucester, is a beautiful figure, of humble fidelity and noble troth. He does not fear to protest against the cruelty of Lear's treatment at his daughters' hands.

> " If wolves had at thy gate howl'd that stern time
> Thou should'st have said, Good porter turn the key,
> All cruels else subscribed : but I shall see
> The winged vengeance overtake such children."

He himself, at last, blinded, impoverished and outcast, recognises in his catastrophe the act of God as punishment for his own old unclean half-forgotten sin, of which Edmund was the fruit, and which was, still, not only unrepented of, but remembered with unpleasant mirth.

As Edgar puts it to Edmund—

> "The gods are just, and of our pleasant vices
> Make instruments to plague us:
> The dark and vicious place where thee he got
> Cost him his eyes."

The character of Edgar is unsuspicious, and, through the very candour of its nature, gets him into positions of the most tremendous risks. Finally it makes him, through the skilful manipulation of circumstances, at the hand of Edmund his bastard brother, an exile from society and home, saving his life only through disguise. At first, one is driven to think of Hamlet, that other son upon whose head, in similarly disordered times and circumstances, the duty of revenge for a father's wrongs had fallen; but Edgar's is not that vacillating nature which will not readily respond in action to the promptings of an outraged soul. His is the character of a genius, ready and clever, Protean, indeed, in its cleverness and resource; as, when, by pretended madness and bedlamitism he succeeds in masking himself beyond discovery even by his father. We find from his mutterings, what temptations his flight had dragged him through—

> "The foul fiend [1] hath led through fire and through flame and through ford and whirlpool, o'er bog and quagmire; hath laid knives under his pillow, and halters in his pew; set ratsbane by his porridge; made him proud of heart to ride on a bay trotting horse over four-inch bridges, to course his own shadow for a traitor."

Nothing in any poesy has equalled or can eclipse the beauty of his relations to his outraged sire, nor can any scene transcend the pathos, the true humane touch of that in which he pretends to lead his father to the precipice at Dover; while the imaginative description of that crag is unexcelled.

> "How fearful
> And dizzy 'tis to cast one's eyes so low.
> The crows and choughs that wing the midway air

---

[1] The names of fiends mentioned by him,—Flibberdigibit, Smolkin, Modu, Maho, —are found in Bishop Harsnet's "Discovery of Popish Impostors," published in 1603.

Show scarce so gross as beetles : half-way down
Hangs one that gathers samphire, dreadful trade,
Methinks he seems no bigger than his head :
The fishermen, that walk upon the beach,
Appear like mice ; and yond tall anchoring bark,
Diminish'd to her cock ; her cock, a buoy
Almost too small for sight : the murmuring surge,
That on the unnumbered idle pebbles chafes,
Cannot be heard so high.   I'll look no more ;
Lest my brain turn, and the deficient sight
Topples down headlong."

Again, how cleverly he becomes, to the frenzied man on his
recovering from his swoon, a dweller by the shore, pretend-
ing he has found him, after his fall, unhurt, though led to
the verge by a fiend. He is now "mad Tom," cowering,
shivering, maundering, comrade of a frenzied king and
a crazy jester with a breaking heart, half-naked in the
tempest-driven moor, and now a champion, nameless and
unknown, vindicating the wrongs of his house on his false
base-born brother ; and yet, ever, through it all, Edgar
himself, the brave, the candid and the true.

The daughters of Lear are terrible creations. Goneril
has a masterful soul, dominating Regan, and quickening the
harsh ragged-edged cruelty of her nature. Goneril has a
nobler husband, Albany, while Regan has the merciless
Cornwall, as mean as herself, who does not hesitate to rip
the eyes out of Gloucester with his own hand. Goneril is
twice cursed by Lear, with the curse of either utter barren-
ness or ungrateful children, a greater curse and bitterer than
that of Œdipus upon his sons.

"Hear, Nature hear ; dear goddess, hear.
Suspend thy purpose, if thou didst intend
To make this creature fruitful,
Into her womb convey sterility.
Dry up in her the organs of increase ;
And, from her derogate body never spring
A babe to honour her ; if she must teem,
Create her child of spleen ; that it may live,
And be a thwart disnatured torment to her ;

Let it stamp wrinkles in her brow of youth ;
With cadent tears fret channels in her cheeks ;
Turn all her mother's pains and benefits
To laughter and contempt ; that she may feel
How sharper than a serpent's tooth it is
To have a thankless child."

Both of these are led into sins of impiety, and not through
ambition alone, for they now have all they could expect to
own ; but rather through ungrateful and unfilial greed, which
makes them feel as though they did not possess what they
had, so long as their father sat at their table, or haunted their
houses.   They clothed their natures first with a disguise of
delicate hyprocrisy, and then with intense, snarling ingratitude; while, towards the close of their terrible life,
seeing the unscrupulous Edmund pressing onwards to
success, their lower instincts dragged them into the creation
of an adulterous compact with his baser soul.   Thus not
only filial impiety, ambition, and greed, but matrimonial
infidelity was their sin, and dragged doom upon them.   They
die without remorse, unrelenting, unrepenting, like their kind ;
and Cordelia alone is left to give her father's soul repose.
Beautifully has she that power, with her touching fidelity,
and her voice gentle and low.

Cordelia is, indeed, a unique creation.   Her quiet submission to her father's passionate expulsion, because her love
refuses to fall into fluent phrase ; her indignation when she
hears of the cruelty of her sisters,—are most true delineations.

"Had you not been their father, these white flakes
Had challenged pity of them. . . .
     . . . Mine enemy's dog,
Though he had bit me, should have stood that night.
Against my fire."

And when her sorrow for her father's fate moved her, with
what a touch of beauty is it written—

"Patience and sorrow strove
Who should express her goodliest.   You have seen

Sunshine and rain at once : her smiles and tears
Were like a better way : those happy smiles
That played on her ripe lip, seemed not to know
What guests were in her eyes : which parted thence
As pearls from diamonds dropp'd."

Of the husbands, Cornwall meets the doom of heaven in being slain through the honest indignation of a servant who cannot bear to witness the cruelty of his treatment of the old faithful Gloucester, whose very hospitality, besides, they are enjoying in his own Castle. Albany, roused to scorn when he sees the base nature of his wife, nevertheless has himself a dream of power and kingship when he sees opportunity draw near in the possible defeat of Lear and Cordelia.

Kent is a fine portrait of a loyalty that will not take rebuff, but comes and serves in another form and name, and dies with his master's sorrow.[1]

Lear's fool is a great creation,—the pathos of a faithful soul, with mirth upon his tongue, while his heart is breaking. Nothing can eclipse the mad weirdness of the hovel scene, when the three craze-brained creatures try, and judge, with terrible irony, the false unfilial children of the King.

And so the drama leads both Lear and Gloucester to recognise not only the judgment of heaven upon their folly, pride, and sin, but, in their disaster, to look, likewise, through the storm of rain and wind, and think with pity on the poor and needy, whom they had neglected in their own day of power. You hear the house shake with the angry storm, till Shakespeare has to pause and listen to the cry of tortured Nature, ere he writes—

" Poor naked wretches, whereso'er you are,
That bide the pelting of this pitiless storm,
How shall your houseless heads and unfed sides,
Your loop'd and window'd raggedness, defend you

---

[1] Kent and the fool are the only individuals who resolutely spoke to the king that simple truth which is one part of love.—MORLEY.
Does it not hold that the truly great and the truly foolish oftenest speak the truth,—the one fearing not, and the other knowing not the consequence upon friendship ?

From seasons such as these ? O I have ta'en
Too little care of this. Take physic, pomp ;
Expose thyself to feel what wretches feel,
That thou mayst shake the superflux to them
And show the heavens more just."

Wherein now lies poetical justice ? Why should Cordelia
die and Edgar live ? In Holinshed's version of the story the
army of Lear, aided by the French allies, is victorious ; and
Lear is reinvested with his kingship. But Holinshed goes
on to tell that, after Lear died, a bitter warfare was waged
against Cordelia by the sons of Goneril and Regan ; and
that, when Cordelia was taken prisoner by them, she took
her own life, valuing liberty at a higher rate. The ballad
printed in Percy's " Reliques " is of interest in this connection.[1] It says of Cordelia,

> " She, true hearted noble queen
> Was in the battle slaine ;
> But when he heard Cordelia's death,
> He swooning fell upon her breast,
>   From whence he never parted :
> But on her bosom left his life
> That was so truly hearted."

The sacrifice of Cordelia in Shakespeare's play was demanded by the instinct of patriotism. The soldiers of a
foreign kingdom must never tread to victory on our shores.
And, further, Cordelia died a sacrifice to the errors of the
age, and a warning, to all ages, of what the cost of evil
ever must be, in the crucifixion, and the agony of the innocent, the beautiful, the brave and the fair through the
sins and violence of others. It is tragically just that Goneril
and Regan should fall by each other's hands, like the sad
brothers of old. The vengeance of the gods cries out of the
storm and stress, but the monsters of an epoch are always
self-destroying.

The Tragedy is one of the greatest in the world—as in-

---

[1] Probably, however, of later date than the play.

stinct and fraught with doom as any play of the Greeks.
Men, in it, are, at first, apparently, the playthings of
heaven's freak and whim. The world is, to appearance,
but a stage of fools. The wheel of doom goes round, and
human souls are bound helplessly upon it. But, finally, the
truth stands clear, and it emerges that the ills and sorrows
are but heaven's judgments on the deeds of men. The
pain of it all rises as the inevitable consequence of the
rending of the bonds of natural love, and the shattering of
the honourable relations which cement society. The agony
untold, the suffering and terror are not thrown away.
Lear's proud, passionate soul is purged of his blinding pride,
and he learns, and so teaches us, before he dies, the worth
of true love, and the deep power of it, transcending expression,

> " Like a tide that, moving, seems asleep,
> Too full for sound or foam."

CHAPTER XXVI

" MACBETH "

The Tragedy of " Macbeth "[1] very strikingly reveals Shakespeare's method with the historic myth. When King James I. visited Oxford, a Latin play on the subject of Macbeth was acted before him, as his traditional descent was from the murdered Banquo ; a topic which must have been of most exciting interest to a king who dabbled so much in necromantic and antiquarian lore. Whether this stirred Shakespeare towards the same subject for a Tragedy can only be guessed ; but he probably found his material where the Latin writer had got his, namely, in Holinshed's Chronicle. There the whole dramatic stuff was lying, and all that was needed was the master-magician's touch to wake it from its dead sleep, and clothe it with psychological life.

The story is simple and plain. Duncan, a weak king, and, like all weak natures, while kindly, yet prone to cruelty and suspicion, has his kingdom racked by internal treason and external foes. Macbeth, who is his cousin, and Banquo, are the bulwarks between King Duncan and overwhelming destruction. The dramatic contrast is found in the keen ambitious nature of Macbeth, and the candid spirit of Banquo. In the setting there is displayed the unique

---

[1] Seen by Dr Forman on April 20th, 1610. (*Vide* his Diary.) Written probably about 1606 (MALONE). In " The Puritan," a play about 1607, there is an allusion to the ghost of Banquo. The play by Shakespeare was first printed in the folio of 1623. In 1596 a ballad of Macbeth was registered and referred to in scoffing terms by Thomas Kemp in his " Nine Days' Wonder." Dr Forman was concerned, with Lady Essex, in the murder of Sir Thomas Overbury, but he died suddenly in 1611 in a boat on the Thames, before the trial.

Shakespearian imagination both of scenery and persons. The old Highland superstitious weirdness of the desert place stands up naked before you,—the bare moor, where the human foot shrinks in loneliness, and the vast empty spaces, flooded with all kinds of whispering fears, fill the heart with all innumerable fancies. The martlet, "guest of summer," with its pendant nest on frieze and buttress and coign of vantage about Macbeth's castle, the awful apparition of a soul aflame with remorse, a conscience that will not sleep, and the terrible unavoidable destiny dragged down upon a man by his own hands, are only scraps of a noble feast. In the development of the bloody-handed hero, and the terrible companion and instigator of his crimes, there is presented a study not a whit less instructive than the wild madness of Lear, or the metaphysical motive-dissecting gloom of the Prince of Denmark.

There is a breath from Scotland seeking through the play whenever the curtain lifts. In the opening scene one feels the gust across the moor, and eldritch cries are borne on the wind.

We are prepared for the advent of Macbeth by hearing of his valour on behalf of his king, first against the Western MacDonald, whom he slays, and then against the Norwegian invader. Next comes Rosse, with tidings of the treachery of Cawdor, in combination, against Scotland, with Sweno; and Macbeth is raised to the honoured thanedom forfeited by the traitor, who is doomed to die.

And now, again, it is the heath near Forres; and the three Weird Sisters are there, when Macbeth and Banquo enter. They start at the wild creatures they behold, and Macbeth challenges them; when they hail him Thane of Cawdor, with the momentous addition that he shall be king, hereafter. Banquo invites their prophecy, though he neither begs nor fears their favours or their hate; and he is told that though he shall be no king, he shall beget a royal line. No further revelation will they vouchsafe to Macbeth's passionate questionings. The two chiefs, awed from such an interview, are met by Rosse and Lennox, who intimate to him his newly added honour of Cawdor. Banquo is struck with something like fear, but Macbeth at once begins to probe his heart over the weird prophecies: and, probing, he wakes ambition sleeping there. He is in a perilous moment, in the flush of victory, feeling how strong he is; and he is expending his strength on behalf of another, and that other. a weak monarch! But meanwhile he is not murder-rapt.

> " If Chance will have me King, why Chance may crown me
>   Without my stir."

Still, he is already a soul in a corner; and Fate, like a cloud, is shutting out the sun.

The misfortune of Macbeth's soul was that such a weak, kindly, half blind monarch sat upon the throne. Duncan had never dreamed of the internal treasons which, grown to muscular giant-hood without his notice, had all at once threatened his kingdom. Even Cawdor, the archtraitor, who had played and plotted with the nation's direst foes, had been to him

> " A gentleman on whom I built
>   An absolute trust,"

although, but only in regard to what is past, he has learnt that

> " There's no art
> To find the mind's construction in the face."

Would for his own sake that there were,—for one is entering his presence to whom he cries,

> " O worthiest cousin !
> The sin of my ingratitude, even now
> Was heavy on me : thou art so far before
> That swiftest wing of recompense is slow
> To overtake thee."

He raises his own son to be Prince of Cumberland, and
there Macbeth, who has, only that moment, been declaring
that the dearest duty is

> " doing everything
> Safe toward your love and honour,"

is stirred within his heart, to question Ambition and
Temptation.

> " The Prince of Cumberland,—that is a step
> On which I must fall down, or else o'erleap,
> For in my way it lies. Stars, hide your fires :
> Let not light see my black and deep desires."

The temptation grips him hard with unconquerable hands.
The King is going to share his hospitality, and he writes
his wife telling her the mysterious portents that have met
him, and revealing to her the greatness promised them.
At once the message sets her heart on fire.

> " Glamis thou art, and Cawdor, and shalt be
> What thou art promised : yet do I fear thy nature :
> It is too full o' the milk of human kindness
> To catch the nearest way."

She knows his nature well,—how he fears to do evil,
not because it is evil, but for the risk it entails, while yet
he should not hesitate to reap the rewards that might ensue
from evil done.[1]   She cries aloud,

> " Hie thee hither,
> That I may pour my spirits in thine ear,
> And chastise with the valour of my tongue
> All that impedes thee."

She will scourge his conscience into the way it shrinks
from, little dreaming that there are riders waiting in the
dark who will saddle it for hell.

---

[1] He does not strongly seek to do right, for the love of right, but he seeks weakly
to do right for love of the worldly conveniences that right-doing brings. He who
holds by the right for its own sake is morally strong, and lapped in proof against the
Tempter.—HENRY MORLEY.

The messenger, herald of the King's coming, and almost voiceless with his haste, enters and tells her what visitor is drawing near. She feels fate in his advent.

> " The raven himself is hoarse
> That croaks the fatal entrance of Duncan
> Under my battlements."

All the great hellishness of her hungry ambition finds a passionate utterance. She calls on all the spirits,

> " That tend on mortal thoughts, unsex me here,
> And fill me, from the crown to the toe, top-full
> Of direst cruelty."

She dedicates her very soul to darkness and dire deeds, for the sake of pride's reward.

> " Come, thick night,
> And pall thee in the dunnest smoke of hell,
> That my keen knife sees not the wound it makes,
> Nor heaven peep through the blanket of the dark
> To cry ' Hold, hold.' "

When Macbeth appears, her mind begins to work its horrid telegraphy upon him. The sun of no earthly to-morrow must rise, awaking Duncan for his departing journey. The night is the night, and the man must be,—what ? a little more, or all hell's depths less, than man ?

While the King sups, Macbeth holds argument with his soul. His good angel and Sin struggle for life or death on the precipice-edge. He wavers because of his appreciation of right motives, through fear of the life to come, and the fact of judgment even here. These three thoughts are the planks upon which, thus, Loyalty grapples to the death with Treachery and Murder. Had he not been harbouring in his heart the whispers of Ambition, had he silenced the voice of his morbidly excitable imagination, he would have been able to stand firm in honour established. But he had shut his heart to the importance of making his own that habit of righteous thought which alone forms a basis of true conduct, and becomes a defence inviolable against temptation. That surrender, over the verge of which he is being almost unconsciously drawn with open eyes, forgets that evil leads to evil. The flood-gates cannot be shut again behind the one ill deed, and, in the whirl, the difference is lost between the bloody fancy and the bloody fact. He is playing with the serpent, when he should be crushing its head beneath his heel! The fear that all is not ended by the blow of the knife, but that only then do consequences begin their interviews with the conscience, ties up his purpose somewhat. There are dregs in the cup of murder which the soul itself must taste. If only one could "jump the life to come!"

> "But, even then,
> We still have judgment here."

Then, again, his generosity and loyalty plead for the King. He is his kinsman and his guest! And he has been so gentle,

> "that his virtues
> Will plead, like angels, trumpet-tongued,"

against his murder, and all the earth be full of pity,—

> "The sightless couriers of the air
> Shall blow the horrid deed in every eye."

He hesitates. Should he open the sluice of Fate, or wait till it open for him? The evil genius of his own household enters, and grips the wavering soul. What?—she asks, in effect,—is not desire that fears to grow to deed but drunken fancy of a brain elate with Hope that shuts its eyes and will not follow Faith,

> "Letting ' I dare not ' wait upon ' I would? ' "

So, taunting his courage "into the sticking place," she conquers his scruples, and his soul is clay in her hands. Torn between Ambition, that star of a soldier's soul, and the magnetic overmastering cajolements of a woman greedy for honour, he gives himself over to her will.

Now night sinks deeper. Banquo is seen walking, as he fears to sleep, for the prophecies are blown in windy dreams about his brain. Macbeth and he meet ; and Macbeth dissembles. When Banquo tells him how he dreamed last night of the Weird Sisters of the heath, Macbeth pretends he has never given them a thought. And now, while waiting for the summons of his lady, which will be the signal for the awful deed, his brain, inflamed with fate, sees the phantom dagger that draws him on to the perdition of his soul. Macbeth shows early the tendency of his mind to hallucination. His imagination is always "on the raw," and apt suddenly to overstep the limit when judgment is overwhelmed in surmise, and reality loses its distinctiveness altogether. Surely there is no scene on living stage or in printed book so fraught and living with the night terrors of human souls after sin! You feel the still gloom breathless, folding the castle close in horror,—the owl shrieks,

> "fatal bellman,
> Which gives the sternest good-night" ;

while, through the corridor the snoring of the drugged attendants mocks their charge, and Lady Macbeth holds her heart in an agony of anxiety lest the deed of blood miscarry. One human touch breaks from her lips. As she had drawn aside the curtains, a flickering resemblance to her dead father gleamed on her heart from the features of the sleeping King, and stayed her own hand from the deed. Like Clytemnestra, even she has her tender moods ; so inconsistent is the human mind, which has stray gleams of tender light still playing in its darkness.

And now it is over ; and Macbeth, red-handed, enters, shaken to the roots of his being. He had listened as the grooms awoke, and heard one say "God bless us!" while the other said "Amen!" He could not say "Amen." And who had greater need than he, standing with dagger in his grip, at the threshold of the slaughter of conscience

and peace ?   And, in his fancy's ear, he heard the doom cried
with a voice of dread,

> " Sleep no more !
> Macbeth doth murder sleep ; the innocent sleep,
> Sleep that knits up the ravell'd sleave of care ! "

A soul, open-eyed forever, fearing to look ahead, and daring
not to glance over the shoulder, for the shadows it may see
behind it, and all the world dark as the heart's own night
of remorse,—never was such a soul set before men to tremble
at, and to pity, even in the horror of its crime.   But one
half of his task has been forgotten.   He should have laid
the bloody daggers by the grooms, that the blame might
be shifted upon them, and now he cannot take resolution in
his hand and go again into the chamber of the dead.   But
she will go.

> " Infirm of purpose !
> Give me the daggers : the sleeping and the dead
> Are but as pictures.
>   If he do bleed,
> I'll gild the faces of the grooms withal,
> For it must seem their guilt."

And, as she goes, the stillness of the night is broken by the
knocking at the gate.   Genius never broke in upon a crime
more terribly than with that !   She comes again, her hands
as red as his.   She has faith, meanwhile, in a little water,
to wash out the stain, and they retire in haste lest the visitors
who come at such an hour must be interviewed.   Again, the
knocking is heard ; and, as he goes, regret speaks through
Macbeth,—

> " Wake Duncan with thy knocking.   I would thou couldst ! "

Macduff and Lennox enter ; and then Discovery runs
shouting through the castle.   And now Macbeth feels
slaughter and blood less than heretofore.   He slays the
grooms, beside whose pillows the bloody daggers have been
found ; and as Donalbain and Malcolm, Duncan's sons, with

some premonition of their danger at Ambition's hands, have fled, suspicion falls upon them as instigators of the deed. The Weird Sisters' words are realised; the hunger of his heart has found its food: and Macbeth sets his foot on Duncan's throne.

Banquo, anon, enters the circle of Macbeth's interest. The prophecy on the heath at Forres had promised to his children the line of the crown, and often, to Macbeth, he has, in conversation, shown that he has not forgotten the promise. The devil of jealousy enters into activity of the play. He suspects Banquo continually. He feels the very shadow of him darken his whole kingdom; and, to take assurance in his own grip, he forces the hand of Fate. What avails the red blood of Duncan on his hands, if only for Banquo's children was he slain? So Banquo too must go.

> " And, with him,
> To leave no rubs nor botches in the work
> Fleance his son . . . must embrace the fate
> Of that dark hour."

With poison of slander and falsehood poured into their ears the murderers go out to waylay Banquo to his death.

Lady Macbeth does not, meanwhile, know the further bloodplot on which her lord has entered, but she finds Macbeth in one of his wretched moods.

> " Better be with the dead
> Whom we, to gain our peace, have sent to peace
> Than on the torture of the mind to lie
> In restless ecstsay. Duncan is in his grave.
> After life's fitful fever he sleeps well."

The dead, at least, are free from the hot terrors of contemplated sin. That wayward Fancy of his has him always on the rack, yet how differently does she try him, as compared with Hamlet, who, a hundred times before he slay, puts his soul through her catechism, yet after his bloody deed feels no compunction; while this man moping in his palace, steps out at once to murder, and only when the deed is done, sits glaring at the bloody horror he has made.

The villains surprise Banquo; and in this episode the frankness of Banquo's nature flashes through the dark most wondrously—a beautiful touch. He addresses them in one of those phrases which, in a tragic moment, with all the terrible power of the ancient Greeks, has in its very vagueness a sort of potent force,—

> " ' It will be rain to-night.'
> ' Let it come down,' "

they cry, and set upon him; and it rains his life's blood on the ground beneath.

While, in the dark, outside, such a tremendous wrong is being perpetrated, in the palace a banquet is prepared. The grim figure of the assassin suddenly stands at the door and tells his tale in whispers to the King—how the gashed body of the victim lies out in the whimpering night; but Fate has played a disconcerting trick in the game, through the escape of Fleance. And, as Macbeth turns to find his chair, lo, the ghost of the man his spite had slain, has entered, and sits in the monarch's place,—seen only by the flayed conscience of the guilty instigator of his death. The King cannot restrain his emotion. He fancies all the table has seen the apparition, and cannot understand,—

> " the time has been,
> That, when the brains were out, the man would die,
> And there an end : but now, they rise again,
> With twenty mortal murders on their crowns,
> And push us from our stools."

There is a difference here between the banquet scene and that in which the phantom dagger draws him on to crime. He recognised the dagger as a hallucination, but this gory phantom of the murdered Banquo seems to his soul as real as himself. This is no stage ghost like that of Hamlet's father, which is seen by others besides Hamlet. This dreadful figure only the murderer's eye can see. It is silent there at the banquet table. It has no word, like that at Elsinore, to speak to those who care to listen to it. It is no sleuth, out of a spirit-world returned to track down guilt to its lair, but it is the Nemesis of guilt, driving the soul to madness.

The feast is broken up, the guests in confusion all retire, and the King determines to go and try to force the hand of Fate. He will seek out the Weird Sisters and discover all.

> " I am in blood
> Stepped in so far, that, should I wade no more,
> Returning were as tedious as go o'er."

He is walking in a shadow-haunted dream. Conscience is mastering him, that giant whom our crimes and sins awake to dog us through the dark passages of life. Imagination makes his brain a house of ghosts. And so he rushes into the road of Tyranny, which is, to such as he, the road to ruin, for Lennox and the lords set the whisper of rebellion afoot, and tell how Macduff has fled to the English Court of Edward, to bring back Malcolm, Duncan's exiled heir, and rid Scotland from the Usurper's galling yoke.

The Weird Sisters give him answers, double-tongued as any of the ancient oracles. They warn him of Macduff, yet tell him he shall fall by none of woman born, while they reveal the long line of Banquo, with the symbols of the union of the crowns,—

> " Some I see,
> That twofold balls and treble sceptre carry,"—

Kings behind kings, yet not of the blood of Macbeth !

> " Be lion-mettled, proud, and take no care
> Who chafes or frets or where conspirers are.
> Macbeth shall never vanquished be until
> Great Birnam wood to high Dunsinane hill
> Shall come against him."

Their words urge him away from scruple, and from laws of God and man. He has Lady Macduff and her children murdered. He heaps outrage upon outrage like a soul doom-frenzied, laying up much recompense when God's wage-day comes.[1]

And now the tragic retribution pierces the soul of Lady Macbeth herself. Sleep that is no sleep becomes her long night agony. She walks in her slumber, and blabs to the dark, that has listening ears, unknown by her, secrets that have blood upon them, washing her miserable hands, all murder-stained, and washing in vain. And the crown and power that cost Macbeth so much to win grow very bitter to his wretched soul. He hovers on the brink of absolute insanity; but he saves his reason by rushing into action. Chased every foot of the way by the shadow that so often pursues kings, he is never caught by its grip. Yet is he sick at heart. To Seyton he mourns—

" I have lived long enough : my way of life
Is fallen into the sear, the yellow leaf."

Lady Macbeth, on the other hand, while he wades in his sea of blood is left upon the shore alone. Her occupation is gone, and she has neither imagination nor sympathy to enable her to fill the blank in her life. With him passion was explosive ; with her it consumed her own heart. In Macbeth the inward fires found volcanic vent ; in her their pent-up force shook, in earthquake, the deep foundations of the soul. Her proud will became sapped by remorse : and though Macbeth lay " in restless ecstasy," she, with naked fancy stretched upon the rack, lived a long sleepless dream of hell—a miserable woman, whose nerves, all flayed, were scorched for ever by the hot breath of her sin. And round the throne are curses, or lip-honour instead of love, service and friendship.

But, as the avengers draw near, his wavering will takes fire, and all the natural bravery of the man declares for

---

[1] Thus far all his crime has been to win and to secure some earthly gain,—has had a motive with a touch in it of human reason. For the complete perdition of the tempted soul, it must be dragged down to the lowest deep, till it do evil without hope of other gain than satisfaction of a fiendish malice.—HENRY MORLEY,

battle in the stronghold of Dunsinane. And, while they prepare, a cry of women breaks upon them. Macbeth asks what it means. He is not afraid to hear.

> " I have supped full with horrors.
> Direness, familiar to my slaughterous thoughts,
> Cannot once start me."

It was the cry of women over a self-slain queen! Conscience had driven Lady Macbeth to her doom. Even that moves him little. What does anything matter now? To-day, Yesterday, To-morrow—what are they?

> " All our yesterdays have lighted fools
> The way to dusty death. Out, out, brief candle
> Life's but a walking shadow. . . it is a tale,
> Told by an idiot, full of sound and fury,
> Signifying nothing."

Chance suggesting an artifice to Malcolm, brings the appearance of the wood moving towards the stronghold, as each soldier carries a branch to hide the number of the host under Siward and Macduff from the watchers: and Macbeth feels Fate clutching him—

> " I 'gin to be aweary of the sun."

And yet he refuses to bow to Destiny. His manhood rises up in arms against his doom.

> " Blow wind ! Come wrack !
> At least we die with harness on our back."

Young Siward goes down before his sword, and he rushes on declaring he bears a charmed life ; but, when Macduff, fateful with vengeance for his lady and his children slain, confronts him, and declares,

> " Despair thy charm ;
> And let the angel whom thou still hast served
> Tell thee Macduff was from his mother's womb
> Untimely ripp'd."

he feels the double-edge of the weapon with which he has been playing cut his hand.[1] It is no new thing in such oracular foretellings ; and Banquo spoke truth when he said,

> " Oftentimes, to win us to our harm
> The instruments of darkness tell us truths,—
> Win us with honest trifles, to betray's
> In deepest consequence."

Macbeth, too late, feels the danger and the folly of having listened to the juggling fiends,[2]

> " That palter with us in a double sense :
> That keep the word of promise to our ear,
> And break it to our hope."

So he and Macduff go battling off the stage, and all the awful completion of the doom of his blood-stained ambition is realised, when his head, upon a spear, is brought in before the camp.

This tragedy of a human heart clutching at what Fate holds, is lit all through with the lurid glow of destiny and despair. Action follows action with soul-devastating, impetuous force, like wave upon wave of destruction out of the deep. Macbeth is, in reality, a generous nature, talented and brave, but sapped and ruined by ambition. His sanguine nervous temperament, his large capacity and ready susceptibility make him at once the Saviour and the Judas of any cause. Supernatural solicitings overmaster his better nature. And truly, the glimpse of the other world given to us, could a door swing apart and voices come out of it, would shake the foundations of the human mind again, and topple good resolve into awful ruin like his. Once enslaved to pursuit of a " Will o' the Wisp," and with the guiding strings of his destiny in the control of a woman of blazing purpose and

---

[1] See the " Trachiniæ," where Hercules is slain through the instrumentality of the monster Nessus, not of woman born.

[2] There are times when Destiny shuts her eyes, but she knows full well that when evening falls, we shall return to her, and that the last word must be hers. She may shut her eyes, but the time till she reopens them is time that is lost.—MAETERLINCK.

iron will, he that was brave, honoured and honourable, beloved even by his arch-foe Macduff, makes his heart a home of doubled-dyed treasons. Yet had he only resisted more, how well might he have shown the prophecies of Satan to be foolishness, how might he have avoided the bitter chalice of unavailing Remorse, and saved from hell the eternal jewel of his soul !

The gulf between honourable zeal and hungry greed of power may be as deep as hell, but it is easily stepped over by the soul once it allows the light of tempting promises to lure it on. He gets involved in a warfare, first, with his better self, and then with invincible Destiny. Crime after crime tries to block the purposes of heaven, but Justice sweeps them altogether in at the door of his life at last.

It is the Tragedy of Jealousy guided to awful acts by entire absence of scruple, by boastful self-dependence, and audacity measuring its strength against God.

It is the Tragedy of the desolating effect of sin. Macbeth flings away his soul for lands, crown and kingdom; and finds himself all at once, in an absolute desert of his own creation. Following the glimmer of the ghost of his own suddenly awakened desires, he stumbles all of a sudden into Judgment Day.[1]

It is the Tragedy of the man of active spirit, the man with whom the will and the deed jump together, especially after the shudder of the first plunge is over. No spectre, however blood-boltered and dread, can turn him from the course of crime in which he plunges full-sail after power.

It is a weird lesson, yet a true one, that it teaches, how Fate passes over the ambitious and the violent, and calls to power those who neither fear the favour or the hate of the weird potencies of the unseen world.

---

[1] It is a remarkable commentary on the commonly-received idea of Macbeth, that his reign was one of kindness and probity, and he was the first king who in actual history in Scotland gave help to the Church in her civilising work,—though his foot was, in accordance with the too common custom of the time, red with blood when it mounted the steps of the throne.

Lady Macbeth is a Scottish Clytemnestra in cruelty, and force of cold-blooded pride. She brings her own chill atmosphere of freezing fear as she moves. Her heart is a hatching-nest of resolute, clever schemes for ambitious advancement. Her face is a continuous mask, a visor of her feelings. Macbeth cannot dissemble with skill, but she shutters her eyes and cheeks against discovery. No fear of failure raises ghosts for her, and she dominates his soul till he marches into bloody ruin at her command. She knows the flexible steel he is, and what a sure weapon he can be in her grasp; and hers is the sword-hand needed for the dreadful purpose of her spirit. But, alas! once she has thrust the weapon home into murder, the sword begins to slay on its own account! And yet, to her, more even than Macbeth, it all was failure. She does not share his honours, and his horrors are his own also ; till, when she is left alone, the fruitlessness of her crimes breaks down her iron nerve, and the bloody secret of her inmost heart leads her captive on the chain of undying misery.

The question of the relationship of the witches in " Macbeth " to Middleton's play " The Witch," discovered in manuscript in 1779, cannot be easily settled, though it is perhaps only fanciful, and a merely apparent connection.[1]

The witches of " Macbeth " are among the weirdest creations surely of all poesy. The popular idea of a witch was a crude and elementary scarecrow, offspring of the simpler mind's fear of sickness and the dark—the explanation of all that was unseen. Their activity was really the embodiment of the dread of an imprecation or curse, for the inauspicious word is, to the rustic, as fraught with awe as in any drama of the ancient Greeks. Mischief was, according to the superstition, their absolute delight, and their mission was to make all goodness and happiness miscarry, and to perplex

[1] Enough that the play of "Macbeth" was certainly being acted in April 1610, when Shakespeare's age was 46 ; and that Middleton had not then written his play of " The Witch," about which some students of " Macbeth " concern themselves unduly.—HENRY MORLEY.

and annoy, wherever possible, the purposes and desires of honest and industrious people. They were said to sail through the air, to hold obscene midnight revels in holy buildings, to raise wild storms at sea, and to afflict innocent folks with wasting diseases and miseries unspeakable. For example, when James himself was in Denmark, it was believed that Satan had gathered his myrmidons in North Berwick Church to raise storms to prevent the young Queen from coming to Scotland,—a "ploy" of Satan which was supposed to belong to his grim and fell band. One of them was Agnes Sampson, the wise woman of Keith-Marishal.

Now, it matters not, whether Shakespeare's age believed in witches. It is enough that the age of Macbeth did, and in the influence of such ungenerous powers of darker nature on the lives of men, as, till our own day, the Highland spirit, which is the clue of the old-world tale itself, believed, and in some places still believes.

The very period in which this play was acted, and the very monarch before whom or with reference to whom it was written, were perhaps those most deeply interested in witch-hunting and dilettante black-art enquiries ever known, as his own "Dæmonologie"[1] reveals. In 1597, in Aberdeen, twenty-four witches were burned; and, as late as 1643, the Church was passing Acts of great severity against sorcery, while in Fife alone, in a few months, upwards of thirty persons were burnt to death for witchcraft. The Church in Scotland expressed astonishment at the wonderful increase of witches which this revealed, not observing that it was rather the blind superstition of the time that was providing fuel for the fire. With James, the Scottish King, new come across the Border to a greater crown over United Kingdoms, the thought of such a weird theme would come over the Border also, to a mind like Shakespeare's.

Shakespeare improved here, however, on the popular idea. His weird creations, that flit and flicker on the heath, are

[1] Quarto, Edinburgh, 1597. "Dæmonologie, in form of a Dialogue."

more than the mere old women with a broomstick, of the
fireside fears. They are real instruments of Fate, with an
actual spell of terrible doom-provoking, destiny-working
power within them. They are " the Weird Sisters," wild, unhuman and inhuman. The only figures that are on a par of
horror with them are the Eumenides; but these are
tormentors of the human soul after the deed of ill, while
those are evil-whispering, horror-tempting prompters to the
actual initiating sin. They are not destiny, nor are they
fates ; but they have an impelling and impending power
behind and above them. They are not masters of the soul,
but they can waken in the soul what will make it a slave to
meaner things than its best and truest. They are the
passions and shadows of desire within, objectified against the
background of the night.

Macbeth needs no compulsion from without. He only
needs a thought to jostle him, and all the combustible
material of his ambition simply kindles. He had seen himself strong enough to crush rebellion. So much stronger
was he than Duncan, who sat weakly upon the throne, while
that was growing. How powerfully could he have carried
out to triumphant issue the rebellion he had suppressed.
And then, as if in challenge from the gods, thrown down
before his better nature, come the visit of Duncan, and the
lurid whisperings of his wife. But something crossing that
moor set the spark to the flame. And he had seen the
Weird Sisters, sure enough ; and they screamed aloud, with
gibbering laughter, the possibilities that were silent, voiceless, heretofore, in his heart. They were emanations of the
evil kingdom within,—shadows of the lurid flame smoulder-
ing already in the soul.

They are objective, but, at the same time, only so to the
soul that has within itself the evil which they specify. And
such, when they have induced the soul towards the first ill
step, blind and soothe it, and shut from its vision the sin
into whose net they have enticed it.

Their prophecy is sufficient in itself; but Macbeth's heart spoke the same thought first. He can only become King by performing a crime, staining with blood the hand of Ambition, for there is an heir who stands between him and the realisation of his fate. So they tempt Macbeth, in the language of his own thought, in the flush of victory; and they clothe his desire, which can only be won through murder, in the colours of the destiny of heaven. Childless, passionless, fashionless, nameless, except Hecate, they are all that human thought can dream of foul, cruel, vindictive and sardonic. So they put also, finally, into his heart the old curse-breeding sin of the ancient men of Greece,—

" He shall spurn fate, scorn death and bear
His hopes 'bove wisdom, grace, and fear;
And you all know security
Is mortal's chiefest enemy."

CHAPTER XXVII

SHAKESPEARE'S TRAGIC PERIOD

IT is evident that Shakespeare is now in a period of deep contemplative thought. We feel that he has come into a closer contact with humanity, and is giving it a more regular, more searching scrutiny. He is sick of the din of theatrical life: and a certain stigma is attached to the actor's name. There are times, too, when the mirth and wit of the "Mermaid" do not suffice to lift him out of his moody reflections, when he feels that he is "in disgrace with fortune and men's eyes," and when he sits in solitary silence, and broods upon his "outcast state." From his own confession, we know that, in this busy London life of his, bitter clouds of jealousy of the living and of sorrow for the absent and the dead, have swept darkly across his soul. Further, by this time he has become a man of note, and of means. The people of his native town have looked to him as a powerful lever in stirring weighty influences on their behalf; and booksellers in the Metropolis endeavoured to push sales of garbled piracies by affixing his name to the Title-page. He has been honoured, too, with the friendship and society of such noble lords as Pembroke, Essex, and Southampton.[1] Even royalty was kindly to him; and he has lorded it over contemporary literature, from its headquarters at the "Mermaid." But still, he has, all the while, been longing, and making provision for the quiet life of "William

[1] Southampton is said to have presented Shakespeare with £1000, equivalent to five times that amount in our currency, thereby laying the foundation of the poet's fortune. The story rests upon the authority of Davenant, reported by Rowe. In his dedication of the "Rape of Lucrece" he says, "The love I dedicate to your Lordship is without end," and the words ring true!

Shakespeare, Gentleman " ; [1] and that, too, without a grain of charlatanry.   He is looking ever to the free, country life, in preference to the " painted pomp " of city and of court. O for the meadows and woodlands of Stratford, free from the stings and the daggers, that lurk in court apparel, just as surely as the jewels!   Like his own melancholy Jaques, he could pierce through the body of the country, city, court, and view it all with a reflective sadness and pity drawn from his wide and varied experience, and sense of baffled search.

> " When to the sessions of sweet silent thought,
> I summon up remembrance of things past,
> I sigh the lack of many a thing I sought."

The closing years of Elizabeth's reign were dark and disjointed.

> " Those three years have I taken note of it : the age is grown so picked that the toe of the peasant comes so near the heel of the courtier, he galls his kibe."

Thus speaks Shakespeare-Hamlet, and we know it was true.[2] The trio of his great friends have been swept into disgrace, —the head of the most brilliant of them is in the executioner's basket.   The boy Hamnet, his only son, the hope of his house, has passed away.   The heart of Shakespeare must then have become more awake than ever to the dark, sad, and earnest side of human life.   Public and private experience have swayed the turn of his thought.   More and more he has received personal testimony to the fact that, behind all the glitter and glamour of the pageant, there is a hidden Tragedy.   " Pass on, Spangles and Motley,—there's a grave across your path ; and a frost shall snap your music ! "   What is the good of it all, then ?   Is life half worth the struggle ?   We will set up the grim Carle, and spear him with a jest !   Neither does that avail us one whit.

> " In this life lie hid more thousand deaths."

---

[1] From 1599 onwards, such was his designation.
[2] Shrouded in a man's writings are the aspirations and despairs of his personal life.   The wise read them, here a word, and there a word,

Time passes swiftly, surely, what can man do?

> " Like as the waves make towards the pebbled shore,
> So do our minutes hasten to their end,
> Each changing place with that which goes before,
> In sequent toil all forwards do contend."

His works are truer perhaps than those of any other man, thinker or writer, for they bear record within them of the changes of his life-experience,—they keep pace with the march of his soul. His first works are all youth, beauty, and love: then the great figures and projects historical of his country: and at last, the struggles and failures of men; everything steeped in an atmosphere of thought, sounding the depths of the human heart, piercing the night of human existence, dropping the plummet-line over the verge into the Infinite. He has had trial, but he has risen by it,—loss but he has gained by it; and he has learned through it all, that there is more in life than life,—something in all, over all, and around all, governing and divine. He loves to brood now on

> " Old, unhappy, far-off things ";

and Death is sometimes even sweet and beauteous.

> " Amiable, lovely Death,"

tender and to be desired—

> " Come away, come away Death,
> And in sad cypress let me be laid."

He finds behind all—Death. Pierce the king's pasteboard mask, and you see the truth. Thrill on, joyous nerve,— leap gaily, gallant heart,—there is a monarch waiting for your joy. Courtier, flatterer, sycophant,—beware,—beware! The hour is coming when every breath is precious, and your words must then be real. You cannot flatter Death! Beauty and Fashion,—deck yourselves ; swagger and flourish for your little brief season : yours, too, is the pillow of clay,

> " Shall not the worm make merry in the mould
> Heedless of all your glory, pomp, and gold ? "

He has dissected the last moments of men—the deepest things in the world. When he has exhausted life, and counted the bitter dregs in Pleasure's cup, then do we see life turned over, brooded upon, analysed and criticised : and our Shakespeare stands there, like Hamlet, with a brow clouded in sorrowful thought,—in his hand that mouldering clammy Death's head, filling it once more with human soul.

He is the veritable Colossus. Beneath and around him, the business and turmoil of the world, and of human passion, whirl and beat ; but, high up, towering into the depths of Night, with its scintillating orbs wheeling above his head, he stands forever, rapt, grand, immortal. Nevertheless, a share in that passion and trouble once was his ; and, though he has risen above it, he has left his record behind him in living pulsating music. All experience, everything in life is at his command, and within his knowledge,—the strong passion, the deep insight of the heart of man, every phase, every utterance, from the simper of folly to the shriek of despair ; and so he hears the lone boom of the eternal billows, and interprets its meaning.

A man, therefore, with such experience of life—a poet with such knowledge of life's experience,—we should imagine that he would persistently, even from the most joyful thought, come back upon the dark, sad, thoughtful side of Being. The dead are ceaseless pilgrims ; and, returning from his festal meetings, he often gets into such company ; and journeys a little on their way : and we can well believe, that, when such an one recounts his memories of the feast and revel, he will also recollect his other experience of the night, and will talk as one who has seen and heard more than other men.

CHAPTER XXVIII

THE HISTORICAL TRAGEDIES

In the Historical Tragedies we find Shakespeare embodying the poetry of history. These plays are created interpretations, rather than literal transcriptions.

In the English plays, the tragic characters, with their passions, ambitions, failures, triumphs, sorrows and crimes, yet embody and glorify the England of the poet's love. Richard II.'s selfish, black-souled passion, with a great keen brain, and a magnificent power of delicate gleaming phrase, yet absolutely inconstant, and never able strenuously to follow noble acts, is a tragic figure, with tragic companionships of suffering and deed. The pride of Æschylus in Athens finds an echo and parallel in Gaunt's immortal eulogy of England,—

> " This royal throne of kings, this scepter'd isle,
> This earth of majesty, this seal of Mars,
> This little world,
> This precious stone, set in the silver sea ! "

In " Richard III." we see, upon the stage, the ills of civil war at last atoned for, and Richard and the evils he has made fall together. Heartshaking, indeed, is the tragic power and lesson of his last night, before the closing battle of his life, wherein, in paroxysm of battle-fury, like a Berserker, he dies. Richard's victory is the victory and vindication of the cause of good and of the good God, and, above all, the vindication of England. " King John " embodies the English love of liberty and rights, set alongside of the weakness of a king, unworthy of the great period into which he has been born. Faulconbridge stands out well, herein, as a typical patriot, with that political wisdom which bids a true man look to his country, since God himself looks after the world. He sets his fatherland above all other thoughts; and expresses an eternal truth of state-policy for national safety when he cries,

> " This England never did, nor never shall
> Lie at the proud foot of a conqueror.
> But when it first did help to wound itself.
> . . . Nought shall make us rue
> If England to itself do rest but true."

In the Roman plays, in like manner, it is Rome herself that stands forward—idealised Rome, yet, in its idealisation, more truly Rome, than the Rome of the Chroniclers, or of the Romans themselves. Witness the lightning-flash photograph which drags the very character of the man depicted into our vision more clearly than the most learned transcription of any annalist could do—

> " The angry spot doth glow on Cæsar's brow,
> And all the rest look like a chidden train.
> Calpurnia's cheek is pale, and Cicero
> Looks with such ferret and such fiery eyes
> As we have seen him in the Capitol,
> Being crossed in conference with some senators."

In these plays we are now in the region not of error or cruel destiny as the controlling and punishment-bringing powers over man and behind action; but passion and the sins of pride of intellect and heart, blinding, death-impelling, are the influences which supply the tragic end and issue of men's deeds. Antony, led by voluptuousness of a self-indulgent nature, sunders himself from the ties of patriotism. Coriolanus, through self-centred haughtiness of temperament, is impelled to seek and claim an isolation like the gods themselves, and so is driven apart from the deepest influences that bind a man to fatherland; while Cæsar suffers from imperial ambition, whose stride galls the heels and hearts of lesser men until they slay him.

CHAPTER XXIX

THE ROMAN TRAGEDIES

CORIOLANUS [1] is pre-eminently a tragic hero, and entangles himself in all that makes for ruin in a state like Rome. Shakespeare has been blamed for expressing, through this creation, his own scorn for the commonalty. He fetches before us, in his crowd of citizens, now hero-worshipping, now urged into stinging hate by the flaming oratory of unprincipled demagogues, a satirical picture of the clumsy, brainless, shortsighted mob, which, being the sediment of a state in time of peace, becomes, in a crisis of misery and excitement, the scum on the surface of an angry epoch's boiling pot of political passion. I think we are entitled to take it as a not inaccurate representation of the mutable many, even in his own time. And yet it is not a caricature. All voices of its utterance are not voices of cruel hate and envy. The riot is relieved by a man in the street who pleads against the mob,

"Consider you what services he has done for his country!"

Menenius Agrippa knows the people, and shows that they have a heart which can be reached by tactful humorous pleading when occasion arises. But not all the skill of Menenius, his most beloved in Rome, can master and move the soul of Coriolanus away from his sullen establishment of anger. He laughs at the mob, and talks the schemers out of their surly discontent, playing with keen satire and searching humour around their clouds until he make them

[1] About 1608.

smile. And, further, in the play, the unswerving haughtiness of the patrician party is exposed in a manner which prevents a trace of our sympathy going towards them, when Coriolanus exclaims

> " Would the nobility lay aside their ruth,
> And let me use my sword, I'd make a quarry
> With thousands of these quartered slaves, as high
> As I could pick my lance."

The scathing hate and scorn which he feels for the mob finds burning expression when, banished, as an enemy of the people and his country, he faces them with—

> " You common cry of curs, whose breath I hate
> As reek o' the rotten fens, whose loves I prize
> As the dead carcases of unburied men
> That do corrupt my air.
>   Despising
> For you, the city, thus I turn my back.
> There is a world elsewhere."

Mutual incompatibility demands separation, with retaliations and revenges, discontents and obstinacies, the angels and ministers of all destruction,—forcing Coriolanus into the crux between devotion to his country and the satisfaction of his hurt pride, and hatred of the fickle " many-headed beast."

In this play we find ourselves surrounded by the austere atmosphere of Rome. Volumnia the Roman matron, mother of the hero, is a living picture. What pride of an ancient matron in the valour of her son speaks here, as she describes how,

> " His bloody brow
> With his mailed hand then wiping, forth he goes,
> Like to a harvest man that's tasked to mow
> Or all, or lose his hire."

And, again, the wisdom, learned from knowledge of her people, throbs from her words of advice to him,

> " Lesser had been
> The thwartings of your dispositions, if
> You had not showed them how ye were disposed,
> Ere they lacked power to cross you."

And what can exceed the bitterness of a mother's invective when she says to Sicinius the plotter,

> " I would my son
> Were in Arabia, and thy tribe before him,
> His good sword in his hand ! "

Indeed, much of the secret of the pride and obstinacy of Coriolanus lies in this mother's nature, for, filled, herself, with glowing patriotism, she has devoted her whole life to training him to go forward, the strong man of his conquering race. All her emotions centred in him ; she has made him the master of valour, dominant and dominating, with the certainty that he has within him that which makes him a rock around whose feet the fickle furies of the rabble break like frothing waves. And yet he seeks no external honour, except the glory of saving his country from her foes, till, his most vulnerable part, his pride, is hurt and wounded, and then he turns in vengeful wrath against his native land, which, in his blindness, he identifies with the mob that he despises. He is a Prometheus, who will not save himself by suave consents, even from the opposition of his equals ; and the acme of his pride is reached when he repels the right of the state to exile him, but declares—"I banish you." Virgilia, the tender wife, lives upon the stage with a still power like the spell of starlight over stormy souls. She is to him his " gracious silence."

The Tragedy displays the ruin of a brave heart through pride. The people are to him but curs, minnows, objects of unfathomable scorn. It shows the evil and error of cleavage in a state between patrician and plebeian, hindering the growth of empire and the good of the people, while yet that good is hampered by the continual obstacle of the big baby mob, drawn hither, thither by strings of hunger, and by flattering breath. The depth of Tragedy is reached when Pride, deserted by its own class, sees its error.

Coriolanus resolves to be himself all, and in this resolution he ruptures nature, patriotism, and society. He takes up arms against Rome, thus throwing himself open to the horrors of impiety and cancelling his own deep prayer,

> "The honoured gods
> Keep Rome in safety, and the chairs of justice
> Supplied with worthy men,—plant love among us,
> Throng our large temples with the shows of peace,
> And not our streets with war."

Coriolanus is not, however, to be taken as the mere embodiment of brute force and animal courage. He has an elevation of mind that lifts him above these. He has every one of the qualities of greatness, and especially of great generalship, which make him trust, above all, to himself in the determination to be successful. His very sufferings plead for him, but he cannot bear to take from fickle hearts reward for what he has endured, campaigning for his country.

> "I have some wounds upon me, and they smart
> To hear themselves remembered."

Some versions of the tale record that he escaped the jealousy of the leaders of his country's foes among whom he cast his lot,—that he died, honoured, with recognition and reward, and that his name won reverence in Rome itself; but this would not have suited Shakespeare's tragic purpose, or the conception of his art.

His heart is hardened and closed against all his past, and when Menenius, his dearest friend, comes pleading to him, trying to touch his finest sensibilities, he replies,

> "Wife, mother, child, I know not. My affairs
> Are servanted to others."

And when he sees his mother and his wife approaching with his son, he declares that he will stand to his resolution,

> " As if a man were author of himself
> And knew no other kin."

The tragic crisis is accentuated by the knowledge which he possesses, that, when he surrenders his rage, in response to the pleadings of those he loves,[1] it is his own very life that he offers up, upon the altar of popular clamour ; for the plot of Aufidius rouses the Volsci against him, and he is murdered on his triumphant return from the peace he has made with Rome.

The tale invests him with a heroic, almost supernatural, power, somewhat like that possessed by the Wallace of Blind Harry. Single-handed he breaks his way into towns and cities, holds an army at bay, and neither wounds nor weakness can subdue his fire. He cries—

> " What custom wills in all things should be, do't,
> The dust on antique time should lie unswept,
> And mountainous error be too highly heapt
> For truth to o'er-peer."

And yet he pleads as justification of what he does, the privilege of custom, the sanction of use and wont, thus plunging himself into a tragic inconsistency.

This is the Tragedy of egoism, punished, when it sets itself against duty and fatherland. Haughty pride hurt and outraged, impels him headlong into the treason which he despises, and which is alien to his nature. Death is dragged around him by his own impetuosity, and precipitated by the anger kindled by his reception at the hands of Aufidius and the mob.

This is the Tragedy of self-esteem growing till it topples

---

[1] The Tragedy of "Lear" arises from the snapping of all the cords by which we are bound together. The Tragedy of "Coriolanus" emerges from the holding fast of these ties, whereby he is led to go back to be murdered by the Volsci, while Rome rejoices in her own safety. Is there not a great Tragic Irony worthy of the ancients here ?

to over-whelming ruin, of misery acting on ignorance, and high disdain ignoring all, with the inevitable climax of loss of home, country, glory, love and life ; and yet, through the great skill of the immortal art of the Master, he makes us love him, filling our souls with a sympathy like that which moved Aufidius,—

> " My rage has gone
> And I am struck with sorrow,"

while one of the leaders of the city says truly—

> " The man is noble, and his fame folds in
> This orb of the earth."

In " Julius Cæsar "[1] we find the Tragedy of the State feeling hampered by the progress towards kingly power of one man's ambition, and his influence with the people. Hunger for kingship, or its equivalent, with the envy which such provokes in the breasts of lesser men, and the questionings of a great heart, involved in mean enterprise, confronted by an apparent contradiction between public necessity and private duty, while torn and divided by mistrust, Melancholy's child, are the tragic motives of the play. It is the " Hamlet " of the Roman Republic ; and, among the figures of the time, it is Brutus that looms large in Shakespeare's eyes. Brutus, of generous nature, brave and upright, with a passion for liberty and a pride over family achievements for freedom's sake in the past, is the real hero of the piece. Round him the central interest beats, for he is crucified upon the arms of a terrible dilemma,—he loves liberty, and he loves Cæsar, yet bitter doubt as to Cæsar's motives has been cunningly inserted in his mind by Cassius ; and so he argues with himself,—

> " He would be crowned.
> How that might change his nature,—there's the question ! "

Not for what he has done does he slay Cæsar, joining the conspirators, whose prime motive is jealous envy, but for

[1] Produced about 1601. See Weever's " Mirrour of Martyrs," 1601, where an allusion to Cæsar and Brutus points directly to this play.

what the future might hold of risk and danger. He cannot trust what he does not see, and he doubts even the evidence of his eyesight. With no personal grudge, but with a friend's affection in his heart for the man he murdered, he stained his dagger with the blood that was dear to him!

He is impelled, cajoled, challenged into it by Cassius, as Macbeth was tempted, lured and driven into self-destruction by his lady, as Othello was dragged and whispered into murder by Iago. The challenge is,

> " There was a Brutus once that would have brook'd
> The eternal devil to keep his state in Rome
> As easily as a king " ——

a sentiment which appeals to the pride of Brutus, who, himself, so cleverly does Cassius insinuate his sentiments, re-echoes the very thought, ——

> " My ancestors did from the streets of Rome
> The Tarquin drive when he was called a king ! "

And yet Brutus, like Hamlet, dare not at first take this burden on him. Again it is a cry against " the cursed spite " which has selected him to set in equipoise what has been displaced.

> " Brutus had rather be a villager,
> Than to repute himself a son of Rome,
> Under these hard conditions as this time
> Is like to lay upon us."

The conspirators are eager to have Brutus identified with them in their cause, for there is no man more honoured in Rome. As Casca says,

> " Oh, he sits high in all the people's hearts,
> And that which would appear offence in us,
> His countenance, like richest alchemy,
> Will change to virtue and to worthiness ! "

Friendship also, and affection, put both hands round his heart, but at last he yields to persistent suggestion, which convinces him even of the untrustworthiness of Cæsar's attitude in refusing the crown thrice offered at the Lupercal,

> "Lowliness is young ambition's ladder."

And yet having accepted it as an axiom of duty that evil can be done to bring good to the state he finds that friendship's pleading silenced and private honour displaced send his soul out into the realms of unrest.

> "Since Cassius first did whet me against Cæsar
> I have not slept."

With Macbeth, sleep is murdered when his dagger has let loose upon him the ghosts dislodged from the bodies he has mangled; but Brutus finds his brain tortured by haunting shadows, now of resolve, and now of disquieting doubt,—

> "The genius and the mortal instruments
> Are then in Council, and the state of man
> Like to a little kingdom, suffers then
> The nature of an insurrection."

Like Hamlet, and, at the same time, unlike enough, he wavers; but it is friendship and love set against revulsion from ambition, that stay his hand, while, when he does resolve, he stands amongst the foremost, nor disdains the bloody deed. It is not ambition, as with Macbeth, nor revenge as with Hamlet, that is his motive power; yet this man's moods are like the one, and his despairs are like the other. He desired his country's good, and the state of things sadden him sorely. He tells his wife how he is at war with himself; and, further, he hides the secret from her, though she is as dear to him

> "As are the ruddy drops
> That visit his sad heart."

What a rack this soul is stretched upon, for murder is a horrid evil, yet the liberty of the state is the very highest good. Must he do this ill that good may come? Or must he do this evil that a greater evil enter? Mistrust is the shattering curse of his soul, and, at last, the shouting of the mobs, and the proud carriage of Cæsar drive home the insinuating whispers of Cassius, and he joins the deadly plot. Cassius is a striking contrast to this man. He is crafty, with that mean-souled foresight and knowledge of nature which made him a born conspirator. Among the crowd Cæsar discerns him for a lean and hungry dangerous spirit. Jealousy makes him master of the choicest weapons of his trade. He knows the grand stop in the organ of the soul of Brutus, and he plays it with exceeding skill.

> " Honour is the subject of my story.
> I cannot tell what you and other men
> Think of this life, but for my single self
> I had as lief not be, as live to be
> In awe of such a thing as I myself;
> I was born free as Cæsar, so were you.
>   And this man
> Is now become a god.
> He doth bestride the narrow world
> Like a Colossus, and we petty men
> Walk under his huge legs, and peep about
> To find ourselves dishonourable graves.
> When could they say till now, that talked of Rome,
> That her wide walls encompassed but one man ? "

He sees the danger of allowing Antony to escape, when Cæsar is slain, and he feels, too, that Antony's mouth should be kept sealed over Cæsar's body ; but the straight-forward honourable Brutus refuses to peer into motives with narrow, spiteful measurements like this. And so it comes to be, that

> " In his mantle muffling up his face,
> Even at the base of Pompey's statua,
> Which all the while ran blood, great Cæsar fell."

It is, indeed, remarkable, how Shakespeare diminishes the grandeur of Cæsar, whose name shook the world ; and yet I question but that the criticism which condemns Shakespeare's portraiture as rather a caricature than a portrait, is more false than the poet's interpretation, inasmuch as it forgets that

Cæsar here is the Cæsar seen through the eye of conspiring envy, not the great master of the world in pride and power imperial, but only, as ever, through jealousy, reduced in size to the constricted limits of the narrow eye whose retina lets in but little of the white sun. Cassius accentuates his weakness, makes him almost a coward, shows how he, claiming high leadership in Rome, is subject to falling sickness, swoonings, deafness. At the same time, Shakespeare, with the spirit of the ancient dramatist, displays in Cæsar a heart inflated by victory and by praise, till it feels as if it should claim qualities divine, spurning the warning of the soothsayer, and claiming a kind of eternalness, so, finally dragging down upon itself, by its own pride, the anger and destruction of the gods.

Antony is depicted with a master hand. Keen, incisive, clever, he makes the wounds of Cæsar set the Roman mob aflame for revenge against those who slew their idol,—making the hacked mantle of the dead hero a record of the envy and the hate of those who slew him.

What did the deed bring forth? It slew a possible tyrant and created a triple tyranny,—Lepidus, Octavius, Antony; and a triangular contest amongst these for power. Lepidus went to the wall, and then Octavius and Antony looked into each other's eyes to see which was to go. But that belongs to the Tragedy of history.

Yes; it brings its Nemesis. Antony, the voluptuary, unscrupulous, forces the conspirators to flee, with the field they had looked upon, unharvested by them. Philippi is their doom-limit; and Brutus and Cassius die, each by his own sword, the sword that slew Cæsar,—Brutus, for being blinded to the duplicity that pleaded with him against his better self, and doing as a patriot, what was unlawful for him to think of as a man. Collective morality is, however, identical with individual truth.

The shadow of him they murder follows them, their evil angel. To Brutus he appears,—the emanation, naturally, of his suffering soul. Portia his beloved, the daughter of Cato, following her father's plan of liberty, believing that

> " Every bondsman in his own hand bears
> The power to cancel his captivity,"

and that,

> " Life, being weary of these worldly bars,
> Never lacks power to dismiss itself,"

had sent her spirit seeking friendly shades; and now, too, the presentiment of doom makes his candle flicker,—the shadow of his soul puts on the shape of Cæsar, and he feels his hour has come. Defeated at Philippi, and refusing to allow themselves to be led in triumph through the streets where erstwhile they were honourable, they fell upon their swords, and Brutus found from Antony also his eulogy,—

> " This was the noblest Roman of them all.
> All the conspirators save only he
> Did what they did in envy of great Cæsar."

In " Antony and Cleopatra "[1] we see, set in the golden glamour of oriental splendour, the witchery of an unstable and fickle love, and the unsatisfying bitterness of sensuous self-destruction. Behind all its beauty, and the glow and colour, the tragic gloom of a decaying empire lies along the horizon. It is the Tragedy of fascination without affection, and without a heart for love; the Tragedy of a queenly state ruined by lust. In it we see the failure of the worship of pleasure, the loss of judgment, the secret of enervation of a mighty people, and, finally, the despair of satiation, which leaves emptiness, and the ashes of a spent fire. In it we look, with awful eyes, on gaunt Despair at bay.

Cleopatra is a creation of absolute genius, unstable yet irresistible, queen of a passion of voluptuous pleasure, dark-browed as Egypt herself; while Rome, in Antony, lies at her feet, magnificently strong, yet bound in mastering

---

[1] Registered in May 1608.

shackles of weakest passion.[1]   Rome, for him, may go to
ruin, and all the disasters which ring him round are nothing.
The world is not itself a balance for Cleopatra's kiss.   And
yet into their bliss steals questioning discontent.   She knows
he was not faithful to Fulvia, and he knows how she played
her game for Cæsar and for Pompey.   His passion finds its
end when she, to calm his jealousy, sends him word of her
death, and he, in frenzy, falls upon his sword, and is carried
to die at her feet.   Her heart, which cries, at first,

> "Shall I abide
> In this dull world, which, in thy absence, is
> No better than a sty?"

turns away from death.   She tries to parley with Octavius,
and to trick him too; then, learning his fixed resolve to lead
her in a Roman triumph, she gave the aspic to her veins,
and died.

That wondrous grimness of Shakespeare's power which
gives even to a babbling countryman the most intensifying
touch of tragic horror in a play, finds vivid exemplification in
that figure of the rustic, carrying the asp for Cleopatra in
his basket of figs.

Perhaps nowhere has Shakespeare given us a deeper
psychological insight into jealousy, or into the awful self-
destruction of a great spirit, drawn aside by passion, to defeat,
dishonour, and death, having missed, through lust, the mark
which history sets up for the truly great,—wise temperance
and mastery of self.   The Circe charms of Cleopatra win
him to idleness and debauchery; and truly, as himself
declared,

> "We bring forth weeds when our quiet winds lie still."

This luxurious Roman is ennobled by Shakespeare for his
dramatic purposes.   To him this mixture of brutality,
indecency, and debauchery, with generous prodigality and

---

[1] If any spark of goodness were left in him, Cleopatra quenched it straight.
—PLUTARCH.

winsome popular gifts, was a metamorphic character, with chinks for imagination to play in; while Cleopatra in Egypt became to his fancy a figure of dream, as she has still remained to the world.

> " Age cannot wither her, nor custom stale
>   Her infinite variety."

To Antony she was the

> " Day o' the world " ;

while he, by her, was prized for his bounty—

> " There was no winter in't : an autumn 'twas
>   That grew the more by reaping."

She has all the mastering gifts of the queen of hearts, and she displays her trump card in her message,—

> " If you find him sad,
> Say I am dancing: if in mirth, report
> That I am sudden sick."

She is the Lady Macbeth of passion, the siren of the oriental luxury which rotted the manhood out of proud imperial Rome.

CHAPTER XXX

"TIMON OF ATHENS" AND "TITUS ANDRONICUS"

In "Timon of Athens"[1] we have a Satire rather than a Tragedy. The easy voluptuary, whose open hand brings crowds to his open door, suddenly finds that the world is not generous without reward, or liberal without wage. His eyes are opened, and he steps at once into a soul-freezing sphere of dead and shattered illusions, "not accompanying his declining foot." He tests, in his need, all whom his bounty in days past had clothed and enriched; and he finds them all base metal, summer-birds, willingly leaving winter. He cannot settle down into the insensibility of unemotional, practical common sense, for he never had it. He becomes the prodigal, aroused and enraged, flinging the husks at the swine he has been feeding.[2] He sneers all through the play, an agnostic of all good, till he is forced to exclude from the general damnation of universal mankind, his faithful steward.

As winter has, with one fell swoop, whirled all the foliage from his life, he goes out into the woods, cursing Athens, and praying that his hate may widen till it cover all things human. His bitter mood is fed the more by the snappish impudence of the churlish philosophy of Apemantus, a hedge-Diogenes, to whose "barbaric yaup" he answers with rebuke.

> "Why shouldst thou hate men?
> They never flattered thee.   What hast thou given?"

---

[1] Sources: Plutarch's "Life of Antony" and "Life of Alcibiades." Paynter's "Palace of Pleasure" vol. i. novel 28, 1567.   Lucian's "Dialogue," "Timon the Man-hater."

[2] He never discovered that he was giving away his all to wolves and ravens.— LUCIAN.

But he is not long to escape contact with what has been his ruin. Digging for roots, he finds hid treasure underneath a tree. He gives it to thieves, to the harlots of Athens who come with Alcibiades when that brave captain needs to be furnished the better for his revenge against Athens, in return for the banishment which was his reward for pleading for his friend. And, when the Senate send messages of proffered honours to him if he return, in order to divert Alcibiades from his invasion, he offers them the tree, as an opportunity of hanging themselves upon it, to escape the punishment they deserve!

The great, bitter Sorrow, whose pain sweeps round the world's sodden shores, speaks to him of a fitting place of rest, where the voice of the waters shall cry kindred meanings to his spirit, and beat the music of his own scorn against the swinging doors of day and night.

> " I am sick of this false world.
> Then, Timon, presently prepare thy grave;
> Lie where the light foam of the sea may beat
> Thy grave-stone daily."

He who had fought for Athens, and helped her with money and blood, now hating her and all the world, makes ready a place to die.

> " Come not to me again ; but say to Athens,
> Timon hath made his everlasting mansion
> Upon the beached verge of the salt flood,
> Who, once a day, with his embossed froth
> The turbulent surge shall cover."

It was indeed, as Alcibiades exclaimed, a fitting end,

> " Yet rich conceit
> Taught thee to make vast Neptune weep for aye
> On thy low grave, for faults forgiven."

It is a Satire on human selfishness and greed ; yet a Tragedy of disappointed estimates of human nature. But the fault is Timon's own. The man that loves you for a sixpence will not continue to love you for less, and nothing is the measure of his affection, when the wage for his flattery sinks down to the same. Timon can curse more at large and with an infinite variety of greater bitterness than Lear, though the cause, very considerably, is the same,— gifts misplaced, generosity squandered and ungratefulness the recompense for both; but Timon lacks as much in tragic grandeur as he exceeds in scorn and vituperative muscularity of utterance. He is a weird figure, not mad,—too terribly bitterly sane, creeping about the verge of life, in a gloaming of hate, till he creep into his grave, upon the very hem of the sea.

Much has been discussed on kaleidoscopic principles as to the Shakespearian genuineness of this play. It might well be an early creation, with later touches of the hand that had read so truly the pulse of Nature, and the erratic deviations of men's affections. I often think the midnights of his times rang bitter chimes like these. If it be not all Shakespeare's, it is likelier to have owed its difficulties to histrionic interpolations; for the fireside thoughts of Shakespeare in his later days must have been coloured, sometimes, of the hue of Timon's.

"Titus Andronicus"[1] belongs to the period before Shakespeare, the spirit of which is represented best of all perhaps by Kyd's "Spanish Tragedy." Ravenscroft in 1687, about a century after its mention by Meres as genuine, reports a tradition of a Shakespearian retouching. It was evidently a favourite of that time, as we may gather from a reference by Ben Jonson. It is a bloody charnel, reeking with revenge, filled with wanton butchery, mutilation and rape, and yet, at the same time, its incidents are a mosaic of reminiscence of classical readings.

I often fancy it might well have been something like this

---

[1] Date uncertain. Included in Francis Meres' list in 1598, in his "Palladis Tamia, or Wit's Treasury," which is immortal because of its invaluable references to Elizabethan literature. See Arber's "English Garner," ii. p. 94. Three years ago a copy of the first edition of "Titus Andronicus" was discovered in Sweden,

that lay in the poet's pocket as he faced the road to London town, with his head and his heart full of dreams about the players. The young man of Stratford, who had listened in inn-yards, to actors' rant of blood and vengeance, might easily be led to write a 'prentice work of some such nature as this, based on the old play which we know to have been acted in Germany in 1600. Criticism is so often a guess in the dark, and the groping hand may easily miss the clue that it almost touches, without knowing it is there. No poet writes uniformly, and must begin somewhere, often beating other men's cast-off drums and trying their battered trumpets, till he have hints given, out of the infinite, for music of his own. Amid all the roar and riot, Aaron's is a character of some defined anatomy—a sort of " Jew of Malta," Iago, Iachimo and the Devil, brewed together in one cauldron of mortal flesh ; and he goes off the stage of life with a final declaration, tragic enough, and blistering in its red-hot iniquity—

> " If one good deed in all my life I did,
> I do repent it from my very soul."

Marlowe's cry is here, and Shakespeare's touch, and the interest of horror heaped on horror, till the women must have shrieked again ; but never greatness stalked across that stage. The bell had not yet rung the full curtain up.

CHAPTER XXXI

THE ACTOR PLAYWRIGHTS

SHAKESPEARE was not of the University wits. His college was the fields and woods of Stratford: his professors, hunger, and the love of all things, and, very often, misunderstanding. There are no class-rooms like the open temple of Nature, filled with the voices of winds and trees, of running waters and singing birds; and Shakespeare was one of Nature's aptest scholars.

The actors had men among themselves with practical knowledge of stage-craft, and dearly-bought knowledge of the world; and so, as we saw, they looked over the acting library which, by this time, was growing in every theatre, and adapted or improved the old plays whose day of rant and bombast had passed away into silence, in the road to forgetfulness. Under their hands the dramas became practical bits of work. They ceased to be elocutionary *tableaux vivants*. The characters became personalities, not hung around with trappings of poetry, but working out their own lives. The effect of this was the ousting of the literary University men, as we can see from the vivid protestations of poor Greene.

Shakespeare was surrounded by this new body of theatrical workers, himself the chief amongst them, lording it in gentle fashion at the headquarters of their gatherings, the convivial board of "The Mermaid" Tavern. The group around him are strong men, touched by contact with his quick personality, and by the strength of a full period. Ben Jonson, George Chapman, John Marston, Thomas

Dekker, John Webster, Thomas Middleton,—all mingled in friendships and quarrelings, and all under the shadow of the greatest thought-king of literature. Beaumont, and Fletcher, and Thomas Heywood, have the voice of a later period in their work, and are really Stuart dramatists, though they almost allure one to follow them, and listen to their speech. But they are over the rubicon, and are not for our consideration here.

Ben Jonson [1] lived a chequered life. He was a soldier with the army in Flanders, and figured as an actor ; but dearest of all to his soul was the repute he won as a scholar, though he was often tiresomely pedantic with his scholarship. He became Poet-Laureate ; yet his was a struggle-life, and his income was dependent upon the uncertain bounties of fickle kings and queens, ever a source of bitterness to the disappointed men who trusted in them. His strength lay in quick scintillating humour, and he really built a national Comedy in his works. His two tragedies of " Catiline " and " Sejanus," though stiff with classical knowledge, are deficient in pathos and in poetry, being far too much of mere chronicle in verse. Yet he had considerable power of combining the tragic of life with somewhat of the outlook of the comic poet, especially the satiric. He shows Sejanus climbing up in the state by mean practices, despising the gods, while yet he has a shrine to Fortune in his house all the time. He has set the gross before the spiritual, and so is overwhelmed ; and the motive of the play is to warn the selfishly ambitious,

> " Not to grow proud, and careless of the gods."

Chapman [2] was, from the point of view of intellect, near Jonson. He stood free from the base, spiteful, quarrel-provoking gossip, which somewhat disfigured this group. He wrote a series of French Tragedies, and had considerable

[1] 1573-1635. See Symonds' " Predecessors of Shakespeare " : Swinburne's " Study " of Ben Jonson ; " Mermaid " Edition, with introduction by Herford.
[2] 1559-1634. See Wards's " Dramatic Poets," ii. 1-36. Swinburne's Essay, 1875.

influence on Dryden, the Choregus of post-Restoration Drama. Chapman was an early "Spasmodic." His strength lies in selections; and his best poetic life was poured into his electric version of Homer's "Iliad," rather than into the mould of Tragic Drama.

Marston [1] set himself forth in a Byronic masquerade of declaiming scorn against mankind, and made his "Antonio and Mellida" a play of exaggerated vengeance, in which the tyrant's tongue is plucked out, the murdered body of his son is thrown down before him; then, surrounded by conspirators, he is baited with curse and insult, till he is despatched with swords. Marston had a coarse cynical nature, without originality; and the graveyard scene, with the ghost crying "Revenge" and groans coming from the earth, is a travesty on "Hamlet," though seriously intended to be impressive, and doubtless it thundered well enough on the simple stage.

Dekker [2] is one of those writers over whose life the shadow of uncertainty hangs; yet he wrote in conjunction with Ben Jonson and Marston. He lived a life of irregular revelry and passion, and died in poverty.

Webster,[3] among them all, seems to have been mentally formed more in sympathy with Shakespeare. His "White Devil, or Vittoria Corombona," and the "Duchess of Malfi" are both very powerful dramas.

The "White Devil" has some passages only to be eclipsed by Shakespeare himself. Her defence, when it is alleged that she was receiving communications from the Duke of Brachino, is striking,—

> "Condemn you me for that the Duke did love me?
> So may you blame some fair and crystal river
> For that some melancholic distracted man
> Hath drowned himself in't."

The beautiful dirge for Marcello, sung over him by his mother, calling all the wild things of the fields and woods

---

[1] 1575-1634.   [2] 1570-1637.   [3] Writing, 1602 to 1624.

to cover him, is exquisite in poetic feeling, while the picture of the mourners is most touching.

> " I found them winding of Marcello's corse,
> And there in such a solemn melody
> 'Tween doleful songs, tears and sad elegies,
> Such as old grandames watching by the dead
> Were wont to outwear the nights with ; that, believe me,
> I had no eyes to guide me forth the room,
> They were so overcharged with water."

The "Duchess of Malfi" is a full house of tragic emotions, and the effects of pity and fear. The plot is a dangerous one at the period, but it is treated with great delicacy,—the love she feels for her steward Antonio, whereby she is involved in the death-dealing rage of her brothers. Her death by strangling ends the tragic tale. She knows no fear, but rises to it like a queen.

> " I know death hath ten thousand several doors
> For men to take their exits ;
> Yet stay ; heaven's gates are not so highly arched
> As princes' palaces ; they that enter there
> Must go upon their knees."

Her brother cannot look upon his crime.

> "Cover her face ; mine eyes dazzle : she died young."

Middleton [1] lives on in the memory of literature largely owing to the interest in his play, "The Witch," which some have believed to have supplied the supernatural machinery of Shakespeare's "Macbeth." [2] It seems debatable which was first in the field, but certainly in Middleton's there is an airy wizardy, most effective : yet his creations are not the soul-chilling creatures that confront the vision of Macbeth and Banquo on the windy heath at Forres. They are not things of destiny, but the bogies of the common superstitious mind. The others are fateful, evil-originating influences, fraught with the most real destiny

---

[1] 1570-1627.   [2] See p. 301*n.*

and fear. The coincidence is not, in any way, remarkable, but Shakespeare did not need to borrow from Middleton.

All of these suffer, of course, from contiguity to the Monarch of their tribe, and from their imitations of him which, at the same time, not seldom give that rare distinction to their utterances in which, often, they excel themselves. His great productions are alone fitted in their entirety to be put alongside the giant remnants of the glory of the Grecian Stage.

CHAPTER XXXII

THE TRAGEDIAN AND THE MOB

THE soul of man, in tragic moments, has flashing insight into the human heart, and into the heart of Nature.

The tragic character was essentially aristocratic, scorning the mean fluctuating souls, that cringed to the higher powers of men, and to the gods. Thus, in the "Second Part of Henry VI." we find the Duke of York exclaiming,

> " Let pale-faced fear keep with the mean-born man,
> And find no harbour in a royal heart.
> Faster than spring-time showers comes thought on thought,
> And not a thought but thinks on dignity."

Jack Cade's law as the law of England, coming out of his mouth, will be "stinking law, for his breath stinks with eating toasted cheese."

The idea of repugnance at the uncleanliness and unclean familiarity of the mob, the gutter-swarmers, finds expression in the words of Casca in "Julius Cæsar."

> " The rabblement hooted and clapped their chapped hands, and threw up their sweaty nightcaps, and uttered such a deal of stinking breath, that it almost choked Cæsar."

The same notion is repeated in the shuddering horror of Cleopatra, when she contemplates the possibility of joining, as a victim, in a Roman triumph.

> " Mechanic slaves
> With greasy aprons, rules, and hammers shall
> Uplift us to the view: in their thick breaths,
> Rank of gross diet, shall we be enclosed,
> And forced to drink their vapour."

Coriolanus refers also to

> " The mutable rank-scented many."

And we find him pouring the bitterest scorn of contempt upon the populace as,

> " You common cry of curs, whose breath I hate
> As reek o' the rotten fens, whose loves I prize
> As the dead carcasses of unburied men
> That do corrupt my air ! "

Undoubtedly this tragic contempt gave some expression to Shakespeare's own resentment of the prostitution of his great gifts to the pleasure of the public.

> " Alas, 'tis true, I have gone here and there,
> And made myself a motley to the view,
> Gored mine own thoughts, sold cheap what is most dear."

Here we might find a parallel in Burns's description of his occupation as a poet,

> " Stringing blethers up in rhyme,
> For fools to sing."

The voice of Marlowe also says,

> " As for the multitude, they are but sparks,
> Baked up in embers of their poverty."

Ben Jonson called " the million,"

> " The understanding gentlemen of the ground,"

while Dekker speaks of

> " The scare-crows of the yard, who hoot at you, hiss at you, spit at you,"

all thus expressing the actor's unpleasant reminiscence of the mob with their tobacco-reek, and odours of garlic, apples and beer.

Coriolanus again tells the people,

> " Who deserves greatness
> Deserves your hate ; and your affections are
> A sick man's appetite.

> With every minute you do change your mind,
> And call him noble that was now your hate,
> Him vile, that was your garland."

Menenius, the wise and tactful, attributes the exile of his hero to his lack of power to meanly flatter the crowd.

Shakespeare could not play cringing parts to win the favour of the mob; and all the less because, through the smoke of the crowded pit, he saw the giant spirits, the heroic and the godlike, that alone made life worth living, looming large, redeeming humanity from littleness, uncleanliness, and mean pursuing passions.

Thus, also, he showed us the stupid fury of the populace, so easily swayed, in "Julius Cæsar" and "Coriolanus," from the one sympathy to the other, now from Cæsar to Brutus, then swung round again by Antony to the other side.

Sir John Davies also sneers at his "gross-headed judge, the multitude."

In the Ancient Drama we find the expression of this feeling, in the phrase of Ægisthus to the Chorus, when they threaten him on the murder of Agamemnon, refusing allegiance to him and Clytemnestra.   He scorns their protest as the worthless words of those

> " Who labour at the lowest oar."

In the "Suppliants" of Æschylus, we see the King, Pelasgus, pleading with Danaus and his daughters for secrecy on his behalf, lest the mob whom he governs, resenting his generosity, refuse to support him.—

> " Mention me not,
> For liberty gives licence to this folk
> Freely to blame their rulers as they choose."

Sophocles does not feel this so much, but Euripides, the poet who was to taste exile, must often have cleared away the mist of tears from his windows, and looked out upon the common crowd with sorrowing contempt.   Thus in his

" Orestes," the fickleness of their feelings is described by
Menelaus,

> " For when the mob is angry, like a flame
> They burn up all that stays within their path.
> Give way—their violence brings itself to nought.
> The people, like a ship held taut, will plunge and splash.
> Slacken your cable,—'twill ride easy then."

And again we see how they can be played with by the voice
of demagogues—

> " Full of conceit, and noise, how quick they lead
> The fickle crowd to evil, with their din
> Driving good sense away : for the smooth tongue
> Oiled well for mischief, has a spell of power
> The mob can never flee from."

The same ills are denounced again in " Hecuba."

> " False band of favour-seekers, fed on praise
> Of all the market-fools, won by soft speaking.
> Would I had known you not, for what care you.
> Piercing the hearts that trust you, if you win
> Only the crowd's approval."

The denunciation of Sparta by " Andromache " was probably
more general in its spirit than it seems, and gathered into
Sparta the mob at large.

But while, as we have seen, the tragic character does
flash his scorn upon the common ruck of sneaks, cowards and
betrayers, he looks with loving insight upon Nature, and
finds great solace at her feet.

CHAPTER XXXIII

NATURE IN TRAGEDY

THE feeling for Nature has been claimed as largely a modern birth in our literature. It is a fact that you cannot make a volume of selections of woodland poetry as such, in the writings of our poets, in a country like ours, so rich in forest landscape; while the sea, before Byron, ran through gleaming shores of thought, in our language.

There is, on the other hand, in these Tragedians much beauty of Nature-glimpses; as if the soul looked suddenly from the poet's eyes, and cried aloud what it had seen in that full-visioned moment. One cannot forget the invocation in " Prometheus Bound,"

> " Ye powers of Nature. All ye swift-wing'd winds
> Rivers and fountains—countless ocean waves,—
> Rippling with laughter. O thou generous earth
> And all beholding sun ! "

Ever and again through the verse of Æschylus the voice of the sea comes in among heroic sorrows.

> " Hoarse from the hollow deep, the waves reply.
> Answering his lonely mourning, sigh for sigh."

Or, again, when the Titan gives Iö directions for her flight,

> " Turn thy wandering steps
> By the lone waters' ever-murmuring marge."

From the same source also he gets the strong image,

> " Thy words, like waves that dash against the crag,
> Shake me, but never move me."

338

In the " Agamemnon " we find the observations of a watchful heart noting the majesty and sweetness of Nature's night.
How the watchman on the palace-roof has seen, with
varying emotions,

> " The starry hosts that, in the spangled field
> Of heaven, night by night take up their stations."

Or what can excel the descriptive power of the flight of
beacons from the height of Ida ?   How true to reality the
picturesque details.   You see the " surging back of the
Hellespont," gleaming to the ruddy flame, lonely headlands
flash, and die into the dark again, and the shaggy forests
of Erica wave in the darkling blaze, like a torch-race
over a darkened course, of eager runners through the
night.

The herald's description, too, of the storm which delayed
the Greeks, is made up of " words by an eye-witness," when

> " In the mad storm of darkness blown from Thrace,
> In fiercest fury driven, the loud winds roared ;
> Flung by the blinding gusts ship dashed on ship,
> In shattering clash of conflict, or to doom
> Drove out of sight before the winds' wild will."

" The Persians " has the sea again in its lines, and we look
out and note

> " The whitening billows foam beneath the gale."

Sophocles had an excellent eye for Nature, but in softer
moods than those that caught the broad soul of Æschylus.

In " Ajax " we find it reflected, in sweet glimpses of
Salamis, isle of his love ; while in " Œdipus " and in
" Philoctetes " the beauty of it breathes in music.

In Euripides, especially, we find continually that charm of
the sea and the ships which must ever strike an island-lover.
We can see him in his retreat, where legend sets him, listening
to the time-old song among the crags,—mystery, mourning,
and wonder ; and watching the ships, creatures of spell and
poetry, passing along the Sound.

In " Medea " we have our foot upon the shore, and the sea
is our well of poetry.

> " She is deaf to a friend's entreatings,
> As a rock in the deep, or a wave of the sea."

Again, in the " Heracleidæ " we get the same glamour of
an ocean-watcher's• dreamings.   Especially telling is the
image of Hecuba, bowed under her overwhelming sorrows.

> " When the storm sweeps o'er the sea
> Then the sailors strive,
> With all the aids that be,
> To save themselves alive.
>
> One will watch the sailing,
> One will guide the helm,
> Another will be baling
> Lest the wild waves overwhelm.
>
> But, when never peace is given,
> And all hope is past,
> Then, bare poles, sails split, and riven,
> Drift they blind before the blast.
>
> So, my heart, with sorrow dumb,
> Crushed by grief, heaven urges,
> Let what misery cares to come,—
> Bow thy head to sorrow's surges ! "

How sweet a picture, too, is drawn before us by the Chorus
in " Helen,"

> " By the deep-blue waters
> I was hanging robes of purple,
> To be dried in the warmth of the sun.
> Lo, my heart with wonder started,
> When I heard a cry of sadness
> Loud with anguish, like the wailing
> Of a maid among the hills,
> Chased by Pan, among the echoes
> Of the fear-resounding crags."

The beauty of some of the episodal pictures in " Iphigeneia "
is most powerful in its appeal to all for whom these things
and thoughts have charm.

Some touches in the later Tragedians are beyond compare exquisite, revealing the true searching minuteness of the poet's glance. We have seen in Marlowe one or two, and Shakespeare's page is studded with them,—moonlight and starlight, song of birds, all the weird and pathetic whispering of Nature. Even in Apemantus, how we find glimpses of the "moss'd trees, that have outlived the eagle," and "the cold brook, candied with ice," and again, in Timon's phrase, "the beached verge of the salt flood," "the turbulent surge" and "vast Neptune weeping over a low grave"; or in "Hamlet," the peep of the

> "Willow growing o'er a brook
> That shows its hoary leaves i' the glassy stream."

CHAPTER XXXIV

CONSIDERATIONS AND COMPARISONS

In the foregoing I have arranged the plays of the Greeks entirely apart from considerations of chronological sequence, but rather to show how the traditional myth-cycles from which the poets derived their tragic material were handled and expounded by them. When taken apart, the plays of Æschylus show traces of remarkable development.

For example, "The Suppliants" is hardly, in the modern sense, a drama at all, and the characters are really secondary in interest to the Chorus. Their parts are more like shadowy backgrounds than living personalities. So, also, in the "Persians" we find the spirit epic rather than dramatic, though the raising of the ghost of Darius from the grave to hear the catastrophe of his empire, is truly tragic. Through the characterisation of Eteocles in the "Seven against Thebes" and the "Prometheus" we are led, however, by the way of strong dramatic growth. Many causes, of course, would be at work upon the poet, probably the influence of his younger rival's work, but, certainly, the effect is his own, for a man's view widens, and his touch gets surer as he goes along. Thus, in the Trilogy of the Atreidæ, we find a combination of Epic and Tragedy which makes for master-piece work. The signal-fires leap across the intervening water-spaces as if on the winged speech of Homer, while Clytemnestra, Cassandra, Electra, Ægisthus, and Orestes, are living people, and make their passion impassioned, living things.

Clytemnestra, in Æschylus, is a different conception altogether from what she would have been in Euripides the Realist, or in the subtly-psychological modern play. She is a big simple character, whose mother-heart, hurt by the robbery of her daughter Iphigeneia, at the hands of her husband, setting glory above family affection, has treasured the bruise in her heart : and having, in the hour of her indignation listened to her husband's foe, gave away forever any claim to sympathy that might have been allowed to her.

From the surviving fragments of trilogies, we could not with fairness judge the standpoint of Æschylus; but, in the complete trilogy which has survived, we find humanity freeing its feet from the bonds of the ancient curse, shaking the shadow of the gods of hate out of its heart, and lifting its eyes to the full day, shining away along the heights. Destiny begins to work more in conformity with justice in the poet's thought. The god is at infinity, and the two lines which to us seem far enough apart, in all terribleness shall undoubtedly some day be drawn together into one. The blind jealousy of heaven, as in Herodotus, aiming, angrily, at toppling whatever human may be high, is transformed to divine Nemesis, awakened to bring to its true level self-inflating pride, and ambitious pomposity. Expiation, not extinction, is the tragic end. The envy of the gods and their hate have become a divine judgment, the natural, just, and inevitable punishment of heaven upon the unbalanced pride of men.

In the "Seven against Thebes" we see how Æschylus could not escape from the shadow of the hereditary curse. Eteocles fights fearlessly and bravely, defending and saving his country from foreign invasion, yet, even in his bravest fight, his father's curse, in the arm of his angry brother, strikes him down,—the same curse which drags the leal heart of Antigone into death, as the punishment of her piety to her outraged brother Polynices.

Æschylus does not believe in the triumph of evil destiny,

that old faith which lay like a cloud of fear along the horizon of Grecian life.   He felt that, of course, the curse of impiety, revengefulness, and all crime drive sorrow before them through generation after generation, but he believes in an ideal of just retribution, some kind of atonement toward which the gods guide men.

Especially does he seem to have woven that doctrine of evil being overcome of good around the spirit and policy of Athens, so far as these struck out in the direction of the laying of ancient feud, and the unifying of the states of the Hellenic people.

An Eastern and Egyptian influence had crept in upon the Greek religion.   The old polytheism was being gradually remoulded, and the religious sense was perceptibly deepened; especially the sense of the individual in regard to his own sin, to the anger of heaven, and to the necessity for atonement.

Above all, Æschylus is a religious teacher, working through the instrument which was, from the first, the medium of true religious utterance.   Hence, to each age his plays have appealed, as if with force intended for that age alone in particular.

The "Prometheus," as it has come down to us, is a protest against a theology which would make any god supreme over everything, to the exclusion even of justice, mercy and pity.   The poet's Jove is a higher conception than that, though, still, more of the vague Unknown ; yet the god of the wise, and the wise god, the soul's refuge, as in the "Agamemnon," from despair.

But the poet does not for a moment dream that the old, dark, furious things which have ravaged human nature,— the passions of an old past,—are dead. They are rather trained to lie at the feet of the civilised soul; yet, should they break forth again, then woe once more to the world !

Sophocles is marked by the spirit of concentration which is the natural reward of coming after a great pioneer.   The plays which have survived, all belong to his ripest period of life and thought.

His outlook on evil, and its operation in the world, seems to have deepened, within his deepest soul, the faith in a unification of all life's entanglements, in the justification of the suffering spirit, though at present under affliction for the sins and pains of others, and in reconciliation with the highest principles and powers. To him the sorrows of human nature had the certitude of repetition. He felt as a reality the first axiom of the poetic, and especially of the tragic, creator,—

> " This wide and universal theatre
> Presents more woeful pageants than the scene
> Wherein we play in."

The shadow of all the world's experience could not yet look in at the window of his thought, as in Shakespeare's; nor the voices of the twenty centuries of sorrow and pain, triumph and gladness, mingle in his utterance, as in Shakespeare's also; yet pride of race, deep sympathetic insight, and knowledge of humanity unexcelled, bring them often into contact one with another. Though both in spirit aristocratic, with the truest aristocracy of Nature, they yet have a fearless contact with the common sorrows of the race, recognising and acknowledging true goodness every-where. Even in " The Trachiniæ," the old nurse, a slave, speaks in the spirit of the free; and, in " Othello," out of the coarseness and grossness of Emilia, a fearless woman-hood flames at last with scorn of the mean liar whose ruinous hypocrisies have shattered all that was so fair.

Instinctively, and with no hectic colouring, their suffering creations win sympathy, and one would rather stand beside Philoctetes, or Antigone, or kneel by dying Hamlet, whispering brokenly, than be in favour with those who meantime seem the darlings of the gods.

Sophocles, like Shakespeare, takes the fable, the tragic

material, but it drapes itself to fit the tragic character around whom he flings it : and it is filled and fired with the ethical principles that he has grappled out of the dark, when seeking for the clues to life's highest mysteries. The Sophoclean tragic personality sees around him all the ancient griefs, the gloomy questionings to which he finds no answer, here : but he turns away from shadowy past and perplexing present, to the eternal principles of justice, and the retribution of the divine, to which testimony is borne by the deepest instincts of humanity. Obedience to the unwritten laws of piety, mercy and probity, is the secret of blessedness, and he that holds fast to his integrity wins invincible peace. In " Antigone," " Ajax," and " Œdipus " appears this law that is treasured since before all time in the heart of the great God.

It takes the years of earth's growing philosophies to develop self-knowledge to such perfection that the varied moods and passions are seen entering, and passing to and fro, about the house of the soul, as we see them in "Macbeth," "Hamlet," and " Othello " ; yet in Euripides we have voices that have prophetic tones in them ; and many of his creations seem almost to touch the fringe of insight with a pathetically modern feeling.

We see how easily has arisen the general statement that the Greek Tragedian devoted himself to action, to the tragic crisis of a great strong soul tried by the gods, or by circumstances strongly opposing, while the Elizabethan concentrated on character. You have on the Greek stage a Titan or a king, a grief-hardened Electra, or a gentle Antigone, suffering, in a strong light of tragic pathos into which they have stepped, of their own will, or been inextricably involved by others, or by heaven ; yet these are not mere victims of Fate. They have chosen the way that led them into it, though, in that way, often, of course, the curse or the sufferings of others have walked behind them. They are not characterless, nor are they mere types, unindividual.

Neoptolemus is a real living soul, with masterly developments of nature and will; a psychological and ethical conflict raging within him, till his conscience triumphs over considerations of self and ambition, and the true man, ennobled and saved from meaner considerations by the sacredness of friendship, and sympathy for undeserved suffering, wins the day. Philoctetes, too, is a characterised personality, and not a lay figure to be clothed around with meaningless elocutions. Clytemnestra, Electra, Œdipus, are individual, strong in their handling of Fate, though involved in an irresistible tide of sorrows, in the guiding of which they were not uninfluential. Yet, in the Elizabethan, particularly the Shakespearian, Tragedy, most truly, character is destiny. Fate may be working around, but the tragic character takes Fate by the hand, and joins in the race towards catastrophe. Both ancient and modern Tragedy give a human setting and exposition of the apparently incoherent matter of Doom. Character remoulds the myth, and dominates the fable of destiny.

Æschylus saw the contradictions of evil and good; but he saw with a wider vision, and perceived, refusing to see otherwise, an influence of justice which would not allow itself to be mastered by ill.

Sophocles also saw the strangely mingled mass, the strain of the one power against the other, but he discerned the law behind it all, the compensation-balance of eternal justice, which humanised the divine, lifted the human higher, and set hope and patience to soothe the weariness of mortal mystery and pain.

The ancient Tragedy felt Fate and the oracles inevitable, yet the characters, like those of the later Drama, most often suffer from their own passionate errors, playing with the edge-tools of destiny, and helping on the fall of doom. Sophocles had a big heart of mercy for the unfortunate, but, of course, in this, fell short of the possibilities opened up for the tragic teacher by the evolution of the Christian ages which so elevated Tragedy. Æschylus feels the guiding hand without.

> " Ah, 'tis a higher power
> That thus ordains.   We see the hand of Jove,
> Whose will directs the fate of mortal man " ;

but Euripides feels that the gods bring in confusion, as a ground for compelling men to worship them, seeking their favour for the sake of release from the besetting difficulties and contradictions of human life and duty, while also he believes that, amid the ravelments of things, the gods must find a clue.

The early Elizabethans made evil topple with a crash, on the crude basis of an idea that good must not be allowed to be quite crushed ; but Shakespeare lifted suffering out of their region of magic evil possession and crude superstition, showing the self-destroying doomfulness of sin and selfishness, and the nobler developments of the spirit through pain. His time was tuned to a greater music, and a "light that never was on sea or land " was breaking in, with wondrous meaning, across the darkness of the soul's perplexities.

Euripides was uncertain of many things, perplexed by the growing difficulties of the faith and practice of his day, and often grew too weary of the difficulties of his tragic creations to try to extricate them from the sorrows which he could not explain.   Yet was he full of pain for them, and left them to the gods, whom neither he nor they wholly believed or trusted in.

In "Hamlet," the dreadfullest Irony in the world looks often round the shoulder of earth's deepest melancholy. There is, also, a kind of unavoidable Doom that drives this wavering nature to destruction, in which it finds its realisation, and the fulfiment of its being.

"Macbeth," if any be, is destiny-driven, yet his ruin is the result of a will that chose evil, having allowed Ambition first to blind it.

Lear, too, helps Fate ; while "Othello" lets the very love

.hat was his life, dazed and stunned by the choking
atmosphere of jealousy, open the door of his heart to
purposes which murdered love and life together with one
fell blow.

The Irony of Fate is strong in the great Tragedies of
Greece and England, as it is a powerful factor in all true
Tragedies of human life everywhere. The curses on the
unknown, which come back so crushingly on Œdipus himself : the footstep of the destined Avenger in Macbeth,
crossing the threshold just as the soul of the murdered king
is quitting it : Mortimer, strong and confident in the removal
of Edward from his path, while his hired villain is even
then whispering in the young king's ear the secret that
brings royal retribution with it,—there are innumerable
instances of such, reflecting, not the poet's sneer under his
cloak at the vanity of human wishes, but only setting on the
boards what life puts on the stage every day, in the damning
scrap of evidential clue left behind by almost every
murderer that ever was known, though months of planning
beforehand had mapped everything out all right.

The critics take, often, very strange positions in regard to,
say, the action of Creon in the " Antigone," and " Hamlet "
in the play, alleging even as a flaw in these, that, in the one,
Creon is more solicitous to bury the dead, than to liberate
the living, and that, in the other, Hamlet does not embrace
one of the many opportunities afforded him of wreaking his
revenge upon his father's murderers.

But, is it not plain that the King fears all at once, with
sudden impact of panic, the wrath of the gods, which the
prophet has denounced upon him, while he thinks, naturally,
the living will be all right for a little longer, and can wait?
And, at the same time, had Creon or Hamlet done otherwise
than they are represented by the poet, there would have
been no excuse for the writing of two of the finest plays
in literature,[1] and the world would have been so much the

---

[1] *Too late!* had to be written over the action of the King.

poorer for the loss. Besides, is it not just because the tragic character does, under given circumstances, fraught with enormous risk, what the commonplace soul would never think of doing, that the really great Tragedy of a life emerges? A nature like Creon's, dogged, superstitious, and proud, is just the kind that is ruled in crisis after crisis by "swing-swang" of pendulum passion; while Hamlet's, in Hamlet's circumstances, and in the environment of the Court at Elsinore, is just the kind that will smoulder through long oppression and suspicion, till it blaze in a sudden fire, and set all aflame with vengeance, burning down the house!

CHAPTER XXXV

THE UNITIES

THERE is little need to-day to speak of "The Three Unities," which once were the panoply of war of critics. They were flung into the heap of things, by Corneille about 1660, although they were drawn from Aristotle and the Grecian stage. The only Unity Aristotle insisted upon was the Unity of Action, throughout a Tragedy: though he did say that Tragedy, as much as may be, tries to keep its action within one revolution of the sun, or nearly so, which gave a formulation of the "Unity of Time."[1] The "Unity of Place" was apparently Corneille's, for he himself allowed that he found it neither in Aristotle nor in Horace. It found its basis, however, quite naturally in the necessity of the construction of the Greek Stage.

The only Unity that has any reason in it, and that really is observed at all in all dramatic work, is the "Unity of Action."[2] This means, of course, that the interest of the play shall be one throughout. It may have more events than one, but the interest must not be divided; and any subsidiary motive must be purely secondary, lying into the main purpose, and leading towards the general conclusion. In the ancient Tragedy there was no counterpoint. The poet avoided all possibility of divided interest, yet he some-

---

[1] Though both Unity of Time and Place are thrown aside without care when required.—*Cf.* Agamemnon, Trachiniæ, etc.

[2] Lessing says—"The unity of the action was the chief dramatic law of the ancients; the unity of time and place were, so to speak, the natural consequences of it, which perhaps they would not have observed more than was required, had it not been for the Introduction of the Chorus. The French on the other hand, set these up as prime necessities.

times had a subsidiary interest beneath the main line of purpose. For example, in "The Persians" there is undivided interest, up to the lamentations of the Persian Councillors, over the national disaster at Salamis ; and a new potentiality emerges in the rising of the ghost of Darius, out of the sleep of the shades, stirred by the woe of his country,—a true tragic episode. But the interest does not divide itself : it rather passes over into and continues the emotion, deepening it to the close. So also in the "Ajax," the death of the hero is not the end, the close of national interest. The burial of the hero is important, for the pride of the Athenians, who have taken him as their national patron, is therein involved.

In the Elizabethan Drama, especially in Shakespeare, you have a strong unity in many parts, many tides seeking one strait, making the tragic wave which finds resolution at last upon one shore. There may be great complexity of thought and passion, with unity of action. "Macbeth" has the murder of Lady Macduff and her children intensifying the surer under-tragedy of retribution ; while the murder of Banquo deepens the interest, and darkens the certainty of judgment ; yet the one great stream flows on to the door of doom.

The tragic event does not at once subside into stillness. It would be the most untrue imitation of tragic life were it so represented on the stage.

"Unity of Time" even in the Attic Stage, was not observed. Not a day or a month, no limit of years, can be laid upon the tragic movement.

Sir Philip Sidney's famous objection to the movement of the stage of his time is worthy of reproduction.—

" You shal have Asia of the one side, and Affrick of the other, and so many other under-kingdoms, that the Player, when he cometh in, must ever begin with telling where he is : or els, the tale will not be conceived. Now ye shall have three Ladies, walke to gather flowers, and then we must beleeve the stage to be a Garden. By and by, we heare newes of shipwracke in the same place, and then wee are to blame, if we accept it not for a rock.   Upon the backe of that comes out a hideous Monster, with fire and smoke, and then the miserable beholders are bounde to take it for a Cave.   While in the meantime, two Armies flye in, represented with foure swords and bucklers, and then what harde heart will not receive it for a pitched fielde ?   Now, of time they are much more liberall, for ordinary it is that two young princes fall in love.   After many traverces, she is got with childe, delivered of a faire boy, he is lost, groweth a man, falls in love, and is ready to get another childe, and all this in two hours' space : while how absurd it is in sence, even sence may imagine, and Arte hath taught and all auncient examples justified.''

But it could not stem the movement of the Drama towards the truer representation of human life and its passions.   Nor would it have been for the good of Drama had it succeeded ; for it would have shut in Tragedy to episodes, and not to a whole action with all that it involved.

ERRATA

Page 69, line 21.—For " his stars " read " her stars."
  ,, 86, note 1.—For " Acharniars " read " Acharnians."
  ,, 176, line 7.—For " Sea-born Night " read " Sea-born Might."

INDEX

354

INVENTORY '80

PART